Tradigital 3ds Max

Tradigital 3ds Max

A CG Animator's Guide to Applying the Classic Principles of Animation

Richard Lapidus

Routledge
Taylor & Francis Group

LONDON AND NEW YORK

First published 2012 by Focal Press

Published 2017 by Routledge
2 Park Square, Milton Park, Abingdon, Oxon OX14 4RN
711 Third Avenue, New York, NY 10017, USA

First issued in hardback 2017

Routledge is an imprint of the Taylor & Francis Group, an informa business

Library of Congress Cataloging-in-Publication Data
Lapidus, Richard.
  Tradigital 3ds Max: a CG animator's guide to applying the classic principles of animation / Richard Lapidus.
    p. cm.
  Summary: "Applying the 12 basic principles of animation introduced by animation legends Ollie Johnston and Frank Thomas is now easier than ever. With great relevance for today's digital workflows, Richard Lapidus presents innovative 3ds Max controls to the classical principles of animation like squash and stretch, anticipation, staging and more. Move beyond these fundamental techniques and explore both the emotion and technical sides of animation with character appeal and rigging. Finally bridge the gap between software-specific instruction and the world of classical animation with this easy to utilize, one-of-a-kind reference guide, perfect for professionals and beginners alike"—Provided by publisher.
  Includes index.
  ISBN 978-0-240-81730-9 (pbk.)
  1. Computer animation. 2. 3ds max (Computer file) I. Title.
  TR897.7.L376 2011
  777'.7—dc23

2011032054

British Library Cataloguing-in-Publication Data
A catalogue record for this book is available from the British Library.

ISBN 13: 978-1-138-40073-3 (hbk)
ISBN 13: 978-0-240-81730-9 (pbk)

Typeset by: diacriTech, Chennai, India

Contents

Start to develop the basics of visualizing animation in a 3d program

Understand the different ways to create and control animation

Have several choices in selecting and editing keys

Control how you see and control motion

Animate modifiers and limits

Create clones

Use the Set Key mode to jump to previously created keys

Scale and offset ranges of keys in the Track Editor

Set keys with the right tangent type

Learn how to locate and identify the location of key
frame information

Use the Key Info of a keyframe to adjust the position of an object

Use the Curve Editor to access curves

Use the Parameter Curve Out-of-Range Types to create
repetitive motion

View and adjust the timing of an object's motion

Use World Space Modifiers and space warps

Link and bind to space warps

Create secondary motion using noise

Use path deformation

IK (Inverse Kinematic) HI solvers

Creating dummy helpers

Contents

Acknowledgments

When I first started thinking about writing this book, the last thing that I wanted to provide the reader with was a series of instructions which required extra plug-ins or scenes so complex that it couldn't render. In addition, I wanted to avoid long detailed technical explanations which couldn't be immediately applied to providing solutions. That really is the key to learning such a power program like 3ds MAX. Instead of merely learning a new tool by clicking through a tutorial, you need to understand along the way why things work the way they do. I've lost track of the number of professionals that have entered my classes looking for an explanation of how to go beyond the tutorials. In a nutshell… "it's always just one button". Many tutorials out there instruct the reader to make changes without an explanation of why it is being done.

I've been developing my college credit classes over the last 15 by paying close attention to the problems that professionals were encountering in the field. Having the opportunity to work as a Certified Instructor in an ATC and as a college professor has been truly invaluable. Hopefully you will develop an understanding of a few new methods for animating within 3ds MAX, and the workflow for problem solving your own unique solutions.

Special thanks to Chris Tedin for stepping in toward the end of this books production to coauthor several chapters. Murphy's Law kicked in several times with family emergencies and a trip to hospital myself with a broken collar bone.

About the Authors

Rick Lapidus, Author

Rick started his art career with a BFA in Sculpture from Washington University. Having spent the last 25 years immersed in the 3d world using animation programs, his recent artwork is a synthesis between the sculpture and 3d visualization. Currently he is pursuing an MFA in Electronic Media at Governor State University.

Rick started his career in 3d animation back in the early 90's with the first 3d studio program.

Currently working as an Associate Professor teaching 3d animation at Moraine Valley Community College. In addition to credit courses, Rick has been providing training to professionals in a wide variety of fields including Instructional Design, Broadcast, Interactive Media, Forensic Animation, Architectural Visualization, and Product Design.

His basic philosophy of teaching is to approach each lesson from a problem solving standpoint rather than merely clicking through a tutorial.

Chris Tedin, Co-contributor

Born in Sitka, Alaska, Chris Tedin started his career as a painter and sculptor. He has been working as an illustrator, graphic designer, and most recently as an art director in Chicago, Illinois. He has been teaching game design and animation for over 15 years. His students now work as animators and professional game designers at Blue Sky Studios, Digital Domain, Aardman/Sony, Microsoft, and as freelance independent artists. Many of his students are now college teachers themselves. He started in the early days with Strata StudioPro, then 3ds MAX version 1.0, Maya 2.0, Softimage 3.8, Houdini, before finally settling on Softimage XSI, beginning with version 4.0 Foundation. Chris still sculpts and paints and teaches part-time at Tribeca/Flashpoint Academy in Chicago.

About the Website

Visit the companion website for *Tradigital 3ds Max* at www.tradigital3dsmax
.com for the source files for many of the examples in this book and hands-on
skill development to accompany the techniques and practical skills featured
in the chapters!

CHAPTER 1

Introduction to the Interface and Seeing Animation in a New Way

Richard Lapidus

After Completing This Chapter, You Will be Able To:

- Start to develop the basics of visualizing animation in a 3d program.
- Understand the different ways to create and control animation.
- Have several choices in selecting and editing keys.
- Control how you see and control motion.

Every few years a study is done that correlates the benefits of playing computer games and improved learning skills. I will wholeheartedly agree that there are benefits that may include improving memory, problem-solving abilities, and motor skills. Unfortunately, the areas that generally need work have to do with visualization, perception of space, and a good sense of timing. The goal is to create a world in which the viewer will be drawn in

FIG 1.1

and immersed with in the reality presented to them. As we journey through this book together, hopefully you will develop the skills or at least a basic understanding of how to start "perceiving" motion and using those skills to create animation. Anyone can create motion with keyframes, but a true animator will breathe life into a character and give it some level of realism relative to its own reality. As a starting point, we will cover some of the basic tools you need to control the 3d environment you are working in. Try to think of the first few chapters as a quick start to understanding the basic workflow of 3ds MAX. Instead of giving you a fully extensive explanation of every single icon and command to start, I want to "pull you in" and get you moving toward seeing how things work. The best analogy I can give you for not expounding for 10–15 pages of parameters is relative to learning how to drive a car. Although I know one or two people who have, most of us didn't sit down and read the owner's manual of a car before learning how to drive.

The first thing I want you to do is change the user interface to look similar to the images in this book. The "dark" version, which is the default, is nice in a low-light environment, but it is hard to see the subtle changes to some of the interface as you work.

1. Start up 3ds MAX and go to the Customize Menu. Choose User Interface and select the AME Light Version. Hit OK to accept and the next time you start 3ds MAX, it will be the default color scheme.
2. Notice how some of the icons and parts of the interface have a yellow background or border. This indicates an active state. You should see the Select icon; create geometry and the perspective view as being currently active.

3. Let's start by maximizing the perspective view. There are actually three ways to do this. Those are with keyboard shortcut ALT+W, the min\max icon, or dragging the upper left corner of the viewport. You will find that there are usually three to five different ways to accomplish the same thing with the program.

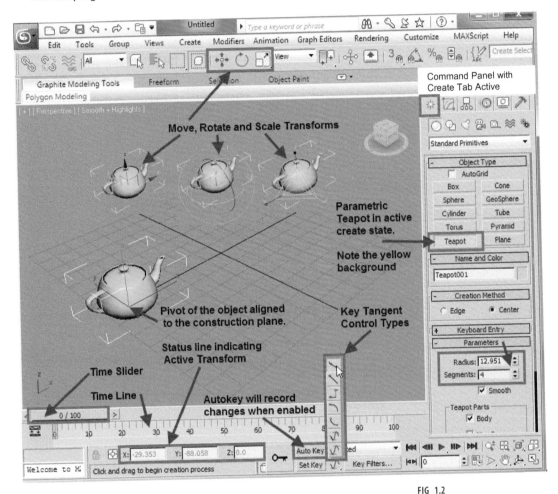

FIG 1.2

Refer to Fig. 1.2 for steps 4–9

4. In the Command Panel, enable the Standard Primitive called teapot and drag out an object of about 30-unit radius.

5. Right click the screen or choose one of the selection modes. (If you don't turn off Create mode, it is still active and you might endlessly be creating objects.)

6. Left click on the three select transform icons in the main toolbar and then finally on the Select and Move transform. Notice how the transform gizmo changes depending on if you are in Move, Rotate, or Scale mode.

3

The program gives you visual feedback as to what is active in a number of ways. The color red represents active animation state, the "X" axis, and the move transform. After creating keys (keyframes) in the next several steps, the transform keys will appear with the three basic color representations (red, green, and blue) much the same way it shows on the transform gizmo.

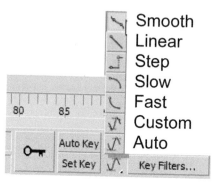

Tangent Types
for Keyframes

FIG 1.2a

7. Make sure the tangent control is set to Smooth which is its default tangent type.
8. Turn on the Auto Key and move the time slider to frame 100.
9. Move the teapot across the screen on the "X" axis. (Note: You could also drag the "X" spinner down in the status line. This is preferable when an object is selected and you want to avoid having to grab the transform gizmo.)
10. Move the time slider to frame 50 and then move the teapot up on the "Z" axis.
11. Play the animation.

You will see that there are three red rectangles now located in the timeline at the bottom of the interface. Keys on a straight line represent, at least in my mind, linear motion, tranquility, or death. One of the rules of thumb for starting to breathe life into your object or scene is to start looking for the curves. Living things tend to move on curves while mechanical motion is more linear or too precisely repetitive. The best analogy for this is a heart monitor you might seem in some TV drama. What happened when the EKG line goes flat? It means the patient is dead. The inverse is also true. Ever notice when the stage has been set to see if someone can be revived? The blipping does not come back all at once. There is an irregularity in the tempo of the graphic until it reaches some moment of repetition before the camera cuts to another actor or scene. Let's look at a few ways to visualize the motion.

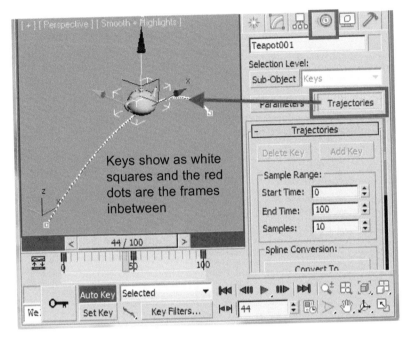

FIG 1.3

12. With the teapot still selected, go to the Motion Panel. It is the fourth tab in the Command Panel. Please see Fig. 1.3.
13. Click the trajectory tab.

What will appear is a red line with three white squares. The squares represent a value of the X, Y, Z position for the object in time, and the dots represent the frames in between the keys you created. Normally I will turn on the trajectory in the Object Properties because this way of displaying the motion of the object visually is only temporarily on while the object is selected. It is nice to note, however, that the motion of the object can be converted to a path which can be used for generating a 3d object or as a path constraint as just two examples. This will be done in a later chapter, but this is how I created the motion in Fig. 1.5 for one of my colleagues teaching a complex calculus problem his students were having difficulty visualizing. For any instructors using this book, a good exercise for practice is creating visuals for other curriculum.

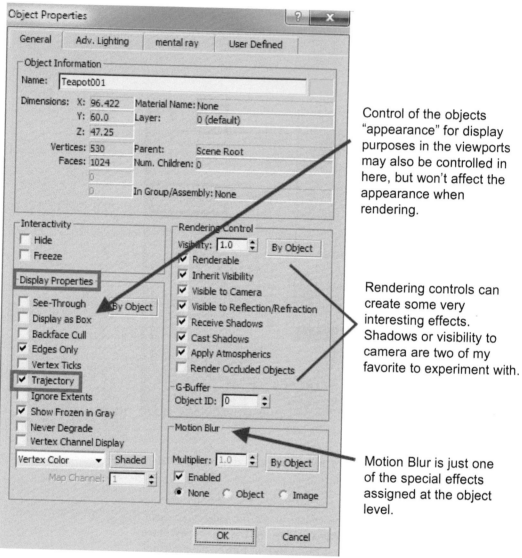

Control of the objects "appearance" for display purposes in the viewports may also be controlled in here, but won't affect the appearance when rendering.

Rendering controls can create some very interesting effects. Shadows or visibility to camera are two of my favorite to experiment with.

Motion Blur is just one of the special effects assigned at the object level.

FIG 1.4

14. Right click the viewport and when the Quad Menu shows up, choose Object Properties. Then on the left side of the Dialog in the Display Properties area, enable Trajectory.

The Quad Menu and Object Properties are two tools you will want to get very well acquainted with. The Quad Menu will change and is customizable as you make changes to your objects. Since the teapot is still parametric, only half of the menu appears. If it were converted to an editable object or had a modifier on it, you would see all four panels. The Object Properties Dialog has more uses than we would want to explore in an introductory chapter, but will be explored in more detail in later chapters.

15. Leave all these preferences in the default state for now except the trajectory on and hit the OK button.

Select the key at frame 50 and drag it to frame 70. Notice how the trajectory changes. There is a built in smoothness and stretchiness to the default tangent controller for the keys created. Move the key to frame 40 and examine the trajectory again. The teapot seems to go beyond the position it is traveling to and then through the key as it moves to the next position. There are several ways to adjust this…but first you needed to see it to believe it. The next way to see the motion of your object is with a graphic editor. There are actually four other ways to see the motion in numeric, range, or line form. Those are Mini-Curve Editor, dope sheet, and the Curve Editor or key values. We will be using all of them through the book except for the Mini-Curve Editor. I find that it always needs panning or zooming to deal with, so I will only show you it once.

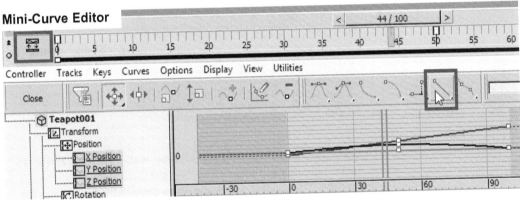

FIG 1.5

16. Click the icon for the Mini-Curve Editor in the lower left corner of the interface. You now see all the curves for your teapot. Drag a marquee around all the keys and then click linear tangent. The curve editor must be closed before the change in motion will show in the viewport. Notice how the teapot now moves on straight lines.

For changing and viewing the tangent types in the next few steps, refer to Fig. 1.2A, which shows the names of the different tangent types in the flyout. I typically will change the tangent type to the one I want before creating animation keys, but they always need to be adjusted at some point in time anyway. I find it easier to memorize as a vertical rather than horizontal list.

17. Click the Step Tangent with all the keys selected. The teapot stays in position and now snaps in one frame to the next position. Nothing I can think of moves like this except for the second hand on a clock. With the dominance of smart phones, the only second hand in my classroom this year was on the wall clock. Not a single person was wearing a watch with a second hand except for me.

18. Try the custom tangent type and then adjust the grips as you would the controls on a vertex in sub-object.
19. Return the keys to the default smooth and close the Mini-Curve Editor.
20. Hit the "F" Key on your keyboard and change the perspective view to a front view.

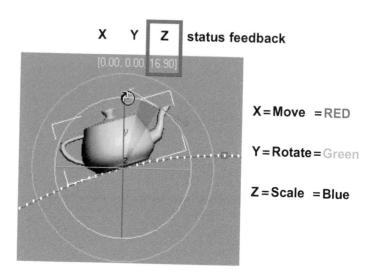

X = Move = RED

Y = Rotate = Green

Z = Scale = Blue

FIG 1.6

21. Move the time slider to about frame 35 and enable the Select and Rotate Tool or right click and select Rotate from the Quad Menu.
22. Drag the "Z" axis that should be the center circle so the teapot looks like it is sitting on its own trajectory. The "Z" axis is shown in yellow in Fig. 1.6. When the Reference Coordinate System is set to View the "Z" axis is always perpendicular to the orthographic viewport.
23. Move the Time Slider to about frame 70 and rotate it forward so it looks like it is sitting on its trajectory on the other side. Play the animation.

The teapot appears to be picking up from frame 0 and then rotates around the apex of the curve. It maintains the rotation all the way through to frame 100. Since a key isn't out in the future to interpolate to, the motion stays all the way through from 70–100. Also notice how the Rotation Keys are in green. I've shown you a key concept here that is "bracketing" your keys. By not having the Rotation Keys on the same frames as the move, you are getting a more complex and realistic motion. Everything doesn't happen at the same time. There has to be some pre- or postmovement to telegraph the action. It's like head turns and eye movements. Linear rotation would not work well with turning a head, and the eyes typically always start moving toward a target before the head. Let's take a look at another really core tool for controlling your keys. We could grab the keyframes at zero and make a copy at frame 100 with the Shift Key. But the Move Key would copy also. We will do it selectively and then I'll show you two more key features for controlling what you see.

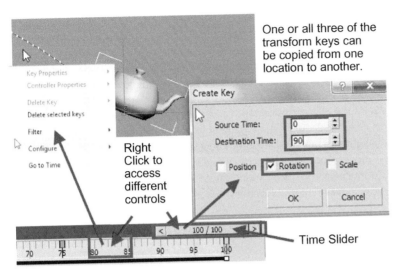

One or all three of the transform keys can be copied from one location to another.

Right Click to access different controls

Time Slider

FIG 1.7

24. Move the time slide to frame 100 and then right click the Time Slider. A Create Key Dialog will appear.

25. Uncheck the Position and Scale Radial button and then enter 0 for the source and 90 for the destination. Hit the OK button and you will see that the Rotation Key from frame 0 has been copied to frame 90.

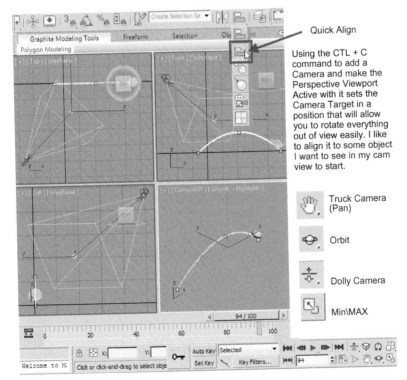

Quick Align

Using the CTL + C command to add a Camera and make the Perspective Viewport Active with it sets the Camera Target in a position that will allow you to rotate everything out of view easily. I like to align it to some object I want to see in my cam view to start.

Truck Camera (Pan)

Orbit

Dolly Camera

Min\MAX

FIG 1.8

9

26. Change back to the perspective view by hitting the home button on the navigation cube and then execute a CTL+C command. This will create a camera view out of the perspective view.
27. Min\Max the viewport for a moment and notice the placement of the camera and target. If you orbit the camera right now, it would be quickly out of view.
28. Hit the "H" Key to select the camera01 target by name.
29. Drag the flyout for the alignment tools for quick align (looks like a lightning bolt on the slanted cubes) and then left click the teapot. The target is now set so you can rotate around it to get a better view. Adjust your view with the icons indicated in your viewport controls to get a nice diagonal motion across the viewport.

One of the things that I like to do for visualizing motion in a still image is to take an objects trajectory and make it visible in the scene. I've also used this for creating paths out of moving objects and having these paths grow over time. When you start to think about having things appear or disappear, the options are endless. We will be looking more deeply into aspects of this in the Visibility chapter 16. For now, let's look at converting motion into a spline, which can be rendered.

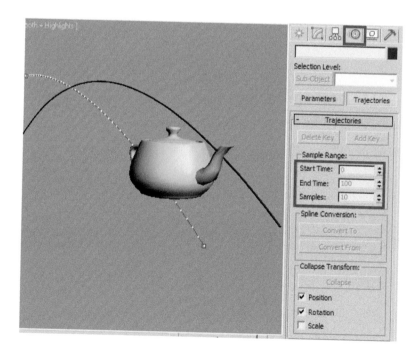

FIG 1.9

30. Select the teapot again either with a left click or "H" and select name.
31. Go into the Motion Tab of the Command Panel and Select Trajectories again.

32. The Start Time and End Time represent the range of keys you want to capture and create a spline from. The number of Samples represents the number of vertices that will be created in that new spline.
33. Hit the Convert To button and then select the spline from your scene called "Shape001".

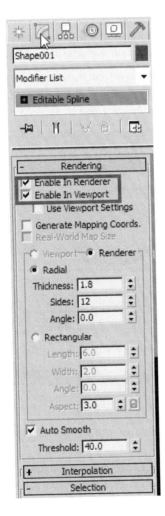

FIG 1.10

There are several things to note about spline objects that will help you in other areas down the line. In the Modify Panel, you will see that the Rendering Portion allows you to enable in Renderer and Viewport. Many modifiers like Turbo Smooth, which add complexity to an object can be set for low resolution in the viewport for navigation and then show when you render. Scene complexity becomes a problem with 3ds MAX, so you want to look for all the ways possible to maximize efficiency. Here is an example of how to save lots of resources. Imagine telephone or cable lines snaking through a scene. Instead of trying to model these as 3d objects, you can merely create splines which are no-poly count and make them renderable. I once demonstrated to a client five different ways to model a chair made out of tubes. In a scene requiring several hundred copies, any version became problematic. We ended up importing the polylines they were using as a base for modeling in another rapid prototyping program and just made them renderable. There was low scene complexity and the splines can even cast shadows. When working in the program, look for these time-saving features. Let's look at a few other ways to visualize motion. Although you probably won't use these tools exactly as shown, it will give you a good overview of functionality.

34. Make sure the Auto Key is off and make sure the teapot is still selected.
35. Hold the Shift Key and move the teapot about 100 units on the "Y" axis.
36. When the Clone Options Dialog appears, choose Copy as the type and hit OK.

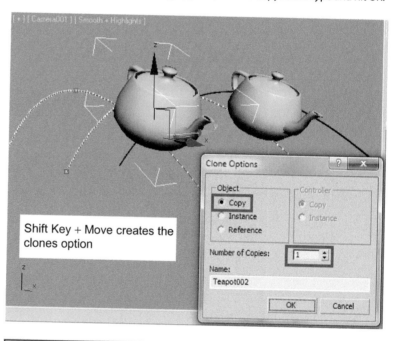

Shift Key + Move creates the clones option

FIG 1.11

Result

The Clone Options Dialog will appear. Shift is used with any transform (Move, Rotate, or Scale) will allow you to create clones of the object. In this case, it creates copies of the keys as well. If the Auto Key were still on, it would allow you to create a clone and create a new keyframe, while leaving the rest in the original position. This is interesting to experiment with. There are three options to choose from: Copy which creates an independent object, Instance which wires the objects together so that changes at the object level controls all other instances, and Reference which is a one-way connection. We will explore these in more detail later.

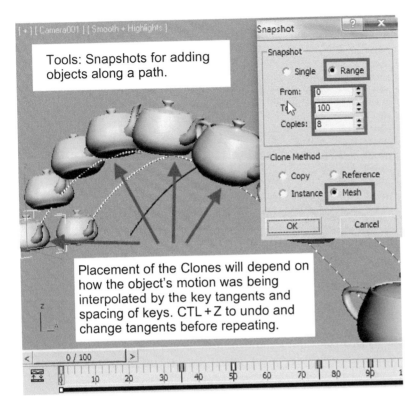

Tools: Snapshots for adding objects along a path.

Placement of the Clones will depend on how the object's motion was being interpolated by the key tangents and spacing of keys. CTL + Z to undo and change tangents before repeating.

FIG 1.12

37. Go to the Tool Menu and try a Snapshot Command. This will allow you to create a number of copies distributed along the objects trajectory.

I will typically use Mesh and then bring the visibility down to 0.2 at the object level in properties or add a material with a value of 15%–20% opacity. For still images once again, this creates a nice easy solution. The next two solutions we will look at will be for getting your objects to show in a little more of a traditional method. The first solution will use ghosting, which is like the onion skin technique used by 2d paint programs to show before and after frames for reference as the animator would draw the frames. The other is motion blur which occurs at render time instead of in the viewport. The ghosting as shown in Fig. 1.13 displays a range of positions before and after the current frame in two different colors. I rarely use ghosting of the objects in wireframe because visually, there is too much information to really see what you may want to be looking at. Consider displaying the object as "box" when you are setting up the ghosting. A good example of what I am really looking to pick up is the swerve of a car through a turn that I want to exaggerate. It's easier to eye up the changes of a simple extent box edge rather than all the complexity of your objects wireframes.

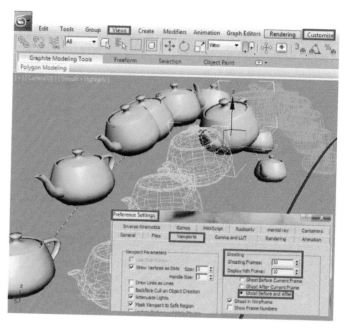

FIG 1.13

38. First go to the Views Menu in the main toolbar and enable ghosting. Ghosting will appear on any object selected in the scene. If you set this up and don't see the effect, you may have de-selected an object.
39. Now go to the Customize Menu and choose Preferences.
40. Try 50 ghosting frames with 10 Display Nth Frame. Turn on Ghost Before and After to see the motion of where your object is coming from and going to.

FIG 1.14

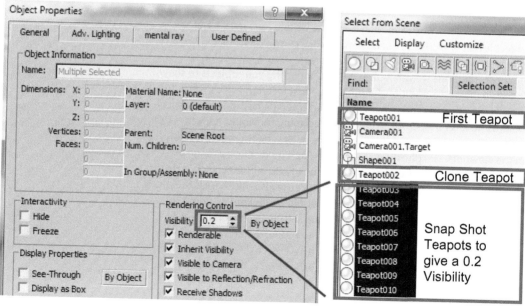

41. Hit the "H" Key and select all of the teapots that were created as snapshots.
42. Right click the screen, and choose Object Properties and change the visibility to 0.2.

Trap

If you use mental ray as the rendering engine, it won't render the object property visibility reduction. You will have to use a material with opacity or transparency adjusted.

43. Hit F9 to render your view. All the snapshots are semitransparent.

Up until this point I haven't mentioned object naming conventions. When an object is created or cloned in some form you have the option of changing the name. As duplicates or new objects are created, they are incrementally named by the primitive. In a decent size scene, you could have several dozen cylinders which became telephone poles, and boxes which were formed into just about anything. In a working environment, collaborating with other animators and merging work together can be problematic if nothing is named. The problem cascades when you think about sending your scene out to a programmer for gaming. If you were playing around with creating extra clones, your selection might not include Teapot003-Teapot010. There are some wonderful options we will explore by assigning attributes later in the book. Your job will be easier if you get in the habit of sticking to a naming convention you can work with. For example: Flying_pot and flying_pot would actually be read as two distinct objects due to the capitalization. I suggest all lower case with an underline between each word. In the DOS days of animating we were limited to eight characters for file names. Keep is short and simple. In forensic cases that I worked on with pick-up truck and a semi-tractor trailer, I used as the main parent: pu_body and trk_body. Each had a listing of parts that started with a prefix of pu_ and trk_. There is even a tool in 3ds MAX that will let you swap in objects for stand-ins. Let's continue to the last rendering option for your viewing pleasure. Let's add some motion blur to the teapot.

44. Select the other teapot, and in the Object Properties, enable Motion Blur
45. Select the Camera01 and in the Modify Panel, go to the Multi-Pass Effect area and enable Motion Blur.
46. Go to the Create Panel and under systems, create a daylight system.
47. Hit F9.
48. Go to the Rendering environment and change the background color to a light gray or white.
49. Create a Plane object in the top viewport for casting shadows onto and then switch your view back to the camera view.
50. Hit the F9 key again and your scene should render something that looks like Fig. 1.1. There are some problems with that image relative to the defaults and the shadows, but we can look at fixing that later on.

Working in the trenches for teaching computer animation at the college and professional levels, I find myself relying on and referring back to traditional animation techniques, which for the most part were my only references when I started learning 3d animation back in the early 90s. Much has changed over the last two decades as to the power of the hardware and capabilities of the software, but essentially it is still a tool. To move toward a goal of being a good animator as one might aspire to be a good writer, you need to keep in the back of your mind that your most important asset needs to be exercised: the brain. A writer is told to write about what they know and then exaggerate it. As an animator, we are wearing many hats. Two of the basic areas that are a direct carryover from the traditional side of the world are to capture how things really move and then to try to figure out how to compose a story. If you aren't drawing what you see every day, then you are missing a world of opportunities to graphically notate the world around you for future use. If you aren't out hunting with a camera, the skills of composition, effects of lighting, and even depth perception may be getting rusty.

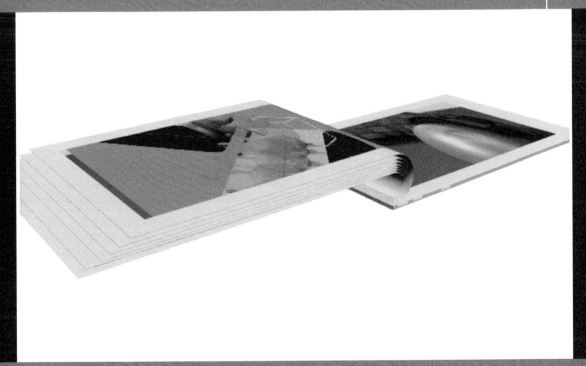

CHAPTER 2

Working with Keys and the Dope Sheet

Richard Lapidus

Rule: Timing

- Animate modifiers and limits.
- Create clones.
- Use the Set Key mode to jump to previously created keys.
- Scale and offset ranges of keys in the Track Editor.

FIG 2.1

Although many of us don't use animated flipping pages of a book in our projects, this is a very simple tutorial for getting your feet wet in the area of animated modifiers that can give your work a more natural and realistic motion. In addition, we will take our first exploration into the timing of motion and making it look more realistic. In a very subtle way, you will also hopefully see that there is an inherent overlap in the timing and even the rhythm of how things are animated as we saw in the previous chapter. Essentially when working on any kind of animation software, you will need to be able to control and adjust the length and speed of an animation segment. We will take a look at this concept through several of the chapters in this book.

I came up with the idea for this tutorial back in the early 90s based on a few problems that kept creeping up during some of my classes. Many of my students were flying a camera though their scenes to end up at a book with images of their drawing ports on the pages. Seemed like a nice idea, but the pages did not bend naturally or seem realistic in the timing of the flipping. Unfortunately, the idea caught on quickly, and most of them were turning stiff boxes, which didn't represent how the pages in a book flip over. The subtle details of the mechanics involved in turning and bending a page eludes most people until they observe you doing it three to four times. It's not really turning a page, but articulating the bend. The other half of the problem is that this is not a precisely timed mechanical motion. Mark your spot in the book and fan the text a few times. Every single time is different based on the amount of pressure applied with your fingers and the force of the bend.

After using this tutorial in classes for close to a decade, most of my students feel very comfortable with utilizing the Dope Sheet to enhance their animations. Think of the first keying or controls you use on your work as broad strokes of the animation and the adjustments you make in the Dope Sheet as a way to control the staging of the timing globally. The software does a great job in interpolating between key positions and doing the "tweening" of translating the object from one position to the next. One of our goals

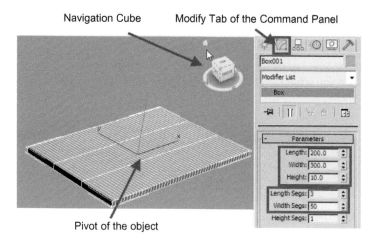

Navigation Cube   Modify Tab of the Command Panel

FIG 2.2

Pivot of the object

18

will be to take the exactness out of the equation and "dirty it up" a little bit. Realistically, although events can be displayed as timelines sequentially, there is overlap and variations in the duration of events. This is something we can control in the Dope Sheet very easily. Although you may not animate a book anytime soon, the ability to control time based on moving or scaling "sets" of keys is an invaluable skill set.

1. Create a box in the top viewport.
2. Go to the modify panel and change the parameters to:

Length 200,	Width 300,	Height 1
Length Segs 3,	Width Segs 50,	Height Segs 1

Note

It's safer to always make the parameter adjustments in the Modify Panel after creating the object. You can very easily create an object, deselect it, and then try to make changes to the parameters while still in the Create Panel, which will result in no changes to the object.

To get the page to bend later on, it needs enough complexity along the width. That's why we are using 50 width segments. To add a picture or text to the page, three extra length segments will be added and adjusted, with a modifier to use a multisubject material in case you want to have a different material, like a picture in the center of the page.

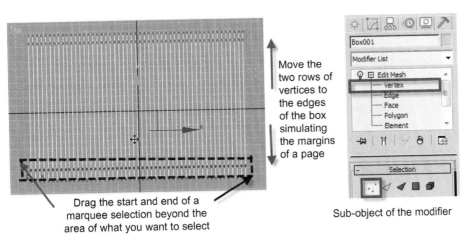

Move the two rows of vertices to the edges of the box simulating the margins of a page

Drag the start and end of a marquee selection beyond the area of what you want to select

Sub-object of the modifier

FIG 2.3

3. Add an Edit Mesh Modifier.
4. Go to the Sub-object Vertex.
5. Marquee select the top middle row of vertices.

19

Note

I have added arrows to the diagram to show you where I click outside of the selection to start and finish the rectangular selection window.

6. Move the vertices up in the "Y" axis.
7. Select the other row and move it down.
8. Turn off the sub-object when you have finished moving the vertices.

Note

To turn off the sub-object of the modifier, you must click where you see yellow in the modifier stack. See Fig. 2.3.

When you have finished the next step, your box should look like the image in Fig. 2.3.

The Length Segs of 3 gives you two extra rows of vertices. To add the Multi/Sub-object material easily, the box is now set up with a center region having low complexity to select and change the Material IDs at the polygon level in a few steps.

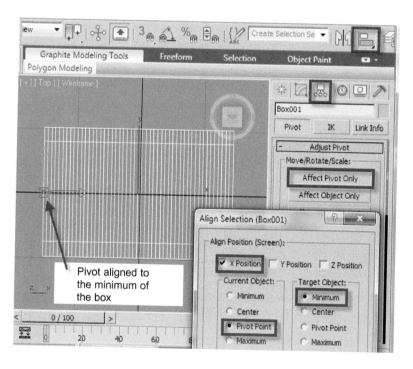

FIG 2.4

9. Open the Material Editor ("M" Key) and assign a Multi\Sub-object Material to the box. Make sure the sub-object is off when you assign the material. Set the number of ID Materials to 3 with three different colors.
10. Name the materials as well.

Note

When assigning sub-object IDs, it helps to use basic colors, so you can see if you have the assignment right. I also like naming the material, so I can remember which one goes where. Try not to use the color red, because sub-object selections are red and you may get confused.

We won't be assigning images into the material in this chapter, but it was a good place to introduce the concept that 3ds MAX is inherently a numeric-based software program. Even though we are working with a graphic user interface that can let you see materials, lights, and shadows in real time, it is all driven by some pretty sophisticated number crunching. It's all numbers. There are numerous opportunities to enhance the workflow when you recognize that the program not only animates by XYZ transform numbers but also records and controls data in other ways as well. We will look more in depth into the Material Editor in the Visibility chapter.

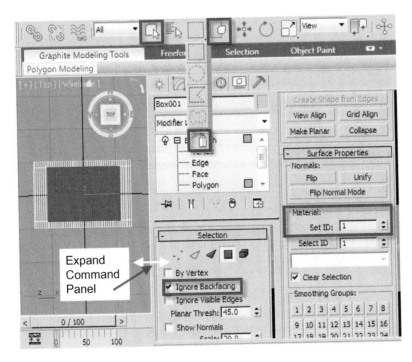

FIG 2.5

21

Refer to Fig. 2.5 for assigning the material IDs in the following steps. By default, all primitive objects created will have a material ID number of 1. For this project, the 1 will be the border, the 2 the front insert area, and 3 the back side.

11. Expand the Command Panel and go into sub-object Polygon.
12. Turn on Ignore Backfacing.
13. Change the Selection mode to Paint Selection Region and drag a selection as you see in Fig. 2.5.
14. Scroll the right part of the command panel to Surface properties.

Note

You can also right click a grey area of the Command Panel and choose Surface properties to get there quickly.

15. If the Set ID number indicates the number 1, then the object by default has a one assigned. If not, you will need to assign the number 1 to all the polygons and then change front center polygons where a picture would be the number 2. The name selection should show front picture as soon as you change the Set ID to 2.
16. Change to a bottom viewport or arc, rotate your view to the backside of the box, and select the same middle section of the box like you did for the top.
17. Change the Set ID to 3.
18. Turn off the sub-object and hit the "T" Key to return your view to a top viewport.

First, we want to change the pivot of the object before adding the Bend Modifier. In this situation where the page would be anchored at the left side like a page in a book, the axis of a bend and the pivot should be aligned here. Unlike traditional animation where the objects have no pivot and the motion is controlled by the person compositing the layers, all objects in the 3d world have pivots you must deal with. I like setting the pivot on an object like this before adding the Bend Modifier because the axis of the Bend Modifier will be set to the object's pivot. Inherently, with most primitive objects, the axis is centered in the middle of the base with the "Z" axis running perpendicular through it relative to the construction plane. Say that five times fast and just remember the pivots aren't always where you want them to be. See Fig. 2.6 for the next steps.

We are going to move the pivot before adding the Bend Modifier. Some modifiers like bend and lathe have centers that align to the pivot of the modifier to the pivot of the object. If you skip this step, the book will bend in the middle and you would have to go to the sub-object center of the modifier and adjust it.

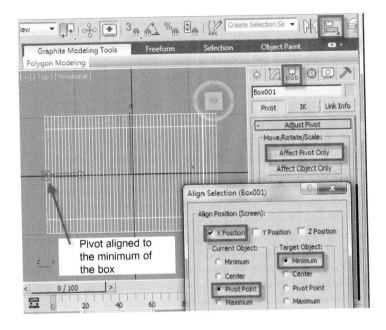

Pivot aligned to the minimum of the box

FIG 2.6

19. Go to the Hierarchy Panel and enable Affect Pivot Only. The Hierarchy Panel is the third tab in the Command Panel. This is the area adjustments and control over linked objects can be easily controlled.
20. Click the Align button in the Main tool bar and then click on the edge of the box.
21. When the Align Selection Dialog appears, enable X Position and set the current object to Pivot Point and Target object to Minimum.
22. Click Ok to exit the Dialog box.
23. Go to the Hierarchy Panel and turn off the Affect Pivot button.
24. Add a Bend Modifier.

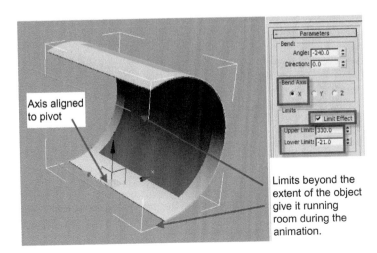

Axis aligned to pivot

Limits beyond the extent of the object give it running room during the animation.

FIG 2.7

23

25. Drag the angle spinner and notice how the object is skewing.
26. Return the angle to 0.
27. Change the axis to "X".
28. Turn on upper and lower limits.
29. Increase the upper and lower limit to:
    (a) Upper limit: 330
    (b) Lower limit: −21

The limits help to control the areas of the modifiers affect on the object. Anything inside the limits gets the effect. When a modifier is added to an object, the amber gizmo that represents the modifier surrounds the extent of the object(s). To make the motion more realistic as the focus of the bend over time is changed, you will give yourself a little "running room" by pushing the limits out beyond the extent of the object. In addition to widening the area of the bend area, the timing is buffered a small amount because it takes a few frames for the limits to start moving in. Effectively, you will be falling off the force of the bend over time. We will animate the limits to a smaller amount over time as well as adjusting the Bend Angle. This will give your page a natural feel of compressing the area of the force over time.

30. The Bend Angle in Fig. 2.7 has a negative angle shown. Make sure you zero this out before going starting to animate the Bend Modifier. This was only shown for display purposes of the limits, Bend Axis, and checking the angle.
31. Turn on the Animate or Auto Key button.
32. Move to frame 10.
33. Increase the angle to −240.
34. Change the upper limit to 260.
35. Change the lower limit to −11.

FIG 2.8

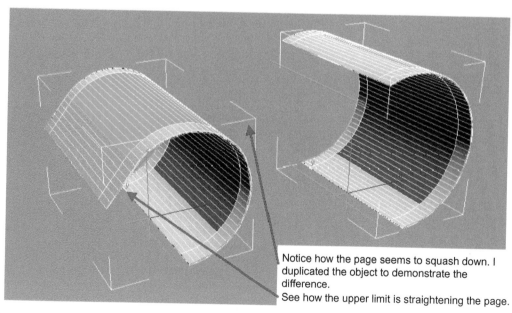

Notice how the page seems to squash down. I duplicated the object to demonstrate the difference.
See how the upper limit is straightening the page.

Your page should look like the image on the left side of Fig. 2.8. Even though the angle and limits are keyed together at the same frame, there is still an overlapping of the motion because the limits are moving in. As we saw in Chapter 1, I mentioned that you want overlapping of actions to create more realistic motion. There are traps to overkeying your work, so this is a nice way to missmatch the timing of the two changes but keep the keys at the same point in time. You will see later in the tutorial when the object is cloned that fewer keys are better.

36. Move to frame 15.
37. Decrease the angle to −200.
38. Change the upper limit to 129.
39. Change the lower limit to −4.

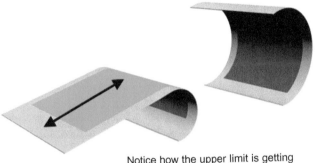

Notice how the upper limit is getting smaller and page is now straight beyond the area of the upper limit.

FIG 2.9

Scrub the timeline back and forth a few times. You will see a bit of a whipping motion start to appear in the bend. As you add more keys, this will accentuate a bit more.

40. Move to frame 20.
41. Set the angle to −180.
42. Set the upper limit to 35.
43. Set the lower limit to 0.

Notice how the page flattens as it reaches frame 40. This is impossible to do without the limits being animated unless you go to a more sophisticated selection of the volume. We will cover that in a later chapter. For now, let's take a look at duplicating the pages and then offset the keys in a more natural fashion. The next few steps will be to create some copies and offset the timing. Pick up a book for a moment and fan the pages. They do not all flutter by evenly over time. Your thumb pressure changes, and there are moments when a page is caught.

44. Go to the front viewport.
45. Turn off the Auto Key and go back to frame 0.

Note

The page is currently 1-unit thick. Before moving on, you could click down in the modifier stack to the box level and make it much thinner. For the purpose of demonstration, I will keep these objects a little thick, so it is easier to see what we are trying to accomplish.

46. Enable the Move Transform, hold the Shift Key and move the book down on the "Y" axis about −2 to −3 units.

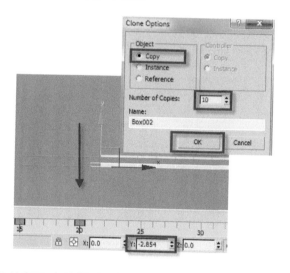

FIG 2.10

Note

You can "eye it" in the viewport or use the status line. You want to have enough distance, so the objects can easily be selected later for adjusting the keys.

47. When the Clone Options Dialog appears, choose Copy and 10 for the Number of Clones.

Note

I'll post a short exercise on the website (www.tradigital3dsmax.com), which I use in my classes for demonstrating and recognizing visually in the modifier stack the differences between the three options. We want to use copies that will duplicate all the current animation, but keep them independent. If you choose Instance or Reference by mistake, the objects will be wired together. Basically if you make changes to one, they all will change to a certain extent. If you did choose Instance for example, merely go into the Modify Panel with it selected and right click the Bend Modifier. When the options appear, choose "Make Unique". This will "un-wire" the objects, and the modifiers will operate independently.

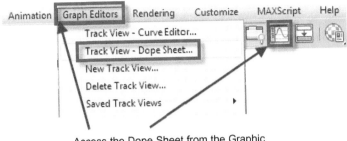

Access the Dope Sheet from the Graphic
Editors Menu or the Icon in the Main Toolbar   FIG 2.11

There are several key points about the defaults that I would like to mention
here. Newer user's to the program often get lost because of some of the
default settings that are very subtle. If you use the ICON to access the Track
View, the default one that appears is the Curve Editor. This version of the Track
View displays the keys and trajectories. The other version, the Dope Sheet,
will show your keyframes as squares or range bars. You will need to use the
MODES Menu in the Curve Editor to switch to the Dope Sheet for this project.
The next thing to be aware of is that only "Selected Objects" appear in the
editors unless you turn this option off in the Display Menu: Filters Dialog in the
Show Only Area. When you created clones with the Shift + Move technique,
only the last object, box10, will show unless you turn off this option or select
all the objects. Look at it, but leave it at the default for now.

48. Drag a Marquee through all of the box objects or hit the "H" Key to use the
Select by Name dialog to select all the objects.
49. Click the Curve Editor icon in the main tool bar or Track View—Dope Sheet
from the Graphic Editors Menu.
50. If you choose the icon to access the Curve Editors, it will default to Curve
Editor. Simply change the Mode from Curve Editor to Dope Sheet.
51. In the Dope Sheet, activate the Edit Ranges Icon. See Fig. 2.12 for the
location.

The goal is to scale and move the ranges of the keyframes to get a more
random animated sequence. Figure 2.12 shows what your animation may look
like after you have scaled some of the ranges longer and shorter. There are a
few rules to follow to get this right:

• Don't move the Top bar directly across from Objects. This will move
everything.
• In this case, the objects are incrementally named in the order they were
created with a negative "Z" offset. Box001 is on the top and Box002 is
directly below it. It follows that no object lower can have its range finish
before the one above it. If it does, it will certainly intersect.
• The length of the range bar determines the speed of the keyframes.
• Any bars that extend beyond the light grey area of the default active time
segment are still there. You will need to enter the Time Configuration to

27

show a longer active segment or hold the CTL + ALT Keys while dragging with the right mouse button to show more time.

- Dragging in the middle of a range bar moves it. When moving a range bar, the cursor will appear as a double arrow. Dragging either end when you see a single arrow scales it.

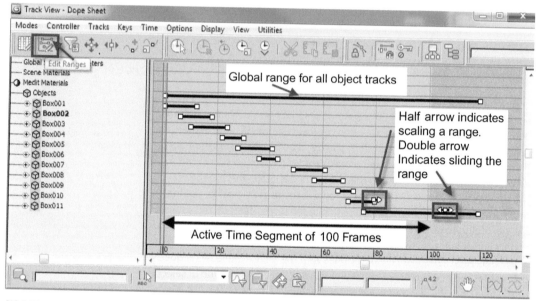

FIG 2.12

Note

The image above already shows the staggered range bars for the animated boxes.

Dragging in the middle of a bar moves it. Dragging on either end scales the sets of keys up or down. Basically evenly spread the animation over time.

52. Enable range bars.
53. Use the zoom extents to bring up all the frames.
54. Adjust and move the range bars.
55. Close the dialog when you are finished and play the animation.

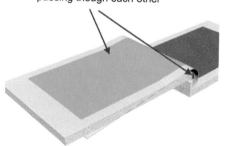

Objects are intersecting and passing though each other

FIG 2.13

Noticed anything funny? The objects are intersecting and dipping through each other as they bend. This is not a big deal to fix and will give us an opportunity to utilize a useful feature near the play buttons. The Key Toggle mode will switch the next and previous frame playback buttons to the next key icons. This will let us snap between previously created keys to make adjustments to existing ones without creating additional keys. Too many keys in close proximity can lead to a lot of overexaggerated motion. Not a bad thing when you want to add exaggeration, unfortunately it causes problems when you least expect it.

56. Turn on the Key Toggle mode.
57. Select the second box and then click the Next Key icon until you see which key is the culprit. Verify that it is not intersecting the first box.
58. Repeat step 57 until you turn on the animate button back, select BOX02, and try to adjust the setting, so the second page does not intersect the first.
59. Notice how the Next Frame button changes to a Next Key button.

Note

This is helpful in letting you toggle to previously created keys to change them without adding new keys by accident.

60. Toggle to the last key on Box02. I changed my upper limit to about 42 or 43.
61. Repeat this for all the following pages.

As we explore timing and motion through this book, I want you to start developing a sense of the inherent inexactness of how living things move and react in the world. Typically, the rule is that living things move on curves, while mechanical devices tend to be more linear. Think of your software as a very precise mechanical device, except when it crashes of course.

62. Create a camera and position it similar to the placement in Fig. 2.1.

It doesn't have to be exact, just try and get a nice close-up of the book while clipping at least one of the edges. Look for a strong diagonal through your composition. Also try adding a few other objects. At this stage of the game, I want you to just practice creating and maneuvering your camera for right now. Most of the books out there don't focus on the camera work until the last few chapters. You may be wearing several hats including that of cinematographer. Do a search on the Internet for rules of 3rds, composition, and photography as a starting point if you have never taken a course in photography. It takes a while to develop the fine art of viewer immersion in a scene. You may even want to pull your favorite DVD off the rack and look at the making of the movie including the directors' point of view.

63. Go to the Tools Menu, choose Grab Viewport, and drag across to Create Animated Sequence File.

This file is a temporary movie file created in the C:\Users\login_name\
Documents\3dsMax\previews folder. There is also a command for renaming
these temporary files (overwritten every time you make a new preview) in the
same Tools\Grab Viewport Drag across area. To save time before rendering, we
will often make previews from the different cameras in the scene and use a
compositing program to slice these together. To get a feel for how the camera
is working with capturing the action in a scene, it makes sense to take a step
back and preview your work to check the flow.

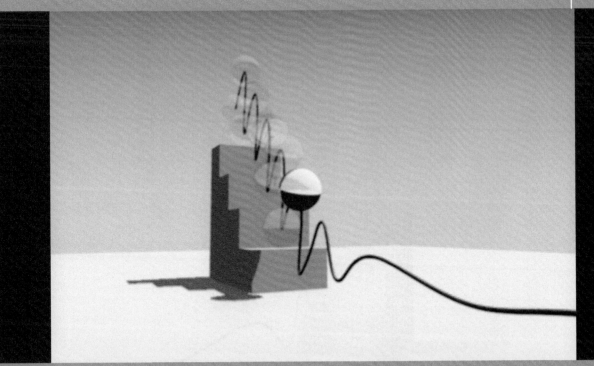

CHAPTER 3

How Do Living Objects Really Move?

Richard Lapidus

Rule: Weight in motion

Rule: Timing

After Completing This Chapter, You Will be Able To:

- Set keys with the right tangent type.
- Learn how to locate and identify the location of key frame information.
- Use the Key Info of a keyframe to adjust the position of an object.
- Use the Curve Editor to access curves.
- Use the Parameter Curve Out-of-Range Types to create repetitive motion.
- View and adjust the timing of an object's motion.

Living objects move on curves and have a certain definable rhythm. When a line goes flat, it either represents calmness and tranquility or that the subject is dead. This chapter will explore a variety of timing factors that will

FIG 3.1

enhance the realism of motion. Some of those factors are affected by weight, acceleration, deceleration, and exaggerated movement. One of the basic exercises in learning the timing of traditional animation is getting a ball to bounce and then trying to give it some life. Following up with the controls we explored in the first chapter, you will be introduced to a few more concepts for managing the interface and the basic functionality of starting to animate. Although this is a very basic tutorial at face value, the ability to "see" animation in terms of how it is stored in 3ds MAX is invaluable. I have developed this tutorial in the past few years based on responses from my students using a 3d program for the very first time. It is essential that you are able to "see" how animation is stored and why things work the way they do. There are more sophisticated ways to rig or script a ball bouncing, but this chapter will give you a good basis for controlling your work.

We are going to start with building a set of steps to for the ball to bounce down. This will introduce you to the Grid and Snap settings as well as some basic navigation controls. This book is primarily based on the creation and adjustment of animation, but I did want to throw in some modeling here and there. Start with a new 3ds MAX file and make sure your Units Setup is at the default of Generic Units. This can be accessed in the Customize Menu. Most of the tutorials will be using Generic Units throughout the book.

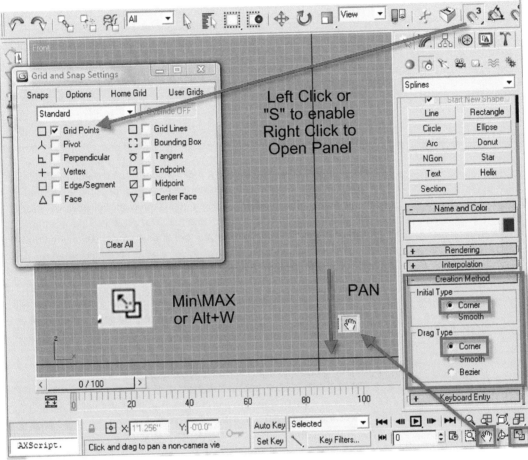

FIG 3.2

Refer to Fig. 3.2 for steps 1–9.

1. Maximize front viewport (Min\Max or ALT + W).
2. Use the Pan Tool and move the construction planes down and to the right.
3. Go to the Create Shapes Panel, choose line.
4. Enable Corner for the Initial and Drag Types.

I love using paths to control moving objects through space. We could also very easily create the motion path for the ball from spline objects in addition to using them to create 3d objects. In fact, that's what we will be doing in

33

the next chapter. There is a distinctive correlation between modeling and animation relative to the complexity used. The rule of thumb typically is that less is more. Fewer keys when animating and less complexity when modeling will impact the success of your projects. This hopefully will increase your chances of creating smoother animation with better rendering times. You can always change the parameters later on, but it makes sense to always think ahead 10–15 steps. The corner option you are selecting will cause straight interpolation in and out of the vertex with every click. Many new users will also click and drag the mouse when setting vertices that allows the user to change the way that the vertex controls the surrounding segment. The drag type will be set to Corner as well just in case you have a "heavy hand" to start with when creating vertices.

Note

Take a moment to open the Interpolation Rollout. The default number of steps is set to 6. Try to keep this number as low as possible unless you notice too many polygons being created in your work. For now, leave it at the default, but make a mental note that it is here. If you like, set the number to 0, which will drop the number of polygons created when the extrude modifier is added. Because no complexity is needed along the flat surfaces of the steps, you may want to reduce it and get into the habit of removing the complexity where it is not needed. You can always go back with an edit poly modifier for example and cut into more polygons. We will be back here several times throughout the book, and it is a key concept to learn.

5. Turn on Snaps and right click the Snap button.
6. Make sure you are snapping to grids.
7. Click from the 0,0,0 position and create a step that is 100 units tall and 100 units wide. (The lighter gray lines are 100 units apart.)
8. Do this four times.

Keyboard shortcut: Use the "I" key to pan the view as you draw.

9. Finish the line by adding one more vertex at the lower left corner of the steps and the last one back at the first vertex created. You will be prompted to close the spline.
10. Click Yes then right click to end the Create Line command.

Note

The Right Click command turns off the create mode. This is an essential skill that I mentioned in Chapter 1. If you don't right click or choose one of the transforms, you are still in the create mode for the last object you were creating.

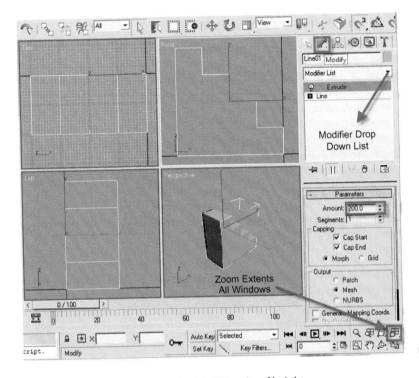

FIG 3.3

11. Add an extrude modifier with 130–200 units of height.
12. Hit Zoom Extents All icon in viewport controls

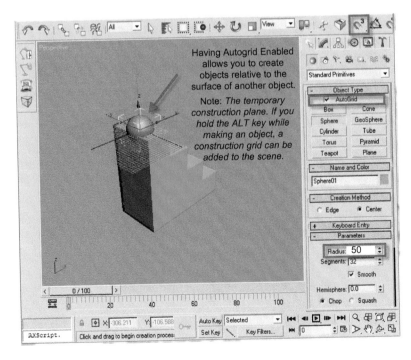

FIG 3.4

13. Go to Create Geometry, select Sphere, and enable Autogrid.

The Autogrid is a great feature for allowing you to snap the pivot of the object being created to the face normal of the object that your cursor is near. You will see the "Z" axis of the new objects pivot pointing 90 degrees from the face. We will talk about the orientations of axes later in the linking and constraint exercises. Aligning in the creation mode will save you a lot of time in trying to move and position objects after you have created them. It is important to note at this point that the sphere is probably one of the only objects that have a pivot set dead center. This makes sense in case you want to create something like a planet or a ball which pivots about the center without having to change it in the Hierarchy Panel. Later on when we look at the trajectory of the ball bouncing down the step, you will see that the trajectory is set in the center and not at the base. There is a work around for that later on in the chapter.

Note

Face normal and axis are two primary components of any 3d program. In 3d MAX, you are always working "X-Y" relative to view, and the "Z" axis is pointed away from the current construction plane. You could repeat that 10 times and still not get it unless you look at the world coordinates in the lower left corners of the viewports. When an object is created in any other orthographic view other than Top or the Perspective, the "Z" axis is pointed straight at you. When you go to move the object, the axis is relative to world again unless you change the pivot coordinate system back to Local to the object. This is not really that important unless you are going to be constraining the object or using it a hierarchy link system. This will be covered in a later chapter when we set up a simple character rig. I have a separate tutorial that covers these basic concepts of the coordinates system and cloning, which will be posted on the web.

14. Turn off Snaps. (Click the Snap button or hit the "S" key on your keyboard.)
15. Create a sphere on the top stair with a radius of about 50.

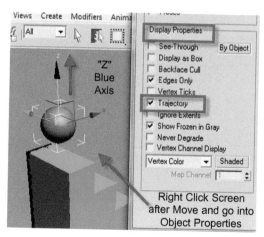

FIG 3.5

36

16. Move it up on the "Z" axis.
17. Right click the screen with the sphere still selected and turn on trajectory in the objects properties.
18. Enable the front viewport and bring it full screen.

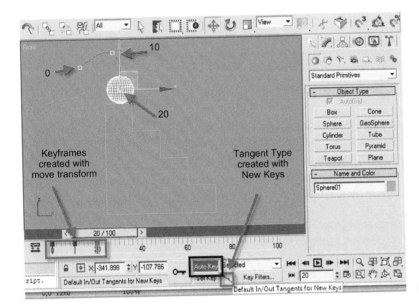

Keyframes created with move transform

Tangent Type created with New Keys

FIG 3.6

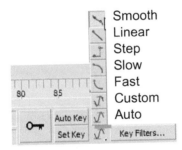

Smooth
Linear
Step
Slow
Fast
Custom
Auto

Tangent Types
for Keyframes

FIG 3.6a

The goal is to create just three keys and then have the software perform repetitions of these keys to bounce down to the floor. You could select the keys and shift move them in the timeline to create copies, but that gets very laborious and hard to control when you start working in longer animation segments. We are going to use the computer to do what it does best—repetitive functions. For this, we will be using the Param Out-of-Range Repeats. This may be your first introduction into controllers, which are very powerful tools in a 3d program. There is a trap to use here, but I will show you how to turn it off and then do some forward animation work. Typically I would use this on an object that spins forever, has a constant motion, or has a way of controlling the speed of some transformations.

19. Change tangent types of keys to smooth. See Fig. 3.6A for a listing of the tangent types in the flyout.

The smooth tangent type will give us a little bit of bend moving into and out of the keyframes. You may notice that the white dots along the tangent of the trajectory that represent the frames in between the keyframes are bunched together a little more as they get closer to each keyframe. This can be exaggerated with other tangent types as well.

Note

By setting the tangent type before you create keyframes, any new keys will interpolate the transition between keyframes using that control. Of course, you will want to experiment with these, and they can always be changed later on in Graphic Editors, Mini-Curve Editor, or key info dialog boxes. Only one of these which I rarely use is the Step Tangent Type. Step will maintain an object property until it reaches the time of another keyframe and will then change to it on that frame. Take a look at the second hand on a clock, it will seem to stay in position and then snap to the next second.

20. Turn on Auto Key.
21. Move the ball up in the air and behind the steps. Make sure you are at frame 0 when you do this. See Fig. 3.6 for the approximate position of the three keys that you will be creating.
22. Got to frame 10 and move the ball up and to the right.
23. Got to frame 20 and move it down onto the first step.

Take a moment to imagine the balls trajectory repeating four more times downward to hit the floor. Unless the offset from the third key to the first key is exact, repeating the keys will result in the ball not hitting the steps or going through them. You will see this in the next step when we turn on the Param Out-of-Range Repeat.

24. Go to the Graphic Editors Menu and open the Trackview; Curve Editor. If you use the icon in the Main Toolbar, that will be the default of the two editors.

FIG 3.7

25. Pan the list of objects until you see the ball that has all three move transforms highlighted in yellow. See Fig. 3.8. By default, any selected object with an animated transform like move will show as selected in yellow.
26. Make sure you expand and highlight all three of the X, Y, and Z Position Tracks.

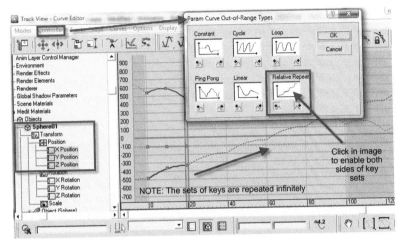

FIG 3.8

27. Go to the Controller Menu and choose Param Out-of-Range Types.
28. Click Relative Repeat graph. Hit OK to exit Dialog and show marquee continued curves.

Notice how the balls trajectory continues into and out of the three set of keys. There are two parts to the repeats represented by the arrows below the small curve diagrams. Those buttons as shown in Fig. 3.8 represent the area before and after a set of keys. By default the Constant is on for both sides of a set of keys. By clicking the diagram image, you are setting both to the same "in and out" type. Let's say you wanted an object to sit in position for a number of frames before moving and then repeating. You would leave Constant on for the left side and choose a different type for the outside. Of course, you would not want a key at frame 0.

29. Turn off Auto Key.
30. Minimize this editor and go to frame 100.

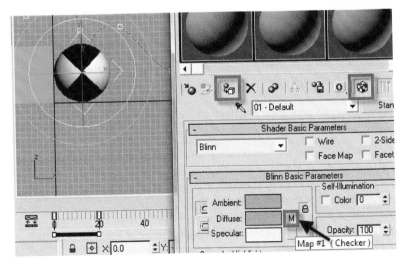

FIG 3.9

31. Hit "M" to open the Material Editor. Go to modes and change to Compact, so it looks like the image in Fig. 3.9.
32. Click the None button for the diffuse map channel. (Fig. 3.9 shows a checker map already assigned.)
33. When the Map Browser appears, choose checker as the map type.
34. Drag the Material onto the ball or use the Assign to select icon. Turn on and show in viewport as well.

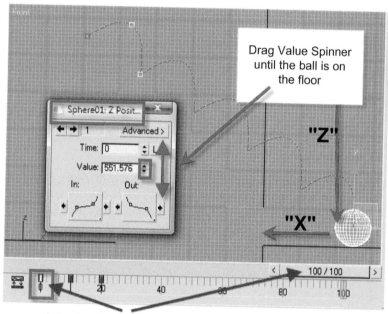

Drag Value Spinner until the ball is on the floor

Adjusting the keyframe of a prior point in time allows you to see the effect of the repeat in the future.

FIG 3.10

Scrub the timeline a few times and notice how the ball misses the steps. The trajectory is on but is no help in visualizing the ball hitting the steps because it is located in the center of the object. Make sure you return to frame 100 before proceeding to the next step. We are going to control the position in the future by adjusting the first key. As you will find in exploring the program in more depth, there are dozens of controls accessible through the right mouse button. The one we will explore next will allow you to access a keyframes numeric value and tangency type.

35. Left click the key at frame 0 to select it. (Selected keys turn white.)
36. Now right click the white key at frame 0 and choose "sphere01 Z position".
37. Adjust the key value spinner until the ball is on the ground at frame 100. Close this Key Properties Dialog.
38. Right click the red key at frame 0 and choose "Sphere01 X Position".
39. Adjust the key value slider until the ball is in front of last step. Close this Key Properties Dialog.

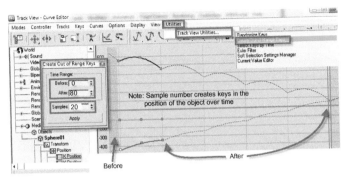

FIG 3.11

In the next few steps, we are going back into the Curve Editor to "bake" some keys in for the range of frames after your hand-keyed animation. If you spin your middle mouse button over the graphic curve of the Editors Dialog, you may notice that the balls trajectory continues on forever. Actually you can't see this in the main viewport because only 100 frames are currently active. A ball bouncing down steps would normally continue bouncing across the floor but not through it. Then again ... there was this time I was playing with a bowling ball at home upstairs ... that's another story for another day. After "baking" in keys where the repeat is working, we will turn off the Param Type and hand key the rest of the animation. This will give you a good opportunity to experiment with the different key tangent types.

40. Go back to the Utilities Menu and drag out to Track View Utilities\Choose Out of Range Tangents. Note the image above.
41. Pick Create Out of Range Keys from the menu.
42. Put 0 in Before, 80 in After, and 20 in Samples. Click Apply.

There are 100 keys in the animation so far with 20 taken up for with the hand keying of the first 20 frames. By adding 20 samples after, you are defining the curves of the "baked" trajectory with 20 keys. See the baked trajectory in Fig. 3.12. Take a moment to experiment with different values if you like. You can undo this operation with a CTL + Z and redo steps 40–42. If the values are too high or low, the motion will be choppy.

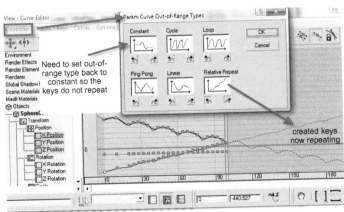

FIG 3.12

43. Go back to Controllers and change the Out-of-Range types back to Constant.
44. Close the Curve Editor.

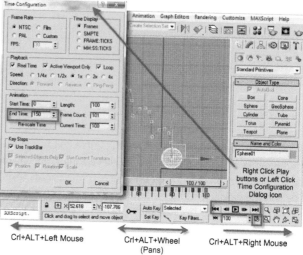

FIG 3.13

Crl+ALT+Left Mouse   Crl+ALT+Wheel (Pans)   Crl+ALT+Right Mouse

There are two basics ways to increase the active time segment, so that your animation will be longer than the default 100 frames. Access the Time Configuration Panel by right clicking the play buttons or left clicking the Time Configuration Dialog icon. My preferred method is simply to hold the CTL + ALT keys and drag the right mouse button until the desired amount of frames is active. Figure 3.13 shows panning and increasing the negative values as well.

Note

If you do show active negative frame values, make sure you do not render them as a single frame to compile later. They will not increment before frame 0, but show as a dash value amount. All work to be rendered should be with positive value keys.

45. Right click any play button to enter Time Configuration.
46. Increase the number of frames to 150.
47. Move the time slider to frame 150.
48. Turn on the Auto Key.
49. Go to Frame 150.

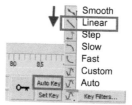

FIG 3.14

Tangent Types for Keyframes

50. Change the Key Tangent to linear and move the ball across the screen. Notice how the ball dips below the floor and note the trajectory curve.

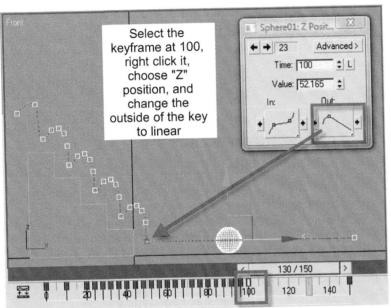

Select the keyframe at 100, right click it, choose "Z" position, and change the outside of the key to linear

Note: The Key Info Dialog shows that you can have different tangent types on the in and out sides of the keyframes. The black arrows on the sides will copy the selected tangent type to the next keyframe.

FIG 3.15

51. Select the key at frame 100. Right click the key, choose "Z" position and change just the outside of the key to Linear.

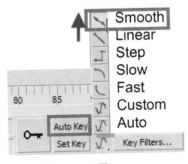

Smooth
Linear
Step
Slow
Fast
Custom
Auto

Tangent Types
for Keyframes

FIG 3.16

52. Now set the Default Tangent for new keys back to Smooth Curve.

Right click the Time Slider at frme 120
and frame 140. Create just position keys.

FIG 3.17

53. Move every 20 frames between 100 and 150 and right click time slider, creating just Position Keys.
54. Go to frames between the right-clicked keys and move up slightly on the "Z".
55. Go to frame 20. Rotate the sphere. Go to Mini-Curve Editor or track view and give the rotation transform track a relative repeat-out-of range.

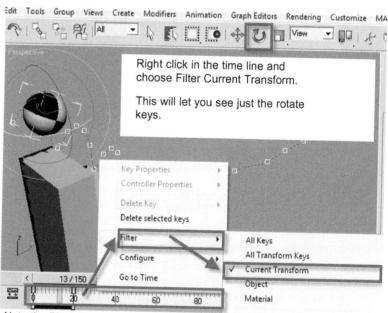

Right click in the time line and
choose Filter Current Transform.

This will let you see just the rotate
keys.

FIG 3.18

Note the Black Range Bar at the bottom of the timeline. Access showing it
with the Configure Command like the Filter\ Show Keyframe type selection

56. Right click the timeline. Choose Filter and then choose Current Transform. This will let you see only the two Rotation Keys.

Play the animation. If the rotation is too fast, move the second key to the right. If it is too slow, move it to the left.

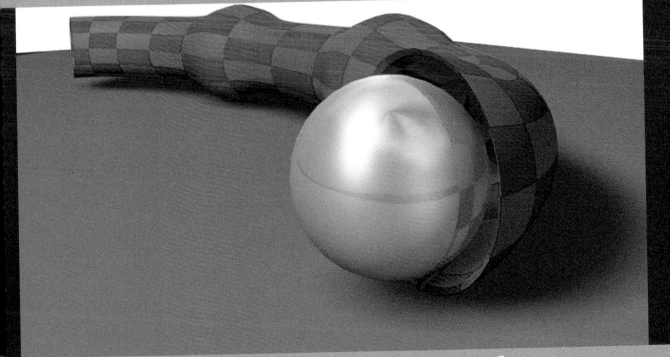

CHAPTER 4

Deforming Objects Based on Motion and Relative to Other Objects

Richard Lapidus

Rule: Weight in motion

Rule: Timing

- Use World Space Modifiers and space warps.
- Link and bind to space warps.
- Create secondary motion using noise.
- Use path deformation.

When getting one object to interact with another, there are a variety of really basic tools that can be utilized to understand how the program works before using the more advanced features of the program. Many times, if you are

FIG 4.1

not using the right axis, a pivot is off, or a single button is not enabled, the results may appear less than desirable. I call this the *"it's always one button"* problem. During the teaching process of a project, I try to get feedback from students relative to what they see happen on the screen and the myriad of possible adjustments that could be made relative to what they know about how things are built and animated. In the early stages of learning this program, they are typically so overwhelmed by the number of buttons and parameters that they forget to reference how things really are in the real world. Animators typically will study motion through interaction, observation, or using some type of media. In the early years of 3d animation, it was not uncommon to use the photography of Eadweard Muybridge. Lately, the motion is captured with 3d suits, high speed cameras, or via video. This, of course, is a starting point. Once we start to imagine how something should act, the next step is to make it believable within the reality of its scene. That might entail exaggerating the motion or overlap of a variety of motions. With a study of motion, the animator must examine how things are built, ranges of motion, and the timing associated with the way real things move. Once we begin to understand that, then one of the goals is to show the intent. We will start by getting a tube to swallow a sphere. The first reference for developing this technique came from watching my son's pet boa constrictor and then an exploration of the ways that the swallowing effect has been exaggerated. In the movies, we have seen at one point in time a character being swallowed by another. In the cartoons, I can remember one eating a stick of dynamite and watching the resulting explosion. Sometimes the character survives it and reacts to the action. In this tutorial, we will explore the exaggerated motion and timing of a large object moving through a small space. That can be a tricky thing to do with straightforward keying of transforms.

Our goal is to get a moving object to go through a curved tube and have it displace the tube as it moves through it. In addition, we will look at a few ways to make adjustments to the keyframes so that we can exaggerate the motion a bit. The tools we will be using are linking, path constraints, binding to space warps, and a look at the difference between World Space Modifiers and Local Modifiers. So as not to build a reference manual at the start of this chapter explaining all those interesting new words above, I'll give you the explanation as they are used.

FIG 4.2

The Create Panel has 7 basic types of objects. The drop down gives you more sub-categories of each type. We will ues the basic ones here to start.

1. Make sure your unit setup under the Customize Menu is set to Generic Units.
2. Activate the top viewport and create a sphere with radius of 20 from the Standard Primitives portion of the Create Panel.
3. Create a tube with 15 and 18 radius and 300–425 height. Also increase the height segments to 45–50 and the number of sides to 30–35.

The variation of these numbers is to give more or less complexity to the tube, which will be deformed by a space warp moving through it. As I will demonstrate in later steps, the complexity can be changed or even animated if you like.

4. Create an ellipse of about 150 units in length and 350 in width from shape types.
5. Switch to the perspective view and click the name of the Smoothing type in the upper corner of the viewport so the Edge Faces mode can be enabled. The keyboard shortcut is F4.
6. Create a Displace Space Warp from space warps types (looks like a wavy icon). Drag out a small rectangle anywhere in the perspective view and right click to turn off Create mode.

Space warps include a wide range of helper objects that represent some type of force emitter or deflector. These are nonrenderable objects used to control a wide variety of parameters relative to the control you want over objects and particle systems. In Fig. 4.3, there are several things I want you to note that will

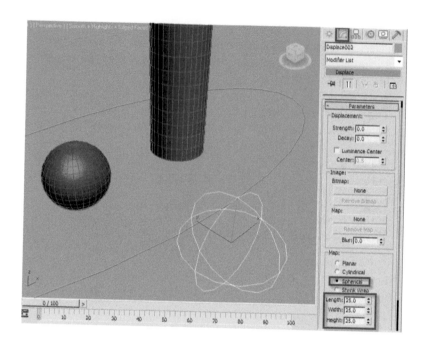

FIG 4.3

affect the success of at least starting to use these in your scene. The first is the Strength and Decay values. By default, they are set to 0. Many new users to this program make the mistake of adding something like a modifier or space warp and then fail to adjust the valves. If something isn't working, select the object and review it in the Modify Panel. Think of yourself as an auto mechanic going through a number of steps testing out the parts. Another noteworthy feature here is the ability to add bitmaps or maps in the Images section of the parameters. I've used this a lot to bulge, displace, or make subtle deformations to surfaces with maps to get scene objects looking more real world and less mechanically precise.

7. In the Modify Panel, change the type of gizmo from planar to spherical and give it dimensions of 25 x 25 x 25 so it is larger than the sphere.

By using even numbers, the dimensional size of the warp is even along all three axes into space. It will also project a force out into 3d space forever unless we control it. If you were to make one dimension longer, you might use that to emulate the effect of the swallowed object becoming squeezed and elongated. The outside radius of the tube is 18 units and the sphere is 20 units. We want to visually see the warp as it moves through the tube so that it is easier to recognize when it is\isn't affecting the tube. In later steps, we will control how far that force affects the tube when it is bound to the warp. Essentially, the size of the gizmo typically does not matter. It emits from the center and the extent is only important if you are using it to hit and react with another object.

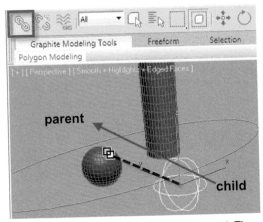

When linking, drag from the child to the parent. The cursor image will change to the one shown when you have a link-able object.

FIG 4.4

8. Using the Link Tool, drag from the edge of the Displace Space Warp to the sphere. This will link the Displace Warp to the sphere.
9. Choose the Select Tool or the Move Transform to turn off linking.

When the sphere is moved through the tube, it will pull the Displace Space Warp with it. You will notice as you dragged from the warp to the sphere, there was a dotted marquee line. This represents that a parent\child relationship was being created. Linking is a common process used in most animation processes involving a complex moving structure. If you hit the "H" Key on your keyboard, the Dialog that appears will show the Displace Warp is indented under the sphere. The warp will now be inheriting any transform for the sphere. As the sphere moves along a path in the next few steps, it will pull the warp with it.

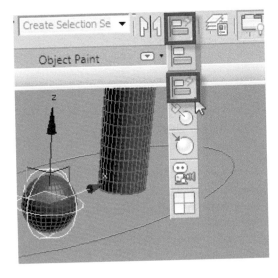

FIG 4.5

10. Quick align it to the sphere.

Note

You should acquaint yourself with the basic navigation of the interface and take some time to memorize the icons. This takes a little time, but I will copy extra images throughout the book of the most common ones for newer users.

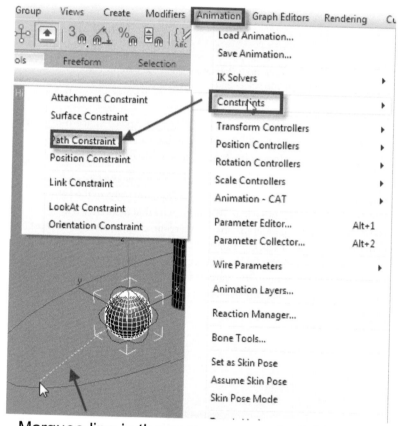

Marquee line is the same as seen in linking, binding to warps, and wiring.

FIG 4.6

11. Select the sphere and from the Animation Menu give it a path constraint.
12. When you move the mouse, a marquee line will appear that seems to be attached to the sphere.
13. Click on the ellipse to set it as the spheres path. The Motion Panel will automatically be active.

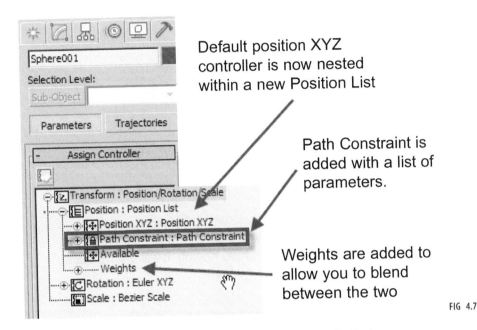

Default position XYZ controller is now nested within a new Position List

Path Constraint is added with a list of parameters.

Weights are added to allow you to blend between the two

FIG 4.7

Take a moment to examine the Assign Controller Frame within the Motion Panel. All objects by default have different kinds of controllers added to the three transforms that may be changed at any time. If you ever add the wrong kind of controller, simply select the track, hit the Assign Controller button and replace it with one of the defaults. The Move Transform is shown as Position and has a Position XYZ controller as the default. By giving you three separate tracks, individual vectors can be animated or controlled individually. For example, you might want to add a little up and down bounce to your object as it moves through the scene. You could add Position List to the "Z" position track, put a noise float on the "Z" axis, and then blend the two. Even though you are giving up hand control of moving the sphere on a path, it is not entirely stuck there.

14. Change the path percent to −35 (negative). This will move the sphere to the middle portion of the front of the ellipse.

You may now notice that there are now two red squares on the timeline at frames 0 and 100. This represents 0% and 100% of the path. The sphere is on the far right side of the ellipse and will move counter clockwise around if you play the animation. The position or move transform is now controlled by a percentage of the ellipses path. The sphere can still be rotated and scaled, but not moved without some adjustment to the controllers.

If the path percent is changed in the Motion Panel with the Auto Key off, the percentages offset to still use 100% of the path. If an adjustment is made with the Auto Key enabled, a new key will be created. We will do this later on to simulate the tube swallowing the sphere.

51

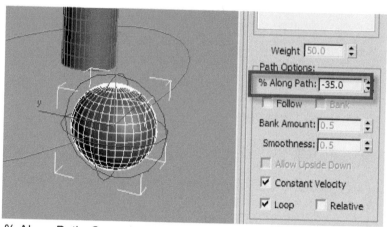

% Along Path: Controls where along the path the object would be. If adjusted with Auto Key off, it will always equal 100% and move through it once

Follow: Makes the object turn with path

Constant Velocity: Ignores vertex number and step value relative to number of keyframes

Loop: If % path is increased to 200, it will go around twice

FIG 4.8

15. Select the tube and go to the Modify Panel.
16. From the Modifier Drop Down List, add a Path Deform (WSM) from the World Space Modifiers Category.

World Space Modifier: This WSM Path Deform is not the same as the regular Path Deform Modifier. WSM Modifiers allow an object to be modified by another object in space that is not a space warp. We will see later on that when the tube is bound to the Displace Space Warp, it looks the same in the modifier stack. Both can be deleted here, but objects are bound to warp with the Bind to Space Warp button in the Main toolbar.

17. Notice that the Path shows <None>. Click the Pick Path button and left click on the ellipse.
18. Hit the Move to Path button. If the object does not fit around the ellipse with "Z" axis … try the "X" axis or "Y" axis as needed.

Most of the time, the "Z" axis will be the right axis unless you created the object with an orientation that did not have that axis pointed up relative to the world. In this case, the tube was created in the perspective view that has the "Z" running up from the construction plane. The "Z" axis pointed perpendicular through the object. This may not always be the case, so it does need to be checked occasionally.

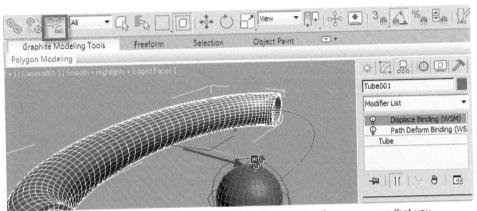

Bind to Space Warps works just like linking. Drag the object to the space warp that you want it to effect. Notice that the Path Deform Bindng and the Displace Space Warp both appear in the Modifier Stack. To remove the effect, delete them from the stack.

FIG 4.9

19. Click the Bind to Space Warp button (next to unlink) and drag to the space warp. Choose the Select Tool once again to turn off Bind to Warp.

20. Move to frame 50 or 70 so the ball is in the tube.

21. Hit the "H" Key on your keyboard to bring up the Select by Name Dialog. Choose the space warp and then go to the Modify Panel. Notice that the strength is set to 0; this is a default that has no effect. Slowly increase the strength by dragging on the spinner (double arrows) until the tube starts to bulge.

Notice that if you go too far the inside surface may push through the outside surface. You will also see that the ends of the tube are bulging off the path. To control the effect of the bulge out into space, you will need to turn on and use the Decay. Depending on where you are in the program, this term can be interchanged with fall-off. They are basically the same. It lets you control how far out into space the effect will go.

Hint

If you put too much of a value on a spinner, just right click it to zero it out.

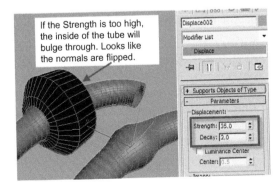

If the Strength is too high, the inside of the tube will bulge through. Looks like the normals are flipped.

FIG 4.10

53

22. Turn on the Decay and slowly move the value up. For the image in Fig. 4.10, an extra tube is displaced on the left with values too high. The one on the right uses 35 Strength and 2 Decay.
23. Play the animation.

Is this motion or animation? Disney defined the term of animation as to bring the illusion of life into a character. The ball is moving and the tube is bulging as it goes through it. Neither is alive and I don't get the feeling that this is not a purely mechanical motion and adjustment. Thinking about the snake for example, it grabs the meal, usually bigger than the opening of the mouth and then slowly works it in. After sometime, it needs to move it through the beginning of the digestive track to a place … well … let's not go into too much detail about that process. If you want the animation to appear to gulp, select the sphere, turn on the Auto Key and move to a frame where the ball is inside the tube. I will show you the fine art of adding the "gain some ground and lose some ground" keying process to show that there is some force at work to get this tube to eat the sphere. If you think about the two original path percent keys, those are the start and end of the path being used. Essentially, the sphere is being pulled into another position. If we think about this as a big rubber band, what would happen if we set another position where the sphere is in the tube and then set another key a few frames later with a lesser path percent value than the previous key? The sphere will move into the tube and then back up a bit before being pulled farther along.

24. Drag the time slider so the sphere is just inside the "mouth" of the tube.
25. Select the sphere, and turn on the Auto Key.
26. Go to the Motion Panel and click the path percent spinner up one click and then down one click.

Notice how the spinner now is bracketed with red corners. This indicates that a parameter has animation keys. Any numeric value in the program can virtually be interpolated. Think about it for a moment … color is numeric, so the colors, opacity, and a variety of other material attributes may also be animated.

27. Drag the time slider 5–10 frames farther in time.
28. Now drag the path percent spinner down until the ball is back outside the tube.
29. Play the animation.
30. Add about two to three more sets of keys and then save your project.

It appears that the sphere is moving into the tube and then coming back out before going farther into the tube. You get the idea now! Move through time and repeat this process. The goal is to have the sphere seem to get stuck and move at different rates of speed through the tube. For some secondary animation, you could also try animating the decay and strength of the Displace Space Warp. Let's look at another way of seeing the motion, adjusting the keys, and even adding some random motion to the bulging of the tube as the sphere moves through it.

31. Make sure that the Displace Space Warp is selected and open the Mini-Curve Editor. It is located at the lower left corner of the interface. See Fig. 4.11. I typically will use the Track View Curve Editors instead of the smaller one because we have dual monitors in our classrooms and it is easy to move to the side. The Mini-Editor allows for quick access but does require some amount of panning once open.

The Curve Editor is where every parameter of the program can be displayed and adjusted. Think of it as the master control panel for your whole 3d world. Everything is accessible from the number of sides of an object to the maps and mapping coordinates on it. It is accessible in a few ways. With an object selected, you can right click the screen and the Quad Menu will appear with access to the Curve Editor. There is also an icon in your Main toolbar that looks like a graph. It is also located in the Graphic Editors Menu.

32. Since the Displace Space Warp is selected, it should be the only object to appear in the list on the right.
33. Hit the "+" next to the object name to expand the tree and see all of the object parameters.
34. Select the Strength parameter and then Assign Controller from the Controller Menu.
35. A list of controllers will display. Select Noise Float.

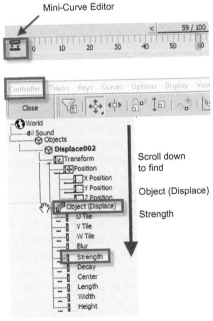

Mini-Curve Editor

Scroll down to find

Object (Displace)

Strength

Control may be assigned to the parameters via the Min-Curve Editors or Graphic Editors These won't show in the Motion Panel.

FIG 4.11

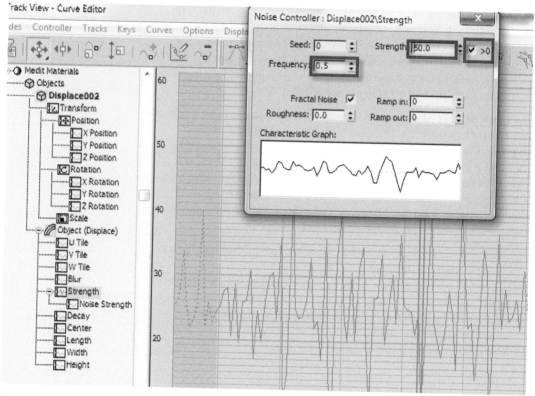

FIG 4.12

36. The Noise Float Controller Dialog will appear.
37. Check the button next to >0.
38. Increase the Strength to 50 and set the Frequency to 0.5.
39. Close the Dialog when you are done.

The controller will put a wave on the values of force, but we need to control it a bit. The strength of the Displace Warp was previously set to about 35. We want the side of the tube to be undulating so an amount greater than 35 should be apparent, but we don't want too much. Somewhere around 50 should give us a distortion that is apparent. Using the greater than zero (>0) control will keep the values from going negative, which would show the ball through the tube. Looking at the graph of the values, you will see the strength is jumping around, but still falling low enough for the ball to show. Before fixing that, let us examine a few more parameters. The frequency will control the amount of repetition of the noise. As a side note, you will see this repeats in forever. The wave doesn't stop and fit within the time frame. That can be controlled. Ramp in and out, which we are not using, will decrease or fall off the wave of the noise much like the Decay did for the space warp. Useful, but it won't help here. We will need to bake the keys and move some of the values around.

Move   Scale

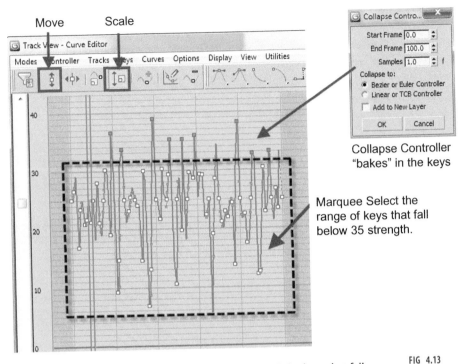

Collapse Controller "bakes" in the keys

Marquee Select the range of keys that fall below 35 strength.

FIG 4.13

40. In the Curve Editor, make a Marquee selection of all the keys that fall below the original bulge level you selected in your project.
41. Use the Scale Key to squeeze these together vertically.
42. Move the keys so the bottom range is 35.

When played back, the numbers will cycle through in the Modifier Panel and you should see some nice bounce to the sides of the tube. If the sphere pokes through anywhere or you see the faces of the tube appearing inverted, simply scrub to that frame in time and move the key down in the graph. The double blue vertical lines as seen in Fig. 4.13 show your current frame.

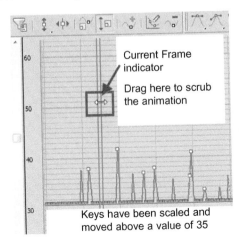

Current Frame indicator

Drag here to scrub the animation

Keys have been scaled and moved above a value of 35

FIG 4.14

If you look at the timeline, it becomes evident that there are a substantial number of keys created by "baking" in the keys from this controller. Sometimes it is hard to see when the Graphic Editor is zoomed out. Let's go and reduce some keys.

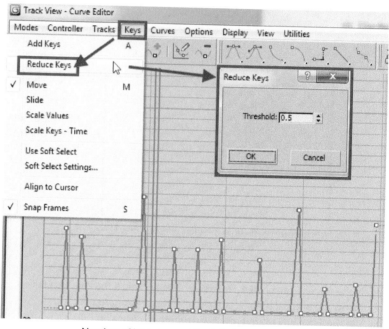

FIG 4.15

Number of keys has subtantially been reduced.

43. Choose Reduce Keys from the Keys Menu. Leave the default threshold at 0.5 and hit OK. You will notice in the timeline that there are fewer keys now down around the 35 value for the strength. Save your work. You may also want to select some of the keys at the top and adjust the tangent values in case the change from the highest value to the lowest is a little too steep.

CHAPTER 5

Chapter Image by George Berlin

Straightforward Animation with a Bones IK Rig

Richard Lapidus

Rule: Straight ahead action and pose to pose

Rule: Exaggeration

After Completing This Chapter, You Will be Able To:

- Create bones.
- Set up solvers to control a rig.
- Link and animate dummy objects.
- Create motion relative to weight and timing.

There are a number of different ways to put together a rig that can be used for animated characters. You can build it by hand, or use a system like biped or CAT that does a lot of the ground work for you. Before getting into one of the systems, I think we need to take a look at working with very simple IK (Inverse Kinematics) rigs to give you a basic understanding of the functionality in working with a controlled structure. There are some very sophisticated ways to maneuver an IK rig, but unless you have a firm grounding in how it works, you will run into problems down the road. For success in creating a character animation, you will need to learn the basic rules of any system you use, as well as to develop an understanding of how you want it to move. We are going to take a look at creating a simple rig with bones, linking these chains together and setting up some constraints to get these to work together. In the first few chapters, we've taken a look into creating keyframes at the object and modifier level. By now, you should have a good understanding of how to selectively control and manipulate keyframes. We'll now take a look at how this works with the more complex motion of a walking character for example. Although used in characters, IK rigs can also be applied to mechanical setups like robot arms and machinery.

This chapter introduces the basic components of an IK rig. To create the illusion that your rig works can walk, for example, you will have to link the bones so that they will move together and also constrain them so they move the way you want them to. In an IK structure that walks on two legs, the hips are typically the parent with the legs branching out from this parent to the feet. We can inversely maneuver the shin and the thigh by moving the feet, but then need to control the motion of the hips from the top down as well. A walk essentially is the interaction of a switch of two pivotal actions. The leg swings at the hips and then when the foot is planted on the ground, the pivoting is in reverse.

Although most character animation is done pose-to-pose, a good starting point is to start to learn about the motion of a walk by creating straight ahead animation by getting a simple rig to walk. In this case, we will set up the rig and test out a few steps. There are more sophisticated rigs you could create, but that will not be covered within this text.

The first step is to create a leg structure starting with the top of the hip. I always like to use the construction planes for placement and alignment of elements when creating a rig. In later chapters, we will also use the construction planes for alignment and check the symmetry of a biped with a character mesh for skinning. The construction planes are easy to see in the viewport and work as a good frame of reference.

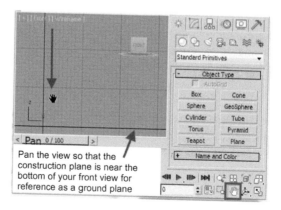

Pan the view so that the construction plane is near the bottom of your front view for reference as a ground plane

FIG 5.1

60

1. Activate the front viewport.
2. Pan the screen so the construction plane is near the bottom of the viewport. See Fig. 5.1.

FIG 5.2

3. Select Systems in the Create Panel and select Bones (Fig. 5.2).

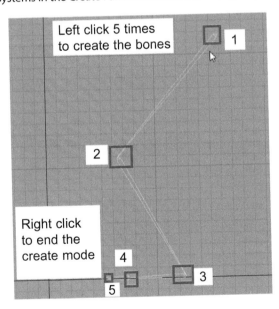

FIG 5.3

4. Start the leg bone by left clicking where you would expect the hip joint to be.
5. Move the cursor down and to the left, and click to create the thigh. Move down to the right and click to create the shin. Move the cursor and click twice more to create the foot and toe bones. Right click to end bone creation. You will see a small bone created at the end of the toe (Fig. 5.3).

61

The length of the bones does not have to exactly match the image in Fig. 5.3. We can edit these later on using the Animation Menu\Bones Tools Command. It is important that you click all the way through the bones you want to create in the chain, otherwise you will need to link the bones together. By default, it will link them together as created. The small nubs at the end of IK chains are for two purposes: one as the end effector and the other as an extra link at the end of the toe bone. When you create a bone, the pivot for it is at the top of the bone. Later on when we add an IK Solver to these chains to assist us in constraining and animating them, you will see that the number of bones is important.

6. Take a moment to rename the thigh bone as rig01_rt_thigh. We will rename the rest of bones in the schematic view after both set of legs are created. I will use this type of naming convention using an underline instead of spaces in case I want to export this to a game engine or work with another animator. Naming is important and you should get into the habit of assigning everything a name.

7. Switch to the left view and notice how the leg has been created centered on the construction plane that was perpendicular to the front view. We will use this as the center line in the rig. Later on when we do skinning, you will see the usefulness of the construction planes for symmetry.

Starting point for marquee selection

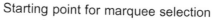
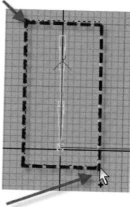

End point for marquee selection

FIG 5.4

8. Enable the Select and Move Tool and drag a marquee around the leg. See Fig. 5.4.

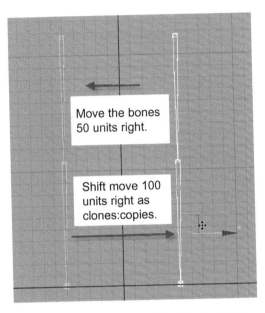

Move the bones 50 units right.

Shift move 100 units right as clones:copies.

FIG 5.5

9. Move the bones to the right along the "X" axis in the left viewport. (Note the offset. You will move the clone double the amount in the other direction so both are lined up on the axis.) I moved about 50 units.
10. Using the Shift Key, move them once more to the left this time. This allows you to have the two leg bone sets offset from the "X" construction plane.

Note

I used a negative 100 on the second move.

11. When the Dialog appears, choose the Clone Option: Copy.

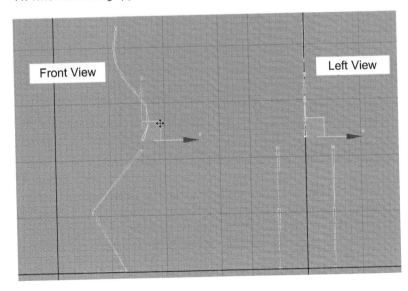

Front View

Left View

FIG 5.6

12. In the front viewport, create a backbone for your character rigging. Start the bone for the base of the spine behind the legs. You do not want to click too close to one of the leg bones because it may attach. Create about five to seven bones. Right click to end the new chain. See Fig. 5.6.
13. Select the base of the spine and rename it as rig01_spine01.
14. Move the spine01 closer to the legs as in Fig. 5.6. As you move the parent in the chain, rig01_spine01, the rest of the chain moves with it. NOTE: The more you create the better the flexibility that can be built into the back. When you right click, the node at the top of the head will be created. Use the picture below as a guide.
15. Create a camera in the top viewport and then change the perspective viewport.
16. Use the keyboard shortcut of "C" to view through that new camera.
17. Orbit the camera view so that you get a good view of the leg structure.

Note

I click to place the camera and drag to place the target. This way, when I orbit the camera, the bones will always be in the center of the view.

IK (Inverse Kinematic) HI Solvers

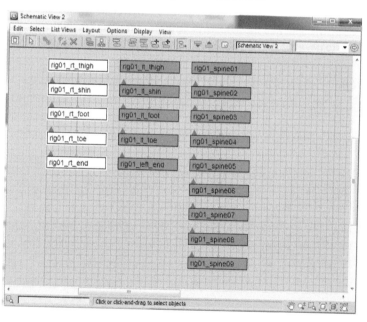

FIG 5.7

18. Open the schematic view from the Graphic Editors Menu and note which icon activates in the Main toolbar.
19. Select all the bones, right click and go into the Object Properties. Turn on Renderable. By default this is off, but I like to render it out occasionally as I work to make notes.

20. Rename the bones in the schematic view as per Fig. 5.7. Assigning the names will make it easier when you get into more complex applications with rigs.
21. After you have named the objects, select the entire right leg in the schematic view and then open the Bone Tools from the Animation Menu.

The Bone Tools will allow us to fix any problems with the chain, color it, and even add fins for depth. Having thicker bones often helps when adding skin to a custom bone setup like this. I like to also color the side of the structure similar to the green and blue coloring scheme with a biped.

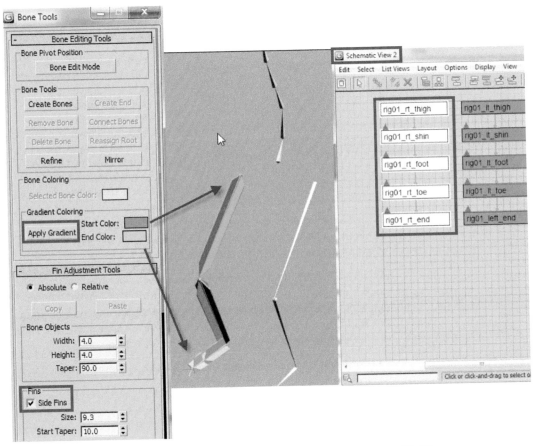

FIG 5.8

22. Change the color of the start and end of the right leg with a variation of green and hit the Apply Gradient Color. Typically, you might want green for the right and blue for the left side.
23. Enable the Side, Front, and Back of the fins and adjust these to add a little depth.

24. Repeat for the other side.

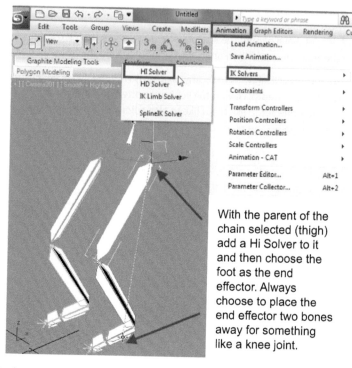

With the parent of the chain selected (thigh) add a Hi Solver to it and then choose the foot as the end effector. Always choose to place the end effector two bones away for something like a knee joint.

FIG 5.9

25. In the camera viewport, select one of the thigh bones.
26. From the Animation Menu, drag down and out to IK Solvers and HI Solver.
27. Move the cursor to the *foot bone* and click it.

As you are moving the cursor, a marquee line appears between the top of the thigh bone and the cursor. When you are done, two white lines will appear: one running through the bones showing the connection and the other from the start to end of the control. An end effector will also appear where the heel should be. This is used for animating the middle of a chain.

28. Do an edit hold before moving the end effector and testing the motion of the leg.

Hint

If you do not let go of the left mouse button and right click, the movement will be negated.

The IK chains need to be two bones as a part because the pivot of each bone is at the top of the object. To have the knee flexing when moving the thigh and shin, the end effector of the chain needs to be at the foot.

29. Select the "rig01_lt_foot" and give it an IK Solver as well, rigging it to the object at the end of the leg called "rig01_left_end".

30. Repeat this for the right leg and also for the spine. You may want to go four to five bones away from "rig01_spine01".
31. Save your work. I'll save a copy of this file and call it ch5_hi_solver.max.

Creating Dummy Helpers

The next step will be to create several dummy objects to work in two different capacities. The first is to create a large dummy between the hips to work as the root or main parent of all the bone chains. It will be located between the top of the thigh bones where the hips would be. The others will be located where the end effectors are. The end effectors need to be animated but are sometimes difficult to select and move based upon their scale. The end effectors will be linked to a dummy for better control.

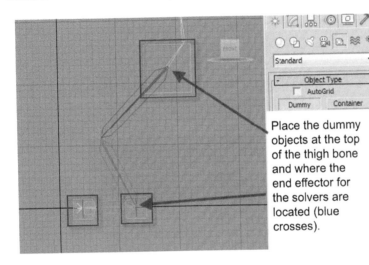

Place the dummy objects at the top of the thigh bone and where the end effector for the solvers are located (blue crosses).

FIG 5.10

32. Activate the front viewport.
33. Go to Helpers Section of the Create Panel.
34. Click and drag three dummy helpers at the locations indicated in the picture.

Note

The hip dummy appears to be centered on the top of the hip bone and the other two on the end effectors (blue crosses).

35. Rename these objects in the Modify Panel as follows:
    hip_dummy
    lt_heel_dummy
    lt_toe_dummy
36. Activate the left viewport.
37. Hit the "H" Key to bring up the Select by Name Dialog Box.
38. Select the two dummies called lt_heel_dummy, lt_toe_dummy.

39. Move these two dummy objects in line with the left leg that should be on the right side.

Note

Make sure you restrict the movement to just the "X" axis. This is done by click and dragging the red arrow head.

40. Hold the Shift Key and move a clone to the center of the leg on the left.
41. A Clone Dialog Box will appear. Make sure Copy is enabled and rename the copied dummy object to rt_heel_dummy, rt_toe_dummy.
42. Save the file as chpt5_hi_solver_place.
43. Go back to the Modify Panel and rename the other dummy.

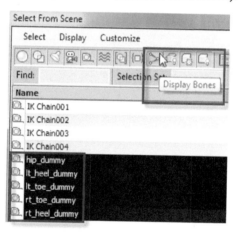

FIG 5.11

44. Hit the "H" Key and select all the dummy objects. You can filter out the bone objects as shown in Fig. 5.11 by turning on the filter. Remember to turn this back on later.
45. Go into the Hierarchy Panel.

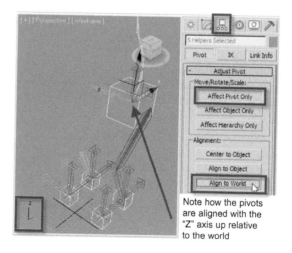

Note how the pivots are aligned with the "Z" axis up relative to the world

FIG 5.12

46. Turn on Affect Pivot.
47. Click Align to world.
48. Turn off the Affect Pivot Only button when finished.
49. Save the file as chpt5_hi_solver_place_dummy01.

Note

We want to align the pivots like this so that the "Z" axis is pointed up relative to the world. When the HI Solvers are linked to the dummy objects later on, they will take on the orientation of the parent. If you forget this step, there is a swivel angle for the solvers that can be rotated at 90° angle. I just like to plan ahead so that there are no unexpected shifts of my objects. The three axes again are colored red, green, and blue. The direction of the vector is X, Y, and Z.

Linking Objects

The next step will be to link all of these objects together. Linking is useful because it makes the job of animating easier. Instead of having to transform the objects separately, we can just move the top or bottom of a chain. For example, right now the first bone you created to build the spine is the "parent" in the chain, and each bone below it is already linked as children. If we move it, the rest of the children in the chain will move with it. Let's see what the chain looks like and then do some linking.

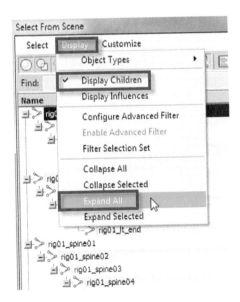

FIG 5.13

50. Hit the "H" Key and bring up Select by Name Dialog.
51. In the Display Menu, turn on Display Children and Expand All.

Note

rig01_rt_thigh is at the far left and each bone below it is indented one space. If we renamed the bones in the leg, it would read something like the picture in Fig.5.13. Take time to rename the objects relative to Fig 5.9 if you haven't already. You can also load the file, chpt5_hi_solver_place_dummy01, to save some time. I just wanted you to see the fully expanded chains at this point so that if you wanted to select by name later on while linking, the object would appear as needed.

Link the end effectors of each chain to the closest dummy object.

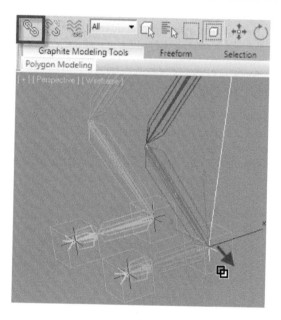

FIG 5.14

52. Zoom in on the left foot area. Select the end effectors of the IK chain (blue cross).
53. Activate the Link button.
54. Click on the end effectors and drag to the edge of the dummy. This will Link the end effectors to their respective dummies.

Note

As you drag from the child to the parent object (IK chain to dummy), the cursor will change to the double square icon as seen in Fig. 5.14. If the choice is valid, the lower square will show in white. If you have problems dragging and selecting the right object, use the "H" Key method. Select the child, enable link, and then hit the "H" Key to select the parent by name. Objects can only have one parent, so if you do choose the wrong one, you can unlink or link to a different parent. Remember we link child to parent.

55. Repeat this linking process for all the HI Solvers to the toe and foot dummy objects.
56. Save the file as chpt5_hi_solver_linked.max.

Link the two thigh bones and the base of the spine to the hip dummy

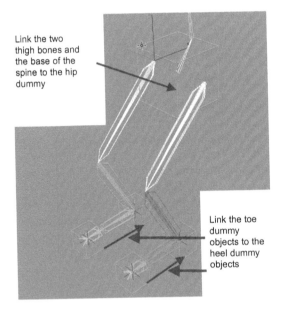

Link the toe dummy objects to the heel dummy objects

FIG 5.15

57. Do an Edit\Hold also and then test moving the dummy objects around. If you don't let go of the left mouse button and right click at the same time, your operation will be canceled. If the objects get moved too much while testing, just do an Edit\Fetch.
58. Link the top of the three bone chains to the hip_dummy as well. Those should be named rig01_lt_thigh, rig01_rt_thigh, rig01_spine01.
59. Link the toe dummy objects to their respective foot dummy objects.
60. Turn off Link.
61. This is a good time to do an incremental file save.
62. Save it as chpt5_hi_solver_linked_all.max.
63. Using Select and Move Tool, move the left heal dummy back and forth on the "X" axis.

Note

Notice how the hip dummy stays in place. That is the end of the IK chain.

Note

The foot moves with the heel. In an IK chain, the end effector is used to move the chain inversely of the hierarchy linkage. In forward kinematics, we would rotate the thigh, then the shin, and finally the foot. In IK, the end of the chain pulls the parents above.

If the linking is correct, the hips when moved will pull the bottom of the spine and the tops of the hips. If you move it really far, you will see the end effectors trying to stick in place.

Undo if you moved it around too much to get back to the original pose.

Adding Position Controllers to Move the Main Hip Dummy

The final step will be to get the main parent (hip dummy) to move and adjust based upon the position of the feet. Traditional forward kinematic techniques required the animator to move the main parent and then adjust the position of the end effectors several times. The illusion of a realistic walk cycle was typically ruined by what is known as "SLIDING FEET". This means that if the feet did not stay put as the main parent moved forward, the feet would appear to slide backward. By using some new controllers to average the position of the main parent "hip_dummy" between the two heel dummies, the hips will pull the top of the legs with it. All we have to do is animate the heels.

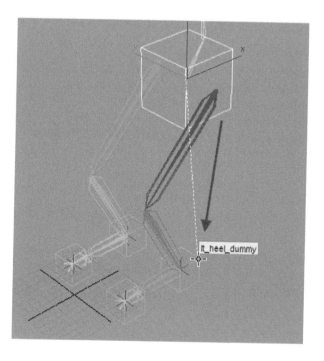

FIG 5.16

64. Select the dummy called hip_dummy. Go to the top menu bar and select: ANIMATION MENU\CONSTRAINTS\POSITION CONSTRAINTS

Note

You could also go to the Motion Panel, open the Assign Controller Panel, and assign a controller to the Position Transform. This is a shortcut.

65. A marquee line will appear attached from the center of the hip_dummy. Move the mouse over the lt_heel_dummy and click on the edge of it.

Note

In wire frame mode, you must click on the edges of objects, not the center of a face.

66. The position of the hip_dummy will be relocated to be centered on the lt_heel_dummy. This is normal. We are controlling the position of this object based upon another.

You will notice that the Motion Panel is now active in the Command Panel. All controls for the constraints you added and may want add in the future are adjusted here.

When a Position Constraint is added, the object will move to the position of the constraining object until you turn on "Keep Initial Offset" which is all the way at the bottom of the panel.

Note: Although we aren't using it here in this example, there are now two layers which can be used for keying or assigning control to other objects.

These of course can switched between by animating the "weight" of the layers. This concept will be explored in chapter 16. If the wrong constraint is added, you can simply enter the Assign Controller panel and replace the errant controller.

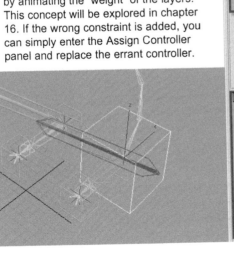

FIG 5.17

73

67. Pan the panel until you find the Position Constraint area.
68. Click on the Keep Initial Offset Toggle.

Result

hip_dummy returns to its initial position.

---

69. Click on the Add Position Target button.
70. Click on the other heel dummy object called rt_heel_dummy.
71. Turn off the Add Position Target.

Note

There is a column in the panel marked WEIGHT. Each Position Target has 50% weighting so they equally affect the position of the DUM HIP. This can be adjusted and animated over time. Think of how a character dragging a foot might lunge forward and catch itself falling in a walk. In a mechanical object, this might be a robot's arm laboring to move into or out of a position with a heavy object.

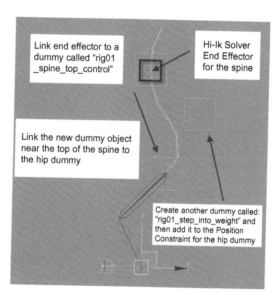

FIG 5.18

72. Create another hi-ik solver for the spine from the root to around the 7th bone.

You will have to add a dummy near the end of the spine where the shoulders would be. We will also repeat the step of linking the end effector to the dummy and then link the dummy to the hip_dummy.

73. Create two new dummy objects in the front viewport as per Fig 5.18. Call these two dummy objects: rig01_spine_top_control and rig01_step_into_weight.
74. Position both dummy objects as per Fig 5.18 and then align the pivots to the world as you did previously in the Hierarchy Panel.

The spine top control will control the near end of the spine chain while the Step to Weight dummy will allow you to have more flexibility in "throwing the weight around" for the whole rig based upon extra movement of the hip dummy. A position constraint could be used on the spine control dummy, but spine tends to move more than the hips. The hips will move the entire spine, yet you will have freedom to animate the top of the chain as you like. Before proceeding to the next step, think about moving the pivot of that spine dummy lower to mid spine or even at the hips. Instead of creating position keys for this dummy, you could create rotation keys which would appear to move on wider swinging arcs. Just a thought.

75. Link the end effector for the spine chain to the dummy near the top of the spine that you called: rig01_spine_top_control.
76. Now link that dummy to the hip dummy.
77. Turn off the linking operation by choosing the select tool. Now re-select the hip dummy and go back to the Motion Panel.
78. Left click the Add Position Target button and then left click on the new dummy for repositioning that you called: rig01_step_into_weight.
79. Turn off the Add Position Target button.
80. Save your work again at this point. Call it chpt5_rigged.
81. Turn on the Animate button, move the Time Slider 10–20 frames and move the heel dummies.
82. Create a few steps.
83. The hip dummy should be at its highest point when one leg is planted and the other is in transition between lifting and planting down. The step weight dummy will allow you to lift the hips up and force it down as you animate the steps.

Hints

You may need to create keys for a foot that needs to stay in place while the other leg is moving by right clicking on the Time Slider button.

CHAPTER 6

Using Ragdoll with Biped

Richard Lapidus

After Completing This Chapter, You Will be Able To:

- Create a shortcut to enable Ragdoll script and set up restrictions on Ragdoll character or biped.
- Animate a biped and use layers to control the exaggerated motion of a fall.
- Control the geometry for mass and simulation.
- Create and save your own custom animated .bip files for mixing.

At some point in time, most of us learn that a person can't fly without wings, and if you fall very hard, something is bound to break. Notice that I skipped the part about using powered vehicles to land you directly with the consequences. Having grown up in the outback wilderness, which is now commonly known as modern Suburbia America, we had a firm belief that gravity could be avoided with the right set of tools or circumstances. It's in our culture for little kids to believe in magic and all the possibilities of a little pixie dust or a magic wand. With the right tools, the effects of that invisible force, which keeps us from soaring in the air, may be counteracted. In my case,

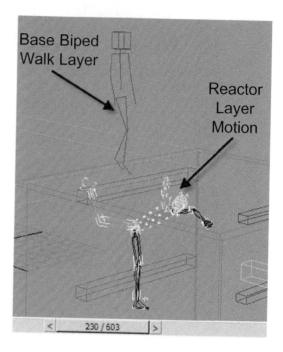

Base Biped
Walk Layer

Reactor
Layer
Motion

230 / 603

FIG 6.1

it was the "Acme Rocket" and the "Bat Utility Belt" which were to blame ... on separate occasions of course.

Yes, unfortunately things do tend to break because of gravity. Actually, there is something else missing. There is a unique state of animation that is necessary to give meaning to a set of actions and reactions. The time when we let the audience know that something is going to happen and get their attention is known as anticipation. After grabbing a viewer's attention, they either have to believe in a theory or agree that it is plausible. Anyone who wants to argue that point can try to rationalize how millions of viewers can believe in the possibility of Death Star with a killer laser beam like the one in Star Wars. With the right amount of planning, and inclusion of details, anything is possible ... right?

Take the case of new software upgrades or plug-ins as being a potential trap. We forget the lessons of our childhood, but also the belief that things don't have to happen in a certain way. All we really need to have is that perfect tool or magical element to make things happen the way we want them to. As a professional working in the field of animation, we tend to be enticed by that shiny new upgrade without paying attention to fact that it's not the plane that flies, but the pilot! The plane moves but is controlled by a living being. It's just a tool, but we have to have something extraordinary kicking around in the back of our minds that we want to create, not the magical combination of controls. We need to let our imaginations run free again.

With a series of commands in the Motion Panel, you can easily create a walk cycle with a biped. This motion will appear a little stiff and inflexible at first.

Not to worry, bipeds have a built-in Layer feature that allows you to build on the base layer motion. We will be using the Rag Doll Utility to constrain the biped so it can be acted on by gravity with the Havok Physics Engine. Normally, bipeds resist anything but sticking to their own footsteps when in Footstep mode. This can be a little problematic when trying to add additional motion, which would require positioning and rotating the structure in unusual positions. This is where layering will be very handy. Think of this chapter as an introduction to creating different parts of an animation.

In the next chapter, we will explore adding a subtle, but necessary detail by layering the motions as separate clips. Instead of having the character fall right down the shaft, a little bit of exaggeration will be added to bring this motion into the realm of animation. I have always liked the cartoon character that can float in mid-air until he realizes his situation. Then the fall comes. Action and reaction without a little anticipation is not only too abrupt but also defies good traditional animation technique. In the next chapter, we will explore in more depth how to control layers, mix, and adjust the timing of these motions to make the scene more believable as an animation piece. When you start to think about capturing what is going to happen and the effects of these movements, something magical will occur. You will be moving out of the realm of simple motion and into that glorious state called animation. Your audience will be drawn in and start to believe.

1. Open the file called "Falling_down_old_shaft.max".
2. Make sure your unit set up is set to US Standard Feet with fractional inches. (This is located in the Customize Menu under Unit Set Up.)
3. Go to Systems and create a biped. Make sure the height is around 5'7" so your project will have similar dimensions as we progress.

In the Biped Rollout, there are four basic icons. The first icon looks like a person and the second a pair of footsteps. We will be using both of these and explore the others later on. Figure mode allows us to change the structure of the character and also set a default position for the starting point of an animation segment. It is also used for setting a pose for skinning a character.

Bipeds are fully rigged systems that allow us to control the movement of two-legged characters in a variety of methods. For our purposes, we are going to use the footstep method in this chapter to immerse you in the process and then refine it in later chapters. Keep in mind that our goal is to utilize just two distinctive motions at this point in time: walking and falling. (Something many of us with two left feet have mastered to the nth degree.) Neither one of these sets of motions can be created with a click or two and look realistic. A good base layer of programming is provided that will simulate the proper positioning of a character but falls short of true animation. Some layering will be added to give a pause in the middle of the sequence, but we will look at layering in more detail in the next chapter. For now, be amazed at the marvel of a programmed walk cycle.

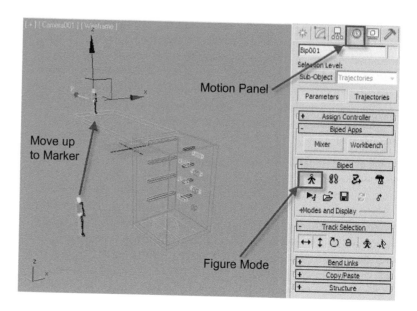

Motion Panel

Move up to Marker

Figure Mode

FIG 6.2

4. Go to the Motion Panel and enable the Figure mode.
5. Move the biped relative to the "X" marker on the second floor box object.
6. Move the biped up so that it is standing just a little above the object called second floor.
7. Turn off Figure mode when you have it in position.

You will only need a small space so that the program does not view the feet and floor object as interpenetrating. There is an "X" spot showing you a good place to start positioning it. Normally, the position of the feet tangent to another surface is not a concern. Bipeds are built from the ground up relative to the construction plane and always oriented along the world axis "Z" space. Try creating one in the front or left view. The program will not allow you to build it starting sideways. That's one of the features of the "system". As you play around with this a little more, you may notice that the feet always want to stay parallel to the ground. This can be annoying, which is why we will be using Ragdoll and reactor to create the free fall in this chapter.

There are a number of great scripts built into 3ds MAX that can be accessed to basically help the animator in quickly performing a series of recorded commands. This can be a real timesaver. If you have ever played around with a biped before, you know that there is no built-in restriction on the joints. Arms, legs, and even heads can all be made to do a 360 spin. Although this seems like a funny move depending on how you rotate the parts, it typically will give you undesirable or unbelievable results. In the next step, we will create a custom toolbar with a command to automatically set up all the constraints on your biped at one time. This could take you 30–45 minutes to add a constraint to each joint and set the proper limits.

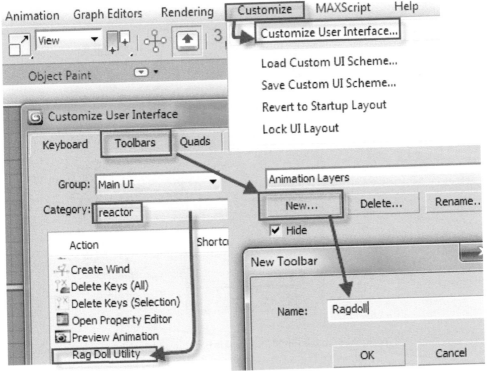

FIG 6.3

8. Go to the Customize Menu and choose Customize User Interface.
9. Enable the Toolbars Tab and click New to create a new toolbar.
10. Call the toolbar Ragdoll.
11. In the Keyboard Tab, Choose Reactor from the All Commands Category, and then drag the Rag Doll Utility into the new toolbar.

Note

There are also Rag Doll Constraints in the Reactor Category and the Reactor Toolbar. These are for creating individual constraints.

12. Click the new utility and the Ragdoll Script will launch.

The script you just ran will create a new floating panel for you to make a selection and apply constraints to all of the biped objects automatically. Any bipeds already in the scene will display in the Humanoids Selection Window. The program looks for biped objects and will list Biped01 in the Dialog.

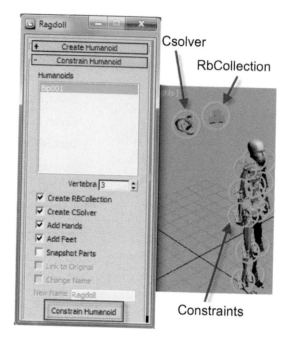

Csolver

RbCollection

Constraints

FIG 6.4

13. Make sure the Bip001 has a blue background and then click the Constrain Humanoid button at the bottom of the floating panel.
14. Close the Ragdoll Dialog.
15. Hit the F9 Key and render the front view.

Note

This will create constraints automatically on the joints, which are part of a CSolver and RBCollection. There are now gizmos aligned to every joint of the biped, and two larger ones floating off to the side slightly. Although you can see them in the viewports, they are nonrenderable helpers. The larger gizmos are special helper objects called collections. To have the reactor physics engine control the falling and interaction of the biped, objects in the scene must be part of a collection. This is how 3ds MAX parses out the scene object to be calculated in the Havok Physics Engine.

16. Select the rigid body collection and go to the Modify Panel.
17. Click the Add button.
18. A Select Rigid Bodies List Dialog appears.
19. In the Select Menu of this dialog, enable Select Children or do a CTL+C.
20. Using the Control Key, select the following objects: plane001 object, shaft, 2nd floor, and boxes, which are linked to the shaft into the rigid body collection.
21. Click the Select button at the lower left corner of the Dialog.

Note

The plane001 object is a reactor helper, which I already located in the bottom of the shaft. You may want to rename it so that if you add a geometric plane to your scene, you don't confuse the two.

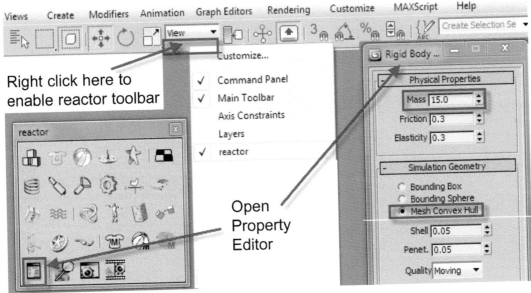

FIG 6.5

22. Hit the "H" Key to select by name and choose all the biped parts.
23. Open the Reactor Toolbar and choose Object Properties. Increase the weight of the object to 15 and set the Simulation Geometry to Mesh Convex Hull.

If you skipped the chapter on Rigid Bodies setup, right click the Main Toolbar below one of the name selection drop downs and click Reactor to show the Reactor Toolbar. After you have set the weight for all of them, leave the Dialog open so another selection of these objects can be made heavier. I like to give all the objects a base weight to start because they will not move with a mass of zero in a reaction.

24. Hit the "H" Key again.
25. Go to the Select Menu and disable Select Children.
26. Click the BIP001 object to select it.
27. Go to the Display Menu and Expand All.
28. Choose just the pelvis, legs, and spine objects.
29. In the object properties dialog, give these objects a weight of 50.

83

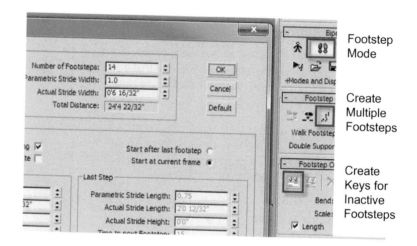

Footstep Mode

Create Multiple Footsteps

Create Keys for Inactive Footsteps

FIG 6.6

30. Select the Bip01 object and go back to the Motion Panel.
31. Turn off the Figure mode and turn on Footstep mode.
32. Under the Footstep Creation Rollout, enable Create Multiple Footsteps.
33. Enter 14–16 footsteps and click okay. If your biped is not 5'7", you will need a larger or smaller number.

Note

Don't worry about all the extra buttons and numbers in the Create Multiple Footsteps Dialog. This is a parametrically programmed system to control the speed and distance a character can walk based upon the height. Your numbers will appear slightly different from the one shown in Fig. 6.6 based upon the height of your character. Since there is no need at this time to increase or decrease the speed of the movement, leave the numbers as they are. If you want to experiment with them, do and edit hold first. You can create some rather painful looking limbo walks by exaggerating some of these parameters.

34. Look at your character's footsteps before you activate them. They should all appear "white" meaning that the footsteps are selected.
35. If there are not enough steps to have the last few hanging in mid-air above the shaft, do a CTL+Z to undo the last create command and then increase\ decrease the number of footsteps. If you have extras, that is okay.
36. Make sure you are at frame 0 before doing the next step. Footsteps will be activated at the frame you are on.
37. In Footstep Operations Rollout, click the Create Keys for Inactive Steps button.

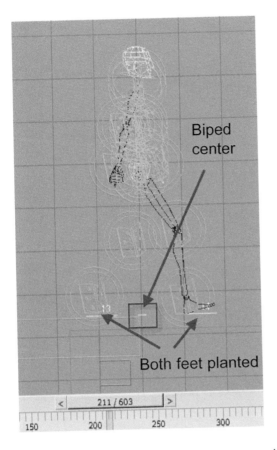

Biped center

Both feet planted

211 / 603

150   200   250   300

FIG 6.7

38. Enable the left viewport and scrub the timeline. Make a mental note when the last two footsteps are hanging in the air over the shaft.

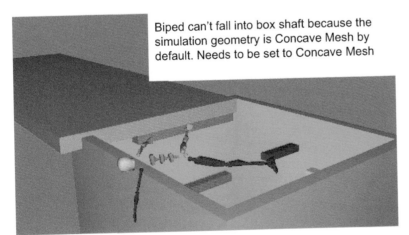

Biped can't fall into box shaft because the simulation geometry is Concave Mesh by default. Needs to be set to Concave Mesh

FIG 6.8

39. Hold the CTL+ALT Keys and then drag on the timeline while holding the right mouse button to increase the active segment by about another 200–300 frames.
40. Go to the Display Panel and in the Hide by Category Panel, check on helpers. This will hide all of the constraints while we set up and check the simulation.
41. Go to the Utilities Panel and activate the Reactor Panel command.

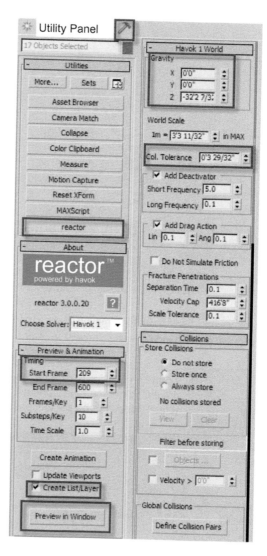

FIG 6.9

42. Open the Preview & Animation Rollout.
43. Set the start time in the Reactor Panel to around the time that you want to create the start of the free fall into the well. I used a start frame of 209. Your start frame may be different based upon how many steps it takes your biped

to get over the shaft and do some viewing of what is\isn't below its feet. Make sure that Create List/Layer is active below the Create Animation button. You will want to have the falling motion added to the bipeds in a unique layer. This layer is like the last one you created for the look around, but is created by the program animating the Ragdoll constraints during the fall.

44. Do a File\Save and incrementally save your file. Also do an Edit Menu\hold at this time. Created keys can't be easily undone.
45. Click Preview in Window.
46. When the reactor Real-Time Preview window appears, hit "P" to play and "R" to reset.
47. We have a problem … the biped does not fall down the well. The beams may also not be falling either.

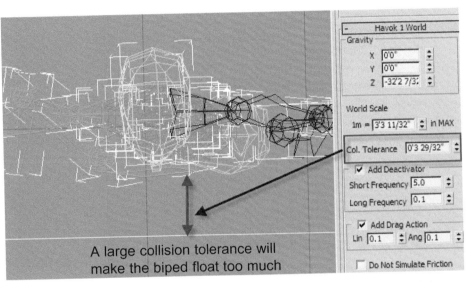

A large collision tolerance will make the biped float too much

FIG 6.10

48. Select the shaft object.
49. Go to the Object Properties Dialog and check the Simulation Geometry Panel.
50. It is set to Mesh Convex Hull. This object is more like a bucket or a cave. Change it to be a Concave Mesh. Enable Unyielding so it will not move.
51. Select all the beam objects and give them a weight of 60. Set these to an Inactive State in the Object Properties as well. This will keep them from being affected by gravity until another object hits them or comes within the range of the collision tolerance.
52. Open the Havok 1 World Panel and check the value for the Col. Tolerance.
53. Bring the value down to less than an inch. If your tolerance is too high, the biped will float up off the second floor before falling and will never really hit the bottom of the shaft.
54. Click the Create Animation button.
55. Scrub the timeline and notice that the base walking motion becomes apparent as a red-stick figure.

The movement of a free fall now appears for the biped after the time you set up for the start of the simulation. Left of the top of the shaft is a red-stick figure in mid-step. This motion can be saved out as a separate file and blended whenever you like.

56. Select any of the biped parts and go into the Motion Panel.
57. Open the Layers Rollout.
58. There will be a new layer created called "Reactor Layer #1" as the current active layer. Layers will blend new motions on top of previously created sets of keys.
59. Click the black arrow to go to the original layer. The biped will now walk 14–16 steps and appear to stop above the shaft.
60. Click the Next Layer arrow and return to the reactor layer.
61. In the Layers Rollout, click the Save button and enable Save Segment at Current Position.
62. Name your layer and save it in the motions folder in the 3ds user's folder in My Documents.

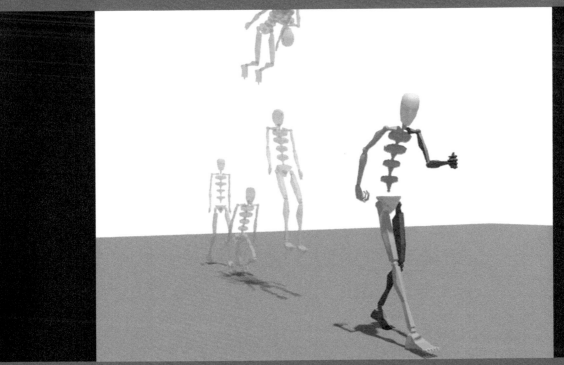

CHAPTER 7

Use of Overlapping Action, Weight, and Drag

Richard Lapidus

Rule: Use of overlapping action

Rule: Weight and drag

After Completing This Chapter, You Will be Able To:

- Set up a biped using the footstep method of animation.
- Use layers to control the biped subtle motion of character.
- Set Keys.
- Utilize Weight.

In this introductory tutorial for starting to animate a biped with footsteps, first you need to create a biped. This is a fully rigged structure used for animating characters. There are several other products that you can use but the one that has been around the longest for 3ds MAX is the biped. Bipeds are created in the Systems Panel of the Create Panel, and then they are controlled and animated in the Motion Panel.

FIG 7.1

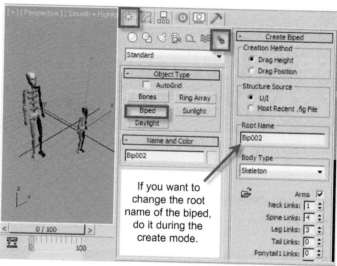

FIG 7.2

If you want to change the root name of the biped, do it during the create mode.

1. Go to the systems portion of the Command Panel, select biped, drag up a biped of any height, it is called biped 01.
2. Drag out a second biped but a quarter the size, this is called biped 02 and right click to exit Create mode.
3. Select the first biped 01, you may click on any part of it, and then enable the Motion Panel.

All changes to the biped as far as its structure and animating it is typically done in the Motion Panel. There are several other modules like Motion Mixer and parts of the Track Editor, which may be used for animating the bipeds. Unlike most other 3d objects, because it is a "system," it will be controlled in the Motion Panel.

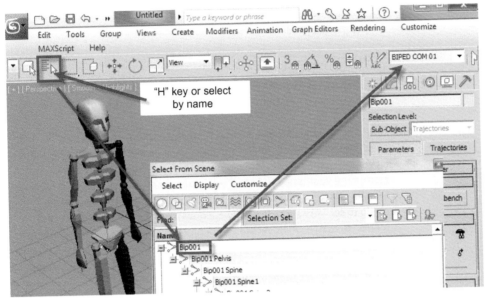

FIG 7.3

If you hit the "H" Key on your keyboard, you'll notice that the biped structure has many joint parts. If you go to the display menu and display the children, they are indented one for every step for which they are linked in the hierarchy. The main COM Object for the control is called BIP 001.

4. Hit the "H" Key and select Bip001. In the Name Selection drop-down box, type in Biped COM01 and hit Enter. You must hit the Enter Key to make it a Selection Set.

You have just created a named Selection Set for that part of the biped. When animating this structure, it is often easier to select it by dragging on the Name Selection to reselect an object. You can also unhide or unfreeze parts of your objects or scenes by reselecting a set and following the prompts. I will often set up a Name Selection for the hand, feet, and spine objects.

5. Repeat this for each hand and foot separately if you like.

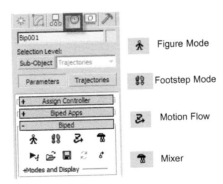

FIG 7.4

6. Select the first biped 01, you may click on any part of it, and then enable the Motion Panel.

Hint

In Hierarchy structures like this, you may also use the Page Up and Down Keys to move a selection to the associated parent or child of the bone.

Notice by looking in the Main Biped Panel that there are four basic methods available to animate a biped. Those are Figure mode, Footstep mode, Motion Flow mode, and also the Motion Mixer. The basic Figure mode allows you restructure your biped to fit to the skin of a character. In creating animation for your character, the size of the biped does not really matter as we are going to see very soon. The software does a great job in retargeting the motion to match whatever scale your biped is. Right now we're just going to take a look at animating it with footsteps and then we're going to layer it to give it some more unique motion and give it some weight for Footstep mode. Here are a couple of rules to keep you out of trouble when working with this system:

- Figure mode is for structuring and not animating the biped.
- If you move the starting position of the biped when out of Figure mode and then reenter Figure mode, the biped will move back a position to the last position you left it in when in Figure mode.
- Save your max and biped files often.
- When animating with footsteps, you can only animate when there are active footsteps.
- If your character will be going through a lot of complex motions, try to break these down into small sets of actions and save to compose with Motion Flow or Motion Mixer later on.

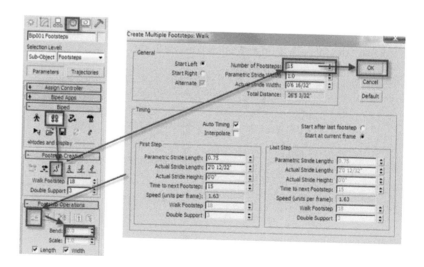

FIG 7.5

7. Enable Footstep mode and examine the new panels that appear. Some of the buttons are grayed out. Refer to Fig. 7.5 for the next several steps. We will be adding multiple footsteps and then having the biped walk around in a circle.

As you look down the panel, only the next logical step of buttons are enabled, and many of them have a yellow asterisks indicating Create\Assign modes for footsteps. When you enable one of the four modes for controlling the structure of the biped or animating it, the tools you need will become available. There are radial buttons with an image of a stick figure doing a run, walk, and jump. The default is set to walk. Leave it as is for now. With further investigation of this module, you will very quickly be able to create the mechanics of a human walk. Following the flow of the diagram in Fig. 7.5, we will create multiple footsteps, set the size, enable the footsteps, and then bend the active footsteps around into a circle. Just follow the buttons down the panel as they become active.

8. Click the Create Multiple Footstep button and the Create Multiple Footsteps: Walk Dialog will appear. Set the number to 15 and hit OK.

The dialog for creating multiple footsteps takes into account the height of your biped and number of steps to calculate how far it could parametrically walk. This happens automatically when you leave the Auto Timing checked. With this interface, you are using a setup that used the biomechanics of a typical walk. Part of this involves the amount of time that both feet are planted on the ground, time to lift and plant each foot. At the beginning of every animation class, I have the tallest guy stand next to me in the center of the room and take 8 footsteps forward to prove this point.

9. In the panel below, Footstep Operations, click the Assign Inactive Footsteps button, which is now active, and the biped will appear to move a little. What has happened is that the feet are locked into those footsteps, and some subtle counterbalancing animation to the arms, for example, is now keyed as well.

Hint

If you deselect the footsteps before activating, they will not be active to assign to the biped. Make sure you do not click the screen until after the next step as well. If the footsteps are not white, they are not selected.

Play the animation. Notice how the number of active frames has also increased to take into account the timing relative to the number of footsteps you activated. There is a little bit of movement of the arm swing back and forth counterbalancing the legs. The hips aren't really moving that much and the whole chest that is made up of four spine objects is actually stiff.

That's where we come in with needing to create layers to add more weight and overlapping movement to the footsteps. Before that let's have a little fun with the bipeds and explore working with the basic footstep motion.

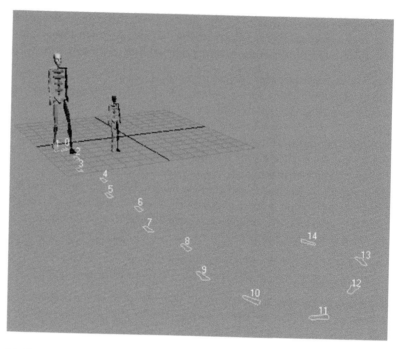

FIG 7.6

10. Go to the Edit Menu and do an Edit Hold.
11. Zoom out your perspective view, so that you can see all the footsteps.
12. Select footsteps 10–14.
13. Drag the bend spinner or type 45 for the degrees and hit Enter. The biped walks and then turns around. Nothing exciting yet!

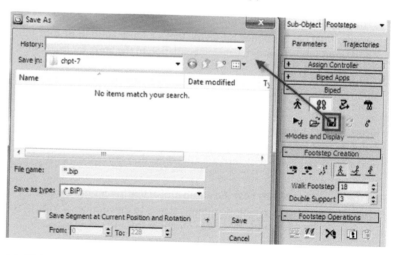

FIG 7.7

14. Click the Save button and call the file biped_walk_turn.bip. This will be loaded onto the other biped. If you enable Save Segment in the Dialog, the footsteps are removed and all objects are keyed. Leave it unchecked for now.

Now that you have saved this six step with eight step loop around as a BIP motion file, it will be loaded onto the smaller biped. You will notice that the smaller biped uses the same number of steps, but relative to it's own size. It will also move to the original starting point of the other biped. It will use the same motion, but relative to its structure. This can create some interesting effects for you later on. As a first step into understanding Biped Motion, I want you to realize that motion can be saved, edited and applied as you want it. Since all character don't start from the same position, we will also use the Move All Mode to position and even set the new file.

15. Turn off the Footstep mode and select the other biped.
16. Select any part of the shorter biped. Now click the Bip File Load button.
17. Navigate to where you saved the first file and load it on the smaller biped. Notice how it moves to the same starting point as the other biped.

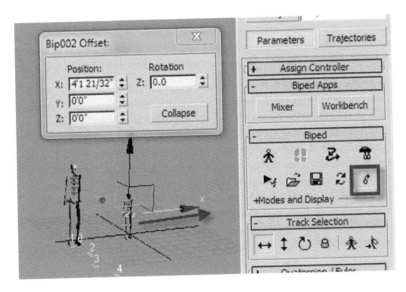

FIG 7.8

18. Turn on the Move all Mode and reposition the biped.

Hint

It's a little easier to use select and move while this is active instead of trying to drag the spinner. There is also a Collapse function in the Move All Mode Dialog. This will offset spinners. If you resave this bip file, it will use the new position instead of the one from the original biped.

19. Play the animation. Both walk 7 steps forward and then loop around in a circle.

The "Move All Mode" also allows you to collapse the changes made to position and rotation. This will remove all the footsteps and generate a keyframe for all the Biped's parts. If you are going to enhance the animation with layers and no longer need the footsteps, this is a good choice. It's very hard to get good looking motion without editing the basic walk/run/jump parametric footsteps.

Re-save this Biped file again with a different name. I use a naming convention of adding "small" to the end of the name. Something like: biped_walk_turn_small.bip works.

If you have done an edit hold, try collapsing the motion in move all mode. After saving the new biped file, turn on footstep mode and delete all the steps. Then turn figure mode on and off to reset the BIP to the original position it was in when created. If you load the collapsed biped file back onto this character, it will have the motion in the place you saved it, but without the footsteps. This is a good technique to use when you are creating animation keys that are not relative to the final placement in space. The motion can be re-positioned when you want and later on we will explore editing separate sequences together as well. The goal is to be able to create your own library of motions if you don't have access to a motion capture system or enough biped files that suit your needs.

There are several rules that you will want to keep in mind when you're working with the biped. Never try to animate the entire sequence of actions from start to finish in one file. It's almost impossible to do a full animation start to finish with your character doing a whole bunch of different ranges of motions. What I mean is if you take a look at the way that they film movies for example, the action is shot several time from different positions and then edited together. I'm always asking my students to take a look at the bonus features on their favorite movies on DVD at home. There is a wealth of resources which these professionals share relative to their craft. When you start to think about each breaking down every major motion into separate pieces of action, and creating separate files for them, the process will be a lot easier. Instead of trying to act out a scene from start to finish perfectly, you will be blending together better segments.

If you think about the editing process of film\video, the concept of leaving some time before and after the action will make more sense. When using footsteps with bipeds, always add a few extra footsteps that you won't be using at the end. The character has a interpolates like any other 3d object and tends to have extra motion beyond the last step which look jerky. It also give you the opportunity to allow time for blending actions together. We will explore this later on when using motion flow and mixer.

20. Save the file and call it ch7_tall_short_walking.max. Then do a reset.
21. Create a new biped and go to the Motion Panel. I've made mine about 5'7".
22. Enter Footstep mode, click Create Multiple Footsteps, enter 10 for the number of footsteps, hit OK.
23. Activate the inactive footsteps.
24. From the Graphic Editors Menu, choose Dope Sheet.
25. Click the "+" button next to BIP 001 footsteps.

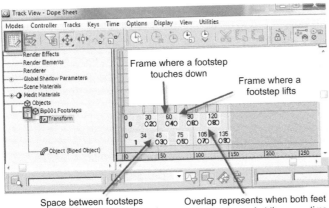

Space between footsteps
represents the foot of the ground

Overlap represents when both feet
are on the ground at the same time

FIG 7.9

You'll now see that your biped has 10 footsteps. The first two being lined up because your biped is starting out from a standing position. Notice how the other footsteps are offset and spaced across the timeline. The spaces inbetween footsteps represents the time that the foot is actually up in the air until the time that it plants. This is how the program interpolates a walk. Footstep lifts, moves through space, touches down, and then plants. The other leg counterbalances and is offset in time. Let's see if we can get our biped to stop walking and then jump in the air. Once this is done, adding a layer to give the biped more of a sense of weight will be easier with an exaggerated motion.

26. Highlight steps 5 through 9 by dragging a marquee around and move those footsteps about 50 keys offset to the right. Based on the height of my biped, the left side of footstep 5 had a value of keyframe 75, so I dragged it to frame 125.

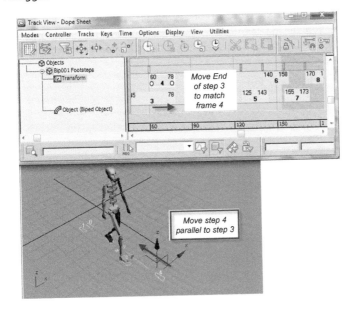

FIG 7.10

97

27. Move the end of footstep 3 to match the end of footstep 4. This will keep both feet planted together until the biped flies into the air. Because we want the biped to eventually jump into the air with both feet together, you will also have to adjust the placement of the footstep.

28. In the viewport, move keyframe 4 parallel to keyframe 3. The biped will now stop with both feet together. Moving footsteps does not affect timing, just the placement.

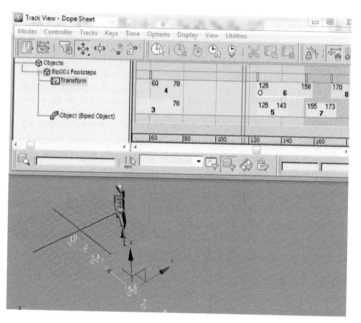

FIG 7.11

29. Repeat these steps for frames 5 and 6. Move 5 to line up with 6 in the viewport and adjust the start of 6 to line up with 5 in the Dope Sheet.

30. Save your file as ch7-freeform-area.max. If you load my file at this point, remember that you must select the biped and enter Footstep mode to see the footsteps in the Dope Sheet.

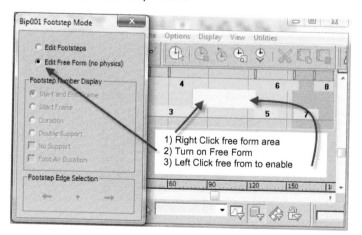

FIG 7.12

98

31. Right click in that large space between steps 3 and 45 and the biped 001 Footstep Mode Dialog appears showing that you're in an edit Footstep mode. There is also a radio button to change to edit free-form, no physics.

When no physics is enabled, the biped is essentially not affected by being positioned in space relative to its footsteps. Notice how it floats way up into space. Part of this is also due to how the program is interpolating a large area of space between the keyframe of the Biped COM Object with a large distance of new uninterpolated space. When activated, you may grab your biped and make it fly through space without it being pulled into the next set of footsteps.

32. Click the Edit Free Form button and then close the Dialog.
33. Click the yellow outline box in the Dope Sheet, so it turns into a solid yellow line.
34. Minimize the Dope Sheet.
35. Play the animation and notice how the biped seems to float off its feet between frames 78 and 125.
36. Move to frame 78 and turn off Footstep mode.

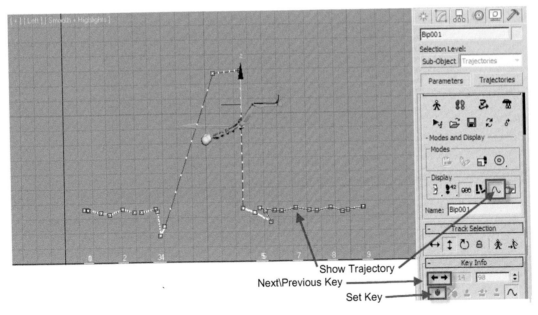

FIG 7.13

37. Open the Key Info Panel and make sure that Bip001 is selected.
38. Turn on Show Trajectory in the Display Area.
39. Move the biped down into a crouch at frame 78 and then hit the Set Key button.
40. Using the arrows for previous keys, move back to the previous Bip001 Com Key. It should be at frame 70. Move the biped into another crouch and then hit the Set Key button.

99

41. Click the right-hand "next" key until you reach about frame 90. Move the biped up in the air higher and also to the right but not exactly over the footsteps at frame 125. Make sure you hit Set Key after ever change or the keys will not be recorded.

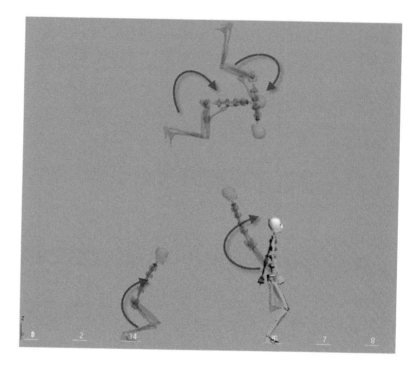

FIG 7.14

42. If you want to have your biped do a flip, you will have to create three to four incremental rotation keys instead of one 360° spin before landing. I added three rotation keys at frames 86, 92, and 105.

Notice how when you play the animation, the biped basically will float up in the air and come down. If you're a fan of any superhero that flies, you may remember that they don't just take off without some kind of characteristic motion prior to lift off. Sometimes it's a pose, a wind-up, or a crouch. In the movies, your favorite actor or actress was probably hooked up to guide wires and then pulled through space. One of the pitfalls of working with a 3d system is that it doesn't have a make me fly like a superhero button.

This is the point that it makes sense to start using Layers in every motion. Real living things not only move curves, but also have a tendency to pose with curves. Here is an example: For a person to jump, there is typically a coiling up of the body before they spring out into space. Unless of course, that is a really cool fact except what we want to do is really take a look at how to control and utilize a little bit more weight in our biped and also how to get this character to look like there's some decent movement on it.

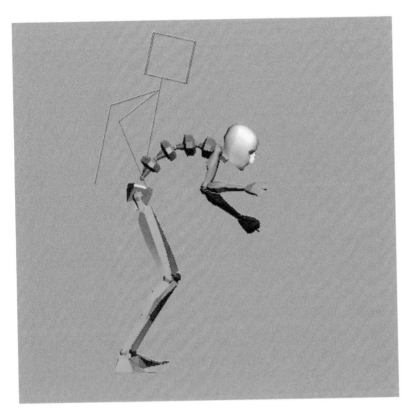

FIG 7.15

When a biped's motion is created by hand, with mocap files or with footsteps as we have seen above, there are keys created for many objects which might not be exactly what you are looking for. Instead of deleting these unwanted keys or creating new ones on top of the existing keys, we can use layers to blend on top of the existing motion. In Fig. 7.15 above, you will notice a red stick figure standing more erect over the crouching biped. This represents base level animation created with footsteps before the freeform area of animation. For our character to jump up high in the air from a standing position, it would need to crouch down and compress like a spring before expanding and flying up into the air. We are going to create a series of layers for the spine to start with. The cool thing about layers is that you can create as many as you want for separate objects and turn them on or off if the motion created is not quite what you want.

43. Hit the "H" Key and select all the spine objects, neck, and head. Create a named selection set called spine-head.
44. Repeat this and create separate sets for the hands.
45. Select the spine-head set of parts and then expand the Layers Panel in the Motion Tab.

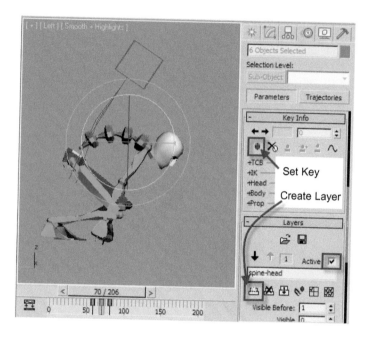

FIG 7.16

46. Create a new selection set called spine-head.
47. Scrub the timeline to around frame 58 where the biped is still standing before the jump.
48. In the Key Info Rollout, click the Set Key button to set a key on this layer for those objects.
49. Scrub to around frame 70 and then rotate the spine and head objects to curl the biped.
50. Hit the Set Key button again.
51. Scrub to frame 80 and rotate the biped parts to uncurl it. Remember to hit the Set Key button after each transform to record the keyframe.
52. Scrub the timeline and notice how the biped will crouch down and then stretch into the jump.
53. Create a new layer and really exaggerate the swinging of the arms back behind the biped and then forward through this action. Make sure that you do not key it exactly on the same keyframes as the other layers. By offsetting the timing of these body part actions, you will get a more natural looking motion.

The feet are held in place by the footsteps outside of the freeform area by the footsteps you originally placed. If you were to try to grab the Bip001 COM Object and move it down in a layer as if you wanted the biped to squat, the entire structure would lower as well in a layer. If you need to reposition the hips down lower at some point in time, it is very simple to de-activate a layer and key in changes to the Bip001 Com on the original layer. You could also leave the layers active and use the up or down arrow keys in the Layers Rollout to make changes to the base layer.

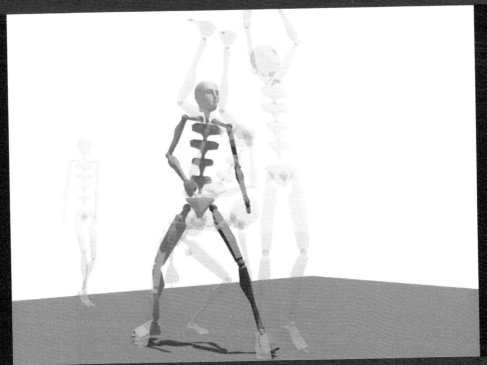

CHAPTER 8

Indications of Speed and Directing Attention

Richard Lapidus

Rule: There is a change of direction when a force meets the character

Rule: Change up the speed of an action to give it more attention

After Completing This Chapter, You Will be Able To:

- Load motions onto a biped using Motion Mixer.
- Add and edit clips.
- Create transitions.
- Mix motion down onto a biped.

In traditional cell animation, there are two basic modes—straight ahead and pose to pose. One of the main concepts that I try to get across to my students when were working with a system like a biped, and this goes for any type of system including your own custom animated rig, is that there are certain limitations to how far you can animate your system without running into problems. The biggest one being that there are built-in dynamics and

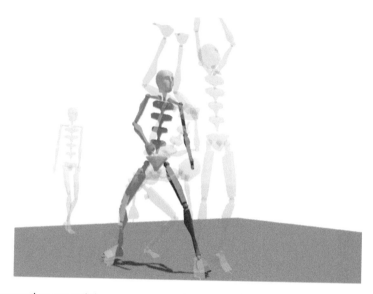

FIG 8.1

curves that control the movement and rotation of parts of your structure that will start working against you when you try to do too much with it. Here's a good example of where someone might get into trouble with straight ahead animating a camera at the beginning of the process of creating their animation. I'll see someone spend weeks creating a scene and animating it without any consideration of how it will be viewed through the camera. The person will finally place a camera in the scene and then, typical to straight ahead animation, will go and start moving it through the scene to catch all of the vital parts from start to finish. This is why in Chapter 1 I introduced you to the concept of the trajectory, so that you do start to think about how your objects are moving. In most animations, when you try to animate the camera all the way through the scene, flying around will create a number of positions where the camera moves too fast or too slow and you don't really have good control over trying to display the action that is happening within your scene. If you've never had the opportunity to work on a production set, in your mind you may think a production is produced seamlessly. You may not be noticing that there are multiple shots and multiple cameras being edited together. Take a look at special features on your favorite DVD at home or go to one of the places that will now rent them or let you download them online, and you can really start to enjoy seeing the process of how a production is put together. The director will have the actors work through setting up the scene and run through the scene several times to figure out how to get the best position for the camera and the actors in the right place. They also have to consider the special effects, whether they're done on site when the production is made or as is typical these days in postproduction with a software like 3ds MAX. It's not that there's anything wrong with straight ahead animation, it's just that you have to be very proficient in anticipating how everything's going to be moving in concert together to have it seamlessly flow together properly.

In the pose-to-pose animation process, the animator has a starting position that can be drawn from and an ending position to be drawn to. Effectively, the whole sequence of action has already been broken down into small pieces and in the pose to pose they're basically now carving those small pieces that will then be edited together. Effectively what you want to be doing is breaking down your animation into those small pieces, animating those small segments, and saving amounts, so that then you can edit them back together.

The purpose of Motion Flow or Motion Mixer is basically to allow you to take your small animated sequences and edit them together. As we saw with the Motion Flow, this editing feature allows you to basically script out which bip files you want to have occur in a certain sequence and then also easily edit the transition between those sequences. The mixer basically does the same job except it shows you the information in a little bit different manner as we will see with bar graphs overlapping in time; but the mixer should go a little bit further in being able to apply additional parts of one animation within another and also being able to slow down or speed up the timing of your bip files with a time warp.

The thing to remember, which most new users to editing motion files find the most frustrating, is that the motion file remembers the position and rotation in 3d space that the files were created in. As I'm going to show you in this chapter, it's very easy to reposition and also change the orientation of your biped files when doing your editing. As we saw in the first biped chapter, the size of your biped doesn't really matter because the motion is targeted relative to the size of the biped that you're adding it to.

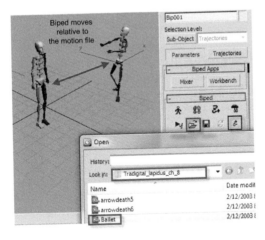

FIG 8.2

1. Create a biped and add a bip file to it. For this exercise, the two biped files that I'm going to use are the ballet and one of the arrows of death which ship with 3ds MAX. The arrows of death files were created by Red Eye Studio in Schaumburg, Illinois. These files are included with 3ds MAX when you do the full installation. You will find a wide variety of motion files in the Autodesk\3dsmax 2011\Samples\Bip folder.

105

2. Load the Ballet.bip file onto your biped.
3. Scrub the timeline and you'll notice that the biped takes a bow from about frame 114 to around 157 and then continues dancing up off. As you scrub the timeline, you're going to notice that the character is on both feet at about frame 182. This is about where I want the next sequence to cut in.

Note

When loading motion files, the X, Y, and Z positions and rotation are saved in the bip file. Use the Move All Mode button as indicated in Fig. 8.2 by the Blue Rectangle outline box to open the Dialog.

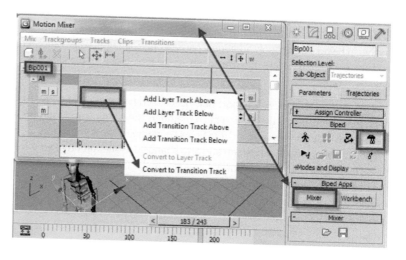

FIG 8.3

4. Enable the Motion Mixer in the Motion Panel for the biped and then also open the Motion Mixer Graphic Editor.
5. Notice how the Bip001 is already loaded into the Motion Mixer Dialog.
6. Right click the layer track and choose Convert to Transition Track.

Note

You're not going to see that ballet bip file automatically in the track. I had you loaded up so that you could scrub through and pick up where you would want to have the transition happen and how much of the action you want from this file. Just because there's animation in the file, it doesn't mean you have to use the whole thing. There's a nice little animation preview window in the Load File Dialog, which lets you scrub through your files to see the basic animation that's in there, but I find it's a little tough to really take your time and examine the file. If you forget to convert this to a transition track, only one file will show when you load and you'll be missing the ability to load in another file to create a transition to.

7. Right click the track again and choose new clips from files. Add the ballet bip file.
8. Repeat and load a second biped file. In this case, I'll use Arrow of death 3.bip. There is a nice preview window in the Load Dialog, which lets you scrub the file before loading.
9. This is probably a good point to save your file and also do edit hold.

Notice that the active time segment only fits the original bip file and not both of them. You will need to extend the active time segment, so that the mixing of these two files is viewable. There is a button in the Motion Mixer Editor to do this for you.

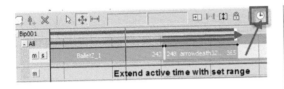
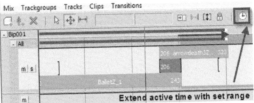

FIGS 8.4 and 8.4a

10. Click the set range button to extend the active time in the interface to match both clips.

FIG 8.5

11. Right click the transition track and choose Optimize all Transitions. By default, the program will create an overlap transition of 20 frames from the end of the first clip and 20 frames from the beginning of the second. This may not necessarily be the best place to transition between the two motions clips. Unlike video, which can be faded, wiped, or cut between, the biped system is driven to move the objects based on the parts. As we will see in the next several steps, you may choose to transition not based on time, but based on position of the body parts, so that there is a smooth transition of the biped through the motions.

107

Note

You need to choose targets you want to program to help hard-hit the biped to match when doing the transition from one biped file to another. We're going to try and keep the feet from slipping around too much, so you're probably going to want to change how the program is going to look at these two files to cut and edit them to match them up. Scrub the timeline again to see how the programs done in matching these up. When I have to go back in and adjust the editing of the transition, the default won't be trying to match both the feet, but to match the COM Object stored. Once you've done this several times, it becomes much easier and you start to really look at where you want to be cutting these together and getting the action to show the way you want. Before optimizing the transitions, you may notice that the biped slides forward and falls at the start of the bow. Not quite what we want.

12. Save the file as trad_ch8_before_optimize.
13. Right click the transition track and choose optimize.

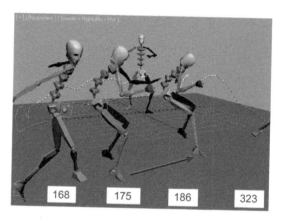

FIG 8.6

The program when it optimizes is actually looking to cut the two sets of actions together based on a logical transition of part of the biped's position in time. In Fig. 8.8, I have created a few snapshots of the biped in time to show you the start and end of the transition. There is also a Dummy Object linked to the Biped001 COM Object to show you the trajectory of the main control through time. Notice how smoothly the hips seem to move from frames 168 to 186. There is very little bounce shown in the trajectory. As you scrub the timeline, you may also see that the right foot slides between frames 175 and 186. This is not very realistic motion. The weight of the biped was actually moving onto that foot into frame 168. What is happening here?

The program will automatically look to focus the transition based on one foot, both feet, and the COM Object to transition the tracks. The Cool thing is that you can view the transitions in other views and then go back to edit the transitions if a problem is detected. Make sure you have the trajectory enabled within the Motion Panel for the biped. All objects may have the trajectory enabled within the object properties, but the biped has a button specifically for this in the Motion Panel. Changing the focus will often times be useful in keeping your character from having sliding feet or even flying unintentionally all together. Right below the focus drop-down is the angle spinner and also preserve height. So if you're not happy with the direction of movement that's inherent in your biped files, you can always change it here within the transition and have your biped go anyway you want.

In the default state, when the program analysis the clips and creates the transitions, it will cut 20 frames from the start and end of a clip. In optimization, it automatically looks to cut the transition down to 10 frames, which may or may not be what you want. That's why it's important to keep scrubbing your animation to try and figure out what part you want to keep and how you want that to be cut together.

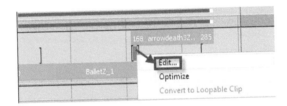

FIG 8.7

14. Right click the transition track and now choose Edit.

What I want to have happen is for the biped to dance across the screen, reach up before the bow portion of this first clip, and then fall backward using the arrow of death. The first time you play this through, the program will search to find the best transition based on using 10 frames and one of the body part(s) mentioned before. There is an easy workaround for this once you scrub the timeline and you figure out what's the best part of the body to focus on. Remember, you can always easily fix the upper body parts by using layers if needed. Let's focus on the feet. I know where I want to end the first clip, so I just basically search the second clip to figure out if it is the right direction and how much of it I want.

When looking at the second clip, I've also noticed that it has a direction that the characters fall into. Let's look at a way to control that as well as we finish up this project. What I want to do is change the direction of the fall, so the are characters actually going to end up moving backward in a different direction.

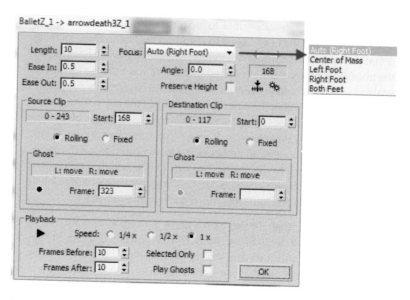

FIG 8.8

Once you determine the ends of your clips and the beginnings, we will go back into the transition and reoptimize it. From Fig. 8.8, please note a few areas that we will be adjusting. The focus drop-down will be set to both feet. The start of the Source Clip will be changed as well as the angle for the Destination Clip.

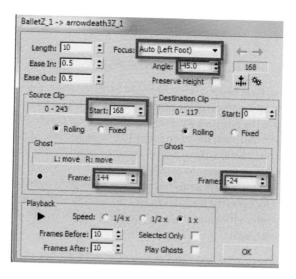

FIG 8.9

15. Right click the transition track and now choose Edit.
16. Set the focus to the left foot. That seems to be the best to have the objects match up.
17. Set the Start transition to 168 for the Source Clip and 0 for the Destination Clip.
18. Bring the angle to −45. This will give your biped a little change of direction from the fall in the A.O.D file.

19. Hit OK and play the animation.
20. If you also adjust the Ghost Frames, part of the Source Clip will show up in yellow wireframe and the Destination Clip in red.

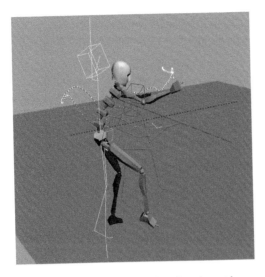

FIG 8.9a

Because the Motion Mixer is just an editor, the clips do not become permanent until the time that they are mixed back down onto the biped. Try turning the Mixer on and off. You will notice that when turned off, the original animation loaded onto the biped is still there. Make sure you have it enabled and now we will look at mixing it onto the biped.

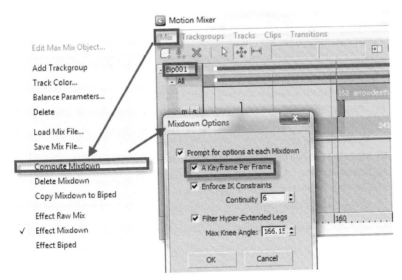

FIG 8.10

21. Select the name of the biped; Bip001 in the upper right hand corner of the Motion Mixer Dialog. If it is not selected with a white background, the Mix Menu items we need will not be available.

22. Choose Compute Mixdown from the Mix Menu.
23. Enable a Keyframe Per Frame because these bip files are mocap and have a keyframe for every frame.
24. Hit OK.
25. Go back to the Mix Menu and Copy Mixdown to bip.
26. Exit the Motion Mixer Graphic Editor and turn off Mixer in the Motion Panel.

Let's try another trick with adjusting the timing of a motion on the biped. This time we are going to have a biped take a few steps and then do a back flip. You could use Motion Flow to do the previous exercise as well as the following one. However, I want the biped to slow down the motion of the clip, so that it seems to float a little while longer. This can be accomplished by adding a time warp to the clip, something that can only be done with Motion Mixer.

27. Load the file called walk_flip_start.max or create a new biped and enter the Mixer again.
28. Change the Layer track to a Transition track.
29. Add your favorite walk file.
30. Add a Backflip file.
31. Select the Backflip Clip and right click it.

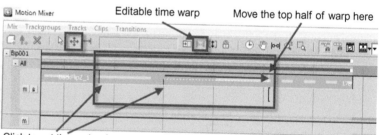

FIG 8.11

32. Choose Add Time Warp.
33. Enable the time warp with the Editable Time Warp icon.
34. Choose the Select and Move Tool and then click on the clip at around frame 120 and 132. This is the time that the biped leaves the ground and is flipping in the air.
35. Move the top half of the left line that appears on the clip to around frame 160.
36. Now drag the end of the clip to around frame 178.
37. Click the Set Range button to set the active time segment to match the new length of both clips.

Result

The biped will now walk at a normal pace and then flip through the air real slow. I've seen this type of slow motion a number of times in the movies or Sunday morning cartoons. The character can defy the laws of physics. Think about.

CHAPTER 9

Freeform Animation

Richard Lapidus

Rule: Squash and stretch

- Create freeform motion with a biped while using a variety of anchors.
- Animate a character to navigate one or more obstacles.
- Incorporate motion inherent adjusting weight.

One of the very important concepts that you want to consider while animating character is how changes in position occur relative to exaggerated motion. For example, if a character is going to apply excessive force to another object, there has to be some momentum built up before the forces are applied. Many people think of momentum in terms of velocity of moving objects, but it can also be viewed as a buildup of energy applied prior to a motion. As you'll see in the image above, I provide you with my classic three obstacles project. In the foreground is a biped facing a fairly odd formed rock. To move the rock up the hill, the biped would simply

walk and gingerly push it. You want your character to crouch down and then release the force of a push as it stretches out against the rock. As a biped doesn't normally squash and stretch like a rubber ball, we're going to consider the squash as the biped crouching and curling up and then stretching out in order to create the illusion that it is moving a very heavy object. The other two obstacles in the scene, one of which is fairly apparent, is to have a biped ascend a staircase with some missing steps and the other is to have a biped climb out of a well. I've included this chapter in the sequence after footsteps, Motion Mixer, and the biped down the well chapters. In my classes, we typically do this exercise first followed by the previous chapters listed above. Because the process of locomotion through walking or jumping can be programmed in I find that many students don't take the time to really study force and motion relative to human motion. Typically, I will give them five weeks to continue working on this exercise after they've had the opportunity to examine motion from footstep driven animations or mocap files. There is always the question of why create animation by hand when you can simply cut and paste captured motion. The answer isn't very simple. I used to answer the question by referring to Michelangelo's David. Yes, there are machines today that can scan and manipulate rapid prototype objects, but it is still the hand of the artist that makes a piece significant. Michelangelo created a work of art with a hammer and chisel, quite possibly the perfect piece of work. Imagine what he can do today with modern tools. Quite possibly he might not want to. He envisioned it, drew it, and removed everything that was not the David within a large piece of marble. Working with the latest tools, might possibly have not given us the same work of art. There's a struggle that occurs in creating art, or animation for that matter. It's not a simple matter of cut-and-paste. Those are simple tools as part of the larger process of perceiving the world and placing them together in order and in some fashion. It might sound like I'm not a fan of motion captured animation. It is in fact quite the opposite. One of my favorite things to do is view the extras included with DVD movies that shows an inside look of the production process. In a lot of the action scenes that require a character to jump, flip, or fly through the air, the viewer is going to see the actor in some type of harness rigged up in front of a green screen. The motion is typically not caught on film or through motion capture devices the first time. The actor, director, and visual artists are working together through multiple takes to get just the right action to pull into use somewhere else.

I have climbed out and over a few obstacles in my time, some of them not so gracefully. I'm going to show you the mechanics of anchoring the hands and feet in order to position the biped through various positions of squash and stretch. Feel free to apply different concepts of how to maneuver through these obstacles using your own creativity. You could of course use footsteps to maneuver the biped walking up the steps, the hill, or out of the well followed by adding layers to complete any of these obstacles. I think you'll find that by taking the time to hand animate all of it; this will give you the opportunity to conceptualize a better animation. In addition to the scene and characters, there are several cameras already created within the scene. There are two reasons for this; one is to quickly view the biped that you will work on, and the other is to immerse yourself within the scene from a particular point of view. Think about and try to imagine having to maneuver one of these obstacles before you start.

Visualization is a very important part of the animation process. The camera, which a lot of people typically use in the end process of creating a project, is very important to view your projects during the entire process because it immerses your mind into the 3d space. Here is an example of why immersion is important. One of my students who chose the "well project" had their biped climbing with the butt sticking as far out from the wall as possible. Since many people have not had the opportunity to climb out of a well or up the face of a mountain before, there are several significant factors that may not be considered. The first one is relative to weight and the result of gravity. Take a look at any movie that has a climbing scene in it. The actor is hugging the rock face as closely as possible unless another support is in place like a rope being held by a friend above. Drama is added to a scene when the character slips or the rope breaks. Then what happens, they are hugging that surface for dear life.

1. Let's start by opening the file called "Chpt9_3_obstacles-start.max".

FIG 9.2

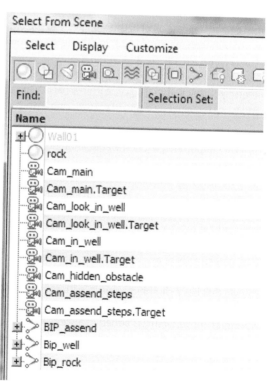

FIG 9.3

2. Click the Edit Name Selection Set icon or drag on the drop-down arrow for Create Selection Set.

You will see that I have already created a selection set for BIP_assend, separate feet, and a set for the back. By creating and naming quick selections for objects, it makes your job easier when trying to reselect an object easily. If you like, select the right hand and make a set for it as well as the left.

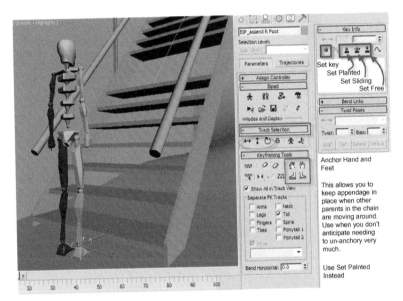

FIG 9.4

3. Enable the camera named Cam_assend steps to view the biped called BIP_assend standing in front of the steps.

I have adjusted the view in Fig. 9.4 in order to see the biped's feet and more of the lower portion of the steps. Note also from the image that the Motion Panel Rollouts have been shuffled around in the following order: Biped, Track Selection, Keyframing Tools, and Key Info. These are the main rollouts we will be using. Under Track Selection, the body horizontal, vertical, and rotation are highlighted with a green ellipse. These three icons allow you to switch quickly to the biped's COM Object if another biped part is selected. In the Keyframing Tools Rollout, the important icons we will be using are to anchor the hands and feet. The area indicated is the Set Key icon in the Key Info Rollout. Since this structure will not be footstep or mocap driven, whenever the main COM Object is moved or rotated the main parent in this hierarchy structure, there is nothing to anchor the feet or hands by default. The key to having planted hands or feet work properly if you are going to need to turn it on or off is to remember to Set Keys before you turn off. The planted option holds a hand or foot in place but does not create keys when you turn off.

We're going to animate the biped walking up the steps, stopping at the top, and then bending over and swinging out into space. I'm going to take this

117

series of steps to have my biped not make it and fall into a hanging position at the first series of missing steps. We're then going to add several layers to control the arm swing, arching back, and any keys that need to be fixed. Because we're using the smooth tangents to animate these keys, the feet and hands are going to have a tendency to move out of position and through the steps at times. This is an easy thing to fix with layers.

FIG 9.4a

4. Select any part of the Bipd_assend and enter Figure mode.

Notice that the biped does not move. I created it and then positioned it here so that if you wanted to change the structure of the biped, it would not move.

5. Increase the number of fingers to five.

I'm not going to increase the number of finger links at this point because I'm not doing subtle hand animation just the broad motion of the walk up, the steps, and a fall.

6. Select the body vertical and click Set Key. Repeat this for the body horizontal.

Notice how a red and yellow keyframe will show in the timeline for the COM Object.

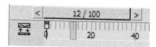

Timeline keyframes

Red indicates a Body
Horizontal Key has been
created and yellow indicates
Vertical Keys for the COM

FIG 9.5

118

7. Make sure the Key Tangent is set to the Default Smooth Interpolation if you changed it in a previous file.

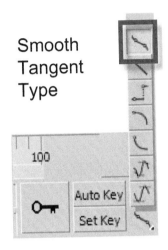

FIG 9.6

8. Now select the right and left foot and click the Set Key button to create keys for them at frame 0. When you animate with the Auto Key off and using the set key method, it will not automatically create keys at the zero key when creating future keys.

Even though we have smooth tangents set, there are so few keys to interpolate a nice move curve at this point. Add a little curve to it so it looks more natural. Finally at around frame 5, add a little rotation to point the foot down. As you scrub the timeline, notice that the foot takes up points down and then rotate back into place to set down on the first step. If you don't want to add the rotations at this point, those can always be added in later on with a layer. Think of this level of animating to be your base layer to get your biped off the steps and prepared to maneuver over the missing steps.

Note

If you find it difficult to be positioning on the "Z" and "Y" axes as we will be through most of the process of animating the steps, you can drag on the spinners for the axis below the timeline in the status area.

At this point, we could anchor the feet, but that becomes very laborious when you need to have the hands or feet move again in the future. If you had a character holding onto something through a long segment, then an anchor would make sense. Instead we will use planted, sliding, and free keys.

119

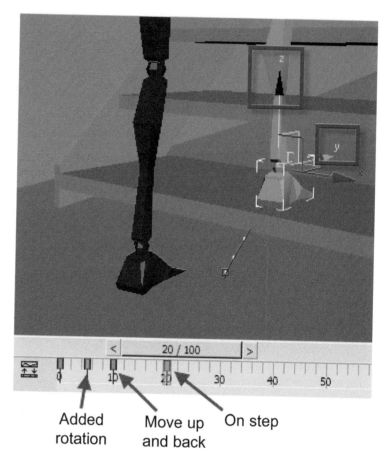

Added   Move up On step
rotation   and back

FIG 9.7

9. Select the left foot and create a planted key. Repeat this for the right foot.

If you move the body vertical, you notice that the feet stay stuck in place.

10. Move to frame 20 and position the right foot up on the first step and created key this time with the sliding key icon. If you try to set a planted key, it will stick. You're going to want to have the foot planted on the first step, but you have to create the key first and then plant later on.
11. Move back to frame 10, adjust the position of the foot a little higher, and set a free key. Move back in time to around frame 5, then rotate the foot down a bit, and set a free key.
12. Select the body horizontal drag to frame 20 and move the body forward. Remember to set a key every time you find a position you like. If you position the biped to high or far forward, you will be pulling the biped off its feet.
13. Move to frame 11 and rotate the left foot a little. Use free keys for setting the positions and rotations. Repeat this at around frame 20. You want to position the left foot so it looks like it's rotating up off the ground.
14. Drag the Time Slider.

15. Move to frame 40 and select the body vertical. Now position the biped to almost standing straight up on the right leg. Since the legs typically are never completely stiff, make sure you leave some bend in the leg.
16. Add a small adjustment to the body horizontal motion as well.
17. Scrub to frame 60 and then back to 40, select the right foot, and set a planted key at frame 40.

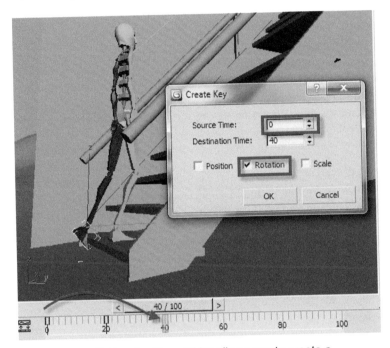

Right clicking the Time Slider allows you to create a key by choosing a different source of time. You can also filter out which keys you don't want to copy.

FIG 9.7a

18. Select the left foot and notice that it's still a little bent. Move to frame 60 and right click the Time Slider. When the Dialog appears turn off position, set the source to be frame 0. This will copy the original rotation from 0 to 60.
19. Now position the left foot up on the second step and create a planted key.
20. Move to frame 40, position the left foot, and set a free key; rotate the left foot and set a free key. Move to frame 50, adjust and rotate the left foot with free keys at frame 60, and then set a planted key.

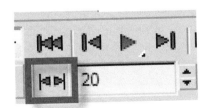

FIG 9.7b

21. When you need to adjust previously created keys, it is always best to use the Key Toggle mode. When enabled, it changes the Next Frame button to a Next Key button so that you are snapping to keys.

The key to making a walk cycle in a freeform mode is to create keys setting the motion into the future like with the step, and then changing it to a planted key before you animate the biped stepping onto it in transferring the weight. You need the planted key when you want the foot to stay in place as you move the bipeds main COM Object.

22. At frame 80, set a body vertical key and then back in time to frame 60, set another body vertical key.
23. Select the right foot and set a planted key at frame 60. Move to frame 70 and set a free rotation key.
24. Scrub the time line and if necessary move the right foot up and set of free key at frame 70 as well.
25. Move to frame 100 where you want to then move the right foot up to the third step. Since you have a Rotation Key at frame 70, the foot will still be bent forward. Right click the Time Slider and copy the rotation from frame 0 to frame 70. Now position the right foot on the third step and set a free key.
26. Move to around frame 90, position the right foot up and back a little bit with a sliding key.
27. Select the body horizontal and at frame 100, try to move the biped forward. Notice how the right foot is sliding. Reselect the right foot and set a planted key.
28. Now position the biped forward and up a little bit setting keys for both.
29. Increase the length of your active time segments because it's going to take more than 100 keys to walk the biped up the steps to the first hazard it must maneuver.

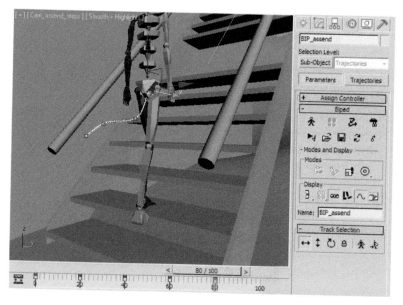

FIG 9.8

Play the animation. As the biped walks up the steps, you're going to see a nice smooth bouncy curve for the trajectory of the BIP COM Object. If it appears that there is extreme peak or valley in this line, you may have animated the biped too far up or down. Turn on your Key Toggle mode and step through the animation jumping from one keyframe position to other keyframe position. The last thing you want to do is add a new position while creating a new key instead of adjusting a previously created key. That's why the Key Toggle mode is such a nice feature, it steps you through from keyframe to keyframe.

30. Orbit the camera to a side view of the steps so that you can see the placement of the feet relative to the individual steps. If the foot is too far into the step, it will clip the next step as it moves up. Take a few moments to readjust the positions of the feet on the steps just in case there is too far into the step.

31. Select the left foot and move to frame 60. Now set a planted key.

32. Move to frame 120 and adjust the body horizontal and vertical so the biped is now standing on the third step with all of the weight on the right leg.

33. Select the left foot, move to frame 140, and animate it onto the fourth step. Make sure you set the position with the free key because if you use a planted key, it will snap it back to the same position that was in the frame 60.

34. Move to frame 100, right click the Time Slider, and adjust the source for the create key to be frame 60. Then set a planted key at frame 60. Now scrub the timeline to around frame 120. Move and rotate the foot into a natural lifted position so that the foot misses the step.

35. Move to frame 160 and set a planted key for the right and left foot.

36. At frame 170, create a new body horizontal and vertical position.

37. Move to frame 145 and adjust the body position as necessary.

38. At frame 140, position the left foot and set a planted key at frame 180, and position the body standing with most of the weight on the left foot.

39. Repeat this series of steps until your biped is standing flat foot on the top step.

40. Save the file and call it Chpt9_3_obstacles_assend _steps.max.

After you've completed the ascent portion of this chapter, we will continue by having the biped reach out and try and maneuver the missing steps. Continue with your previous file or load Chpt9_3_obstacles_assend _steps.max.

41. It should take you somewhere between 260 and 400 frames to have your biped ascend up the steps. It just depends on the speed at which you have your character moving.

FIG 9.9

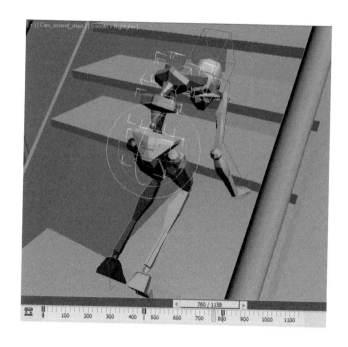

42. Move forward about 50 frames beyond the last point that you keyframed the biped to a standing position on the seventh step.
43. From the name selection drop down, choose the selection set called Bip_assend_back that will select all of the bipeds spine objects. This is one of those sets that I created before I saved the first start file.
44. Click the Set Key button to set position rotation keys at this point in time. If you are a starter animating the program, you would interpolate all the way back to frame 0.
45. Move forward about another 30–50 frames and rotate the spine so the biped bends over set a key.
46. Repeat this for the head and neck as well as making sure to offset the range that is used to set the keys.
47. Want the biped disorder look around a little bit as it's bending down to reach and touch the step that's there.
48. Scrub your timeline and find a position about 20–30 frames after the bend and set positions for the hands now, move forward in time, and rotate the hands so that they are resting on the next step in front of the biped.
49. You should see your biped bend over and touch the step. Take a few moments to rotate forearms and upper arms to get a natural position.

Up until now, we've been doing straight ahead animation. We will continue with that but now we're going to plant the hands and have the biped swing down through the steps. Alternatively, you could have your character swing up and land the feet on the steps. I tried to make it enough of a gap that a normal person couldn't hop over the missing steps. I've seen this done before and it never ends very well for the biped.

50. Now turn and plant the hands and plant the feet.
51. Position the biped into a crouching posture by moving the body vertically down a bit. Set a key.
52. Move forward in time and move the body vertical up and set the key to as if the biped is going to jump up in the air to move through. The hands will be in same position because they're planted, but that's okay because we can fix that later on.
53. Scrub the timeline and you should see your biped bend over touching the step. Crouch down, stand up, and then move through time and pull the body vertically down below the steps and set the key. You should see your biped hanging for dear life below the steps with the feet still stuck there on the last step. Not a very natural position for bipeds or people.
54. Set keys at the time in your animation before the biped jumps and then turn off the anchor for the left and right foot.
55. Scrub your timeline again and add a few rotation keys for the feet as they're pulled off the step and then further in time, position them through to the next step above or down toward the ground if you're going to have your biped fall through the opening.
56. Add a new layer for the biped and call it feet. Create new positions for biped in order to fix any problems which occurred in keyframing the feet. Think of layers as an adjustment on top of the basic motion that subtly allows you to enhance what is already there.

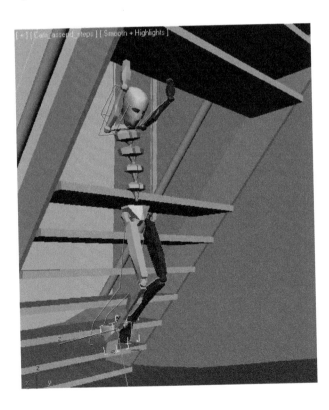

FIG 9.10

57. Create separate layers for the back, head, and even hands. The great thing about layers is that they can be turned off if you don't like them.

FIG 9.11

The best option for you when you're starting to work through fixing animation or adding subtle motion on top of the broad strokes is to create separate layers for the various body parts. For example, when I moved my camera around to the front position after creating the sequence of walking and dropping between the steps, I noticed that the biped had swayed a little too far to the right because I must've added a little bit of X movement on the COM Object. I also noticed that the legs are rotated a little bit far to the right because of my camera angle not catching it. In this case, I would create a separate layer to fix the legs, one for the arm swing, adjustments of the spine, and finally one to reposition the hands after the other layers were created. It's important at least in this animation where we are trying to plant the hands and then move the biped in a drastic vertical position to fix those after adjusting everything else. Any change that you make to the COM, swinging the arms, or curving the back is going to apply some force and possibly reposition the hands since these objects are no longer anchored. Of the three obstacles to work a biped through, this is probably the most difficult. Once you get a handle on anchoring hands and feet, then doing a vertical climb out of the well or steps pushing a boulder up the hill will seem relatively easy. I hope you've found this chapter to be very challenging but at the same time a lot of fun to work with.

It takes some work to successfully handle keying a skeletal structure like a biped through fairly normal activities. There are several useful resources that you can look to in order to add some realism and understand the biomechanics of motion. The first that comes to mind is using the photography of Eadweard Muybridge. In the history of photography, he was the first to use high-speed film to capture the motion of humans and animals. These are a very good resource not only to study the cadence of the walks, for example, but also to understand the motion and positioning of body parts. With the availability camcorders and DVD players, you can also capture motion on film electronically and then step through it frame by frame to do what is called rotoscoping. Obviously, what's going to make your animations look more realistic is to focus on the action that you're trying to capture and then exaggerate a bit.

FIG 9.12

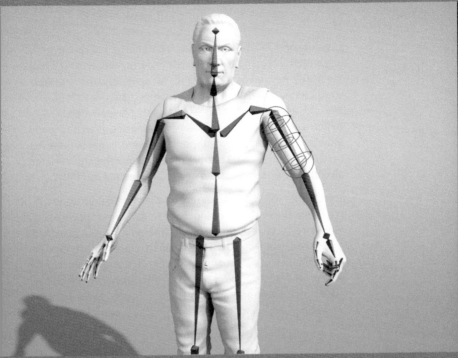

CHAPTER 10

Deforming Objects with Bones—Skinning, Envelopes, and Vertex Weighting

Chris Tedin

Rule: Appeal

After Completing This Chapter, You Will be Able To:

*   Place bones into mesh models appropriately for deformation.
*   Set envelopes with Skin Modifier and adjust falloff.
*   Adjust individual vertex weights using the Weight Editor.
*   Use more advanced deformers to create creases and bulges.

The best way to understand the technique of deforming meshes using bones by enveloping, or "skinning" as it is called in 3ds MAX, is to look at our own bones that lie under our own muscles, tendons, and flesh. Our skin can't move without muscles, and both would simply collapse without the support and

129

structure of the underlying bones. It is important to carefully study nature for inspiration and guidance while creating any animation rig. Every animal on the planet evolved by the demands of nature, and the stresses put on it by the struggle to survive. Whether built for speed, strength, flight, or underwater life, each animal has a unique structure that gives it mobility. There are patterns and similarities between many species, as well as subtle differences. Muscles grow for different purposes, growing leaner or more massive, lighter or denser. Each animal's overall shape is determined by the interplay between all of these different variables and environmental conditions.

This chapter will introduce the concept of mesh deformation through the use of "enveloping" or "skinning." Each vertex on the target mesh is pulled in different directions by "bones", linked together in an animation "rig." Skinning is a very popular technique for animating meshes in 3d and is used for feature films, commercials, and game production. It is a very robust system, allowing for a great deal of flexibility by bending the character's limbs, as well as more subtle chest expansion, and facial deformations. Combined with careful "morphing" style deformations, skinning is a powerful tool in a 3d artist's toolkit.

We will begin this chapter by creating a basic set of bones in a mesh object, in this case a human leg, and use 3ds MAX's "skin" modifier to deform the mesh. The first steps will be to set up and adjust the basic envelopes that "capture" the vertices. These envelopes have falloffs, which allow the artist to smooth out or add creases between the bones. The next steps will go through the "Weight Table," and show how each vertex's weight can be adjusted to follow each bone's influence differently. Finally, we will add a few simple Bulge and Joint Angle Deformers, which will give the character some more subtlety and realism.

The best way to understand skinning is to simply begin the process and work through the techniques step-by-step. I have a sample scene called "Leg_Skinning_Exercise.max", which has the basic mesh (a human leg) and a few simple bones. It is best to begin with a low-polygon mesh to learn the techniques. In fact, it is always best to skin with as few polygons as possible. When the mesh becomes too "heavy" or dense with polygons, the process of adjusting the weight of each vertex becomes more difficult.

This is a typical bone deformation setup. The human leg with three basic bones set inside the mesh. Notice how the bones are placed within the "skin" of the mesh, simulating fairly accurately the actual placement of the leg bones. In some areas, such as the knee, the bones are fairly close to the skin. In other areas, the bone is set much deeper beneath muscle, fat, and skin tissue. Also notice that the foot pivots at the ankle rather than the heel, which is why the bone is set above the ground plane in that joint. Please feel free to use your own models with this exercise but be careful that your mesh density is rather low for this beginning exercise, especially when we dig deeper into the Weight Table.

1. Select the leg's mesh. Go to the Modifier Panel and add a "skin" modifier to this mesh.

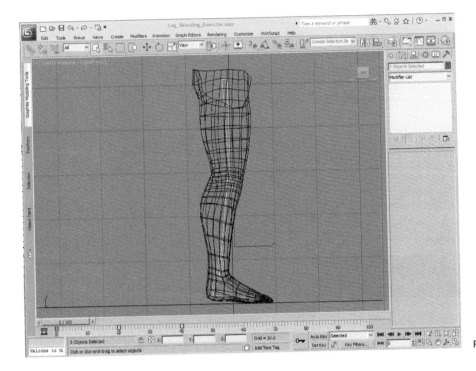

FIG 10.1

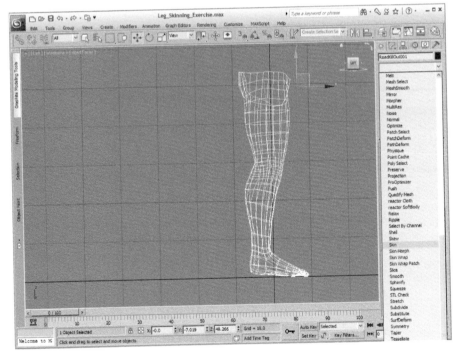

FIG 10.2

2. Click "Bones: Add" button and select all bones in the scene.

131

Hint

It is a good practice to have a proper naming convention for your bone objects. Even non-bone deforming objects should have the name "bone" added to the first part of their name, so that they can be easily selected in this Dialog box.

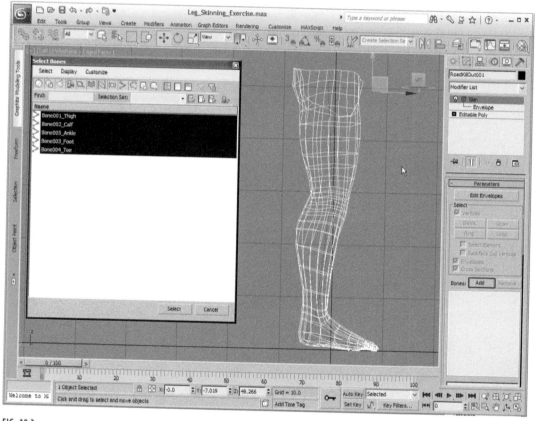

FIG 10.3

3. Slide the animation timeline forward to frame 40. I animated the calf and foot bones to preview the deformations on the mesh.

Hint

This is a great technique for showing problems in the deformation. Rather than deselecting the mesh and moving the bones, which takes time, sliding the timeline takes just a few seconds and never takes you away from the Skin Modifier Panel.

Notice that, with the default deformations, there are some problems with the deformation around the back of the knee and ankle.

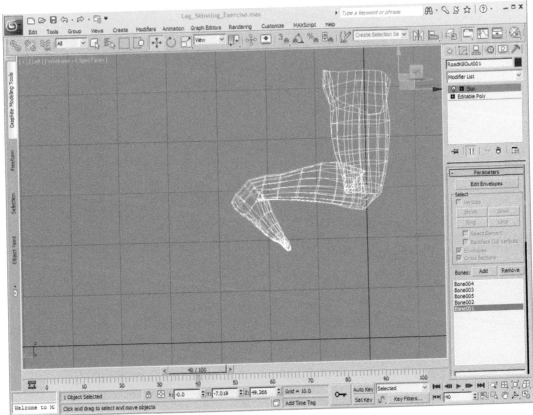

FIG 10.4

We will fix these problem areas with a few techniques, namely envelope adjustment and vertex weighting. I will also introduce the more advanced Joint Deformer as well. It is a good practice to save iterations of your files, so click "Save As" and press the "+" button next to the "Save" button to save an incremental version of the file.

4. The Envelope Adjustment tool is available by clicking the "Edit Envelope" button or by clicking the Envelope Sub-Object. Make sure both the "Envelopes" and "Cross Sections" boxes are checked.

5. Zoom into the top of the main bone, near the hip. Select "Bone 1" in the Bone List Panel. A sausage-shaped "gizmo" appears, which you can use to adjust each bone's influence on the surrounding vertices. Select one of the handles at the top right, linked with a dark red half circle and vertical lines. As you pull this handle (shown in figure below), the colors on the vertices change from blue to yellow, orange, then finally red. Each color represents that bone's influence on that vertex. Red is 100% and will allow that bone to move those vertices exclusively.

133

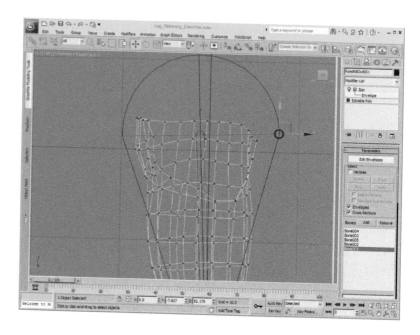

FIG 10.5

6. Pan down near the knee and adjust the bottom part of the envelope. Next, click on Bone 2, or calf bone in the skin modifier's panel and adjust those envelopes as well. Notice how the half circle end of each envelope crosses over its neighbor. This region around each joint will share the weighting influence depending on its distance.

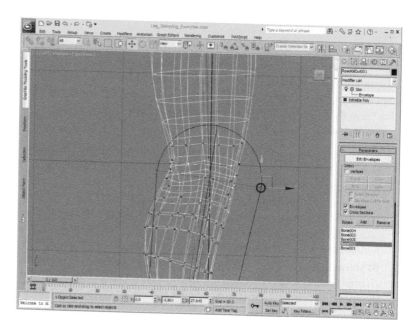

FIG 10.6

134

7. Test the deformation to see the results. You should notice a great deal of "softening" in the joint, which is an effect of a greater falloff distance. This might be suitable for softer regions, or a fish tail, but for a knee, it is a little too soft. We will adjust the inner envelope control to tighten it up a bit more.

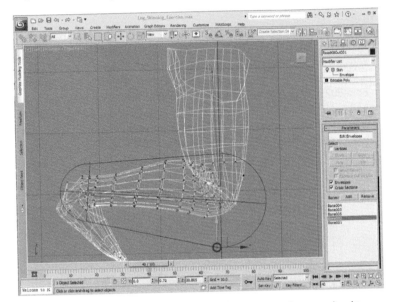

FIG 10.7

8. Next, select the inner envelope control. This may require zooming in closely to see the control points. Expand this smaller "sausage" a little bit to increase the bone's influence by shortening the falloff area to the next bone. Next, increase the inner envelope weight control on the thigh bone as well. The final result should look like this.

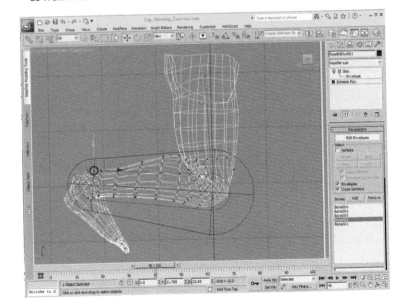

FIG 10.8

135

The effect is a bit sharper, but there are some problems around the inner part of the knee. This is a typical challenge for many animators, which is why you see many characters with tiny, tube-like legs. Thick, stocky bodies are much more difficult to skin without encountering this kind of overlapping problem. Clothing may cover up many of these problems, but these areas can be fixed with some creative vertex weighting.

9. Before we tackle vertex weights, let me show you one more feature with the envelope weights. If you notice, the envelope around the calf is just barely large enough to wrap around the main muscle. Select the Bone002_Calf. Scroll down the Modifier Panel to the Cross Sections and press the "Add" button. The cursor changes to a cross icon. Click midway up the thigh bone, and notice that a new cross section ring has been added. Click the "Add" button again to deactivate and adjust the radius. Notice how this ring changes size to encompass more of the calf muscle's mesh.

FIG 10.9

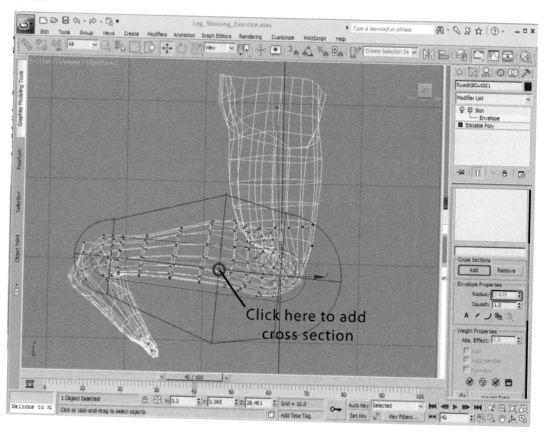

10. Now, onto the Vertex Weight Table! Click the Weight Table button. Intimidating, isn't it?

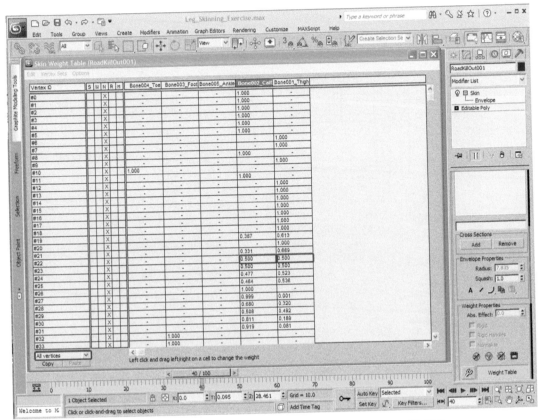

FIG 10.10

It's not really as bad as it looks. All the vertices that are in the model are listed (by number) along the leftmost column. All the bones that are included in the skin modifier are along the top edge. Each vertex can be influenced by any bone in the modifier, and the amount is indicated where they intersect. For example, vertex #22 is influenced by Bone002_Calf by 50% (0.500) and by Bone001_Thigh by 50%. Therefore, this vertex will be equally deformed by both bones.

Now, let's simplify the look of this Weight Table. Click on the rollout below the list of vertices and change it to "Selected Vertices." Notice that there are no vertices showing in the Weight Table. That's because there are no vertices selected. We will now begin selecting vertices and adjusting their weights manually.

11. Minimize the Weight Table, or move it out of the way of the model. We will begin selecting "loops" of vertices around the leg model and adjusting all of the values at the same time.

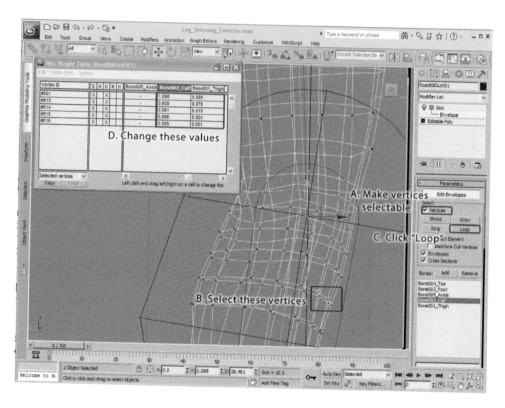

FIG 10.11

12. Click "Vertices" to make the model's vertices selectable. Select a few vertices along a "loop" around the knee, just below the joint. Click the "Loop" button to select all the vertices around the leg. You can simply change the values in each column to adjust the weight influence by each bone. An easy way to do this is to use the "Absolute Effect" field.

FIG 10.12

You will notice that there are a few vertices in the selection that are not influenced by the thigh bone whatsoever.

13. To make a quick change, select the thigh bone in the Weight Table by selecting the top of the column. Then, type a small number, like 0.1 in the "Absolute Value" field. You will notice that all the vertices now share common weight values. It is important to type these values in the bone containing empty fields. If a field has a value of 0, making changes to the other field has no effect. "Normalizing" (where both fields' values add up to 1) can only occur if there are 2 or more bones that influence that vertex's deformation.

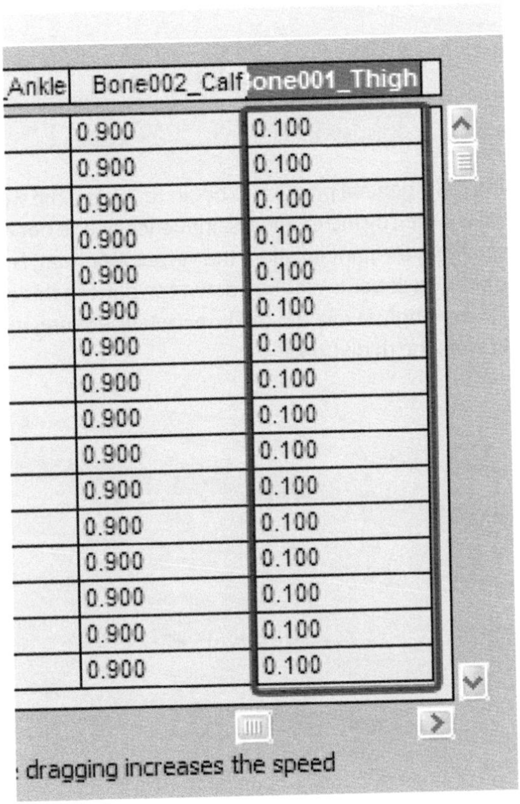

Ankle	Bone002_Calf	Bone001_Thigh
	0.900	0.100
	0.900	0.100
	0.900	0.100
	0.900	0.100
	0.900	0.100
	0.900	0.100
	0.900	0.100
	0.900	0.100
	0.900	0.100
	0.900	0.100
	0.900	0.100
	0.900	0.100
	0.900	0.100
	0.900	0.100
	0.900	0.100
	0.900	0.100

dragging increases the speed

FIG 10.13

14. As you can see, the Weight Table is not as intimidating when you filter just the values you need to adjust. Often, it is easier to type the values in the "absolute" field and confirm the weights in the table. Although it is easy to tweak the values in the Weight Table as well. Simply click in the field and drag the mouse cursor from left to right to make small changes. The vertex will often move interactively while you drag, which is very convenient. This works best when the bone is set to an extreme pose, so the deformation will be visible.

139

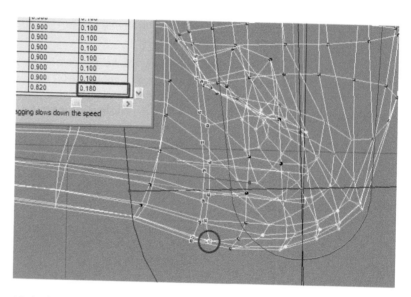

FIG 10.14

15. At this point, it is a general practice to begin to "blend" the weights from one bone to another, by increasing the influence of one bone over the other. Generally, at the joint location, the vertex weighting is 50/50, with equal weight on each bone. Working down the bone in this example, the weighting increasingly favors the calf bone, while working up the leg, the weighting favors the thigh bone.

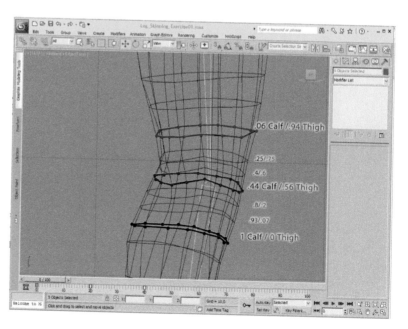

FIG 10.15

These values will, of course, vary with each project. Feel free to use the tweaking technique to begin fixing the problem areas around the inner part of the knee.

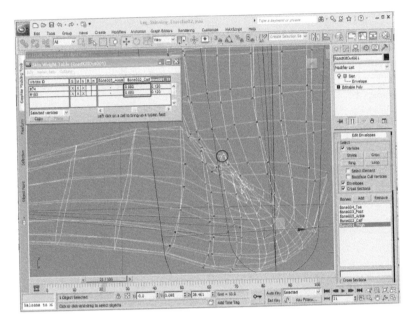

FIG 10.16

16. Select the vertices that intersect unnaturally and begin tweaking the values in the corresponding fields. By "scrubbing" the time slider from frame 0 to 20, you should be able to see the deformation and correct any problems. When completed, the final results should look something like shown in Fig. 10.17.

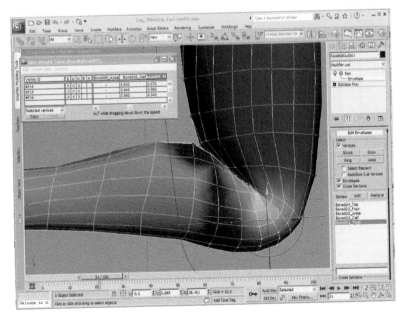

FIG 10.17

I turned on shaded view to see the results more clearly. Notice the nice crease in the back of the leg. All the intersecting vertices have been corrected by carefully tweaking the values of each vertex. This is why it is important to be economical when modeling any character you plan to skin. Inevitably, you will need to tweak these vertices. The fewer there are, the easier it will be to fix.

If you take a look at the Weight Table, you will notice that the total weighting for each vertex will always equal 1. This is called normalizing. The skin system will always level out any vertex's weight to a total of 1, so that no excessive deformation will occur. Of course, you can turn this effect off by unchecking the vertex's box in the "N" column.

FIG 10.18

Vertex ID	S	M	N	R	H	Bone005_Ankle	Bone002_Calf	Bone001_Thigh
#501	X	X	X			-	0.900	0.100
#502	X	X	X			-	0.900	0.100
#503	X	X	X			-	0.900	0.100
#504	X	X	X			-	0.900	0.100
#505	X	X	X			-	0.900	0.100
#506	X	X	X			-	0.900	0.100
#507	X	X	X			-	0.900	0.100
#508	X	X	X			-	0.900	0.100
#509	X	X	X			-	0.900	0.100
#510	X	X	X			-	0.900	0.100
#511	X	X	X			-	0.900	0.100
#512	X	X	X			-	0.900	0.100
#513	X	X	X			-	0.900	0.100
#514	X	X	X			-	0.900	0.100
#515	X	X	X			-	0.900	0.100
#516	X	X	X			-	0.820	0.180

Skin Weight Table (RoadKillOut001)

Edit   Vertex Sets   Options

Selected vertices

Copy   Paste

ALT while dragging slows down the speed

Be careful, however. Unchecking this column while making adjustments could create some unexpected and unpleasant results.

Notice that there are now X's in the "M" column on the left. This indicates that there was some manual weighting being done. If you wish to set the weighting to the default level created by the envelope tools, simply uncheck this column for each vertex you wish to reset to the default value.

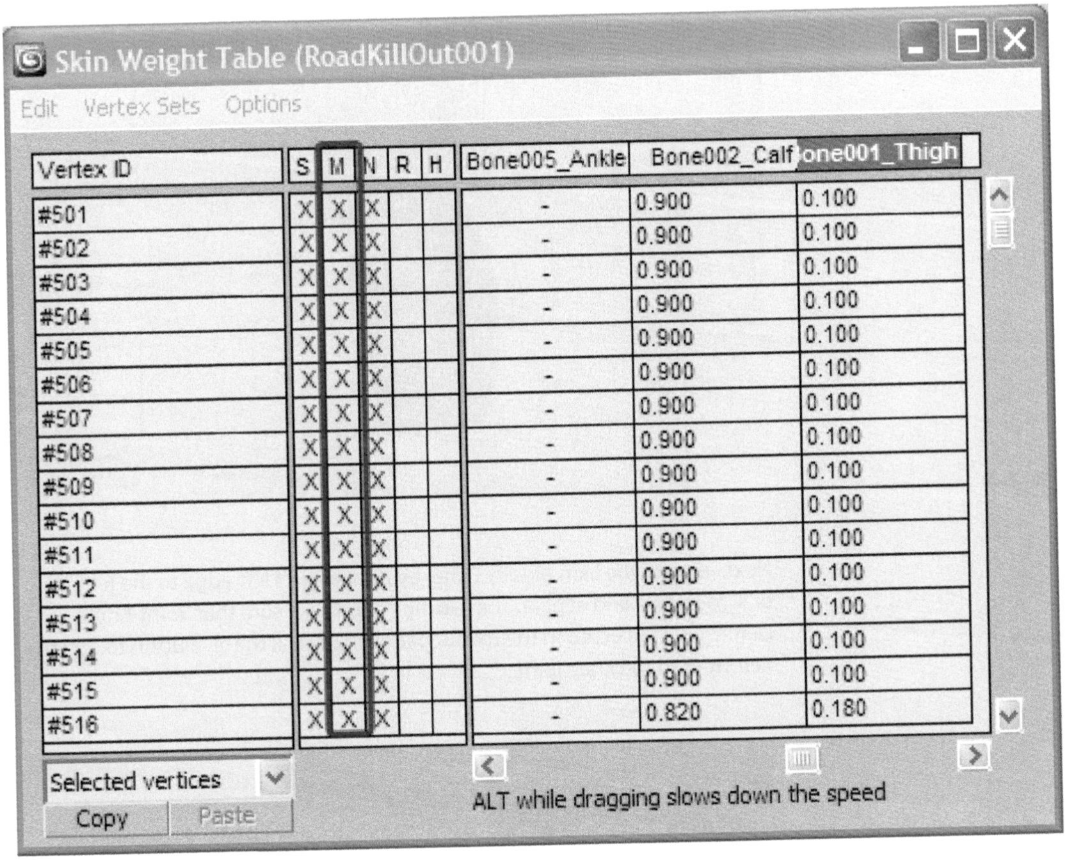

Vertex ID	S	M	N	R	H	Bone005_Ankle	Bone002_Calf	Bone001_Thigh
#501	X	X	X			-	0.900	0.100
#502	X	X	X			-	0.900	0.100
#503	X	X	X			-	0.900	0.100
#504	X	X	X			-	0.900	0.100
#505	X	X	X			-	0.900	0.100
#506	X	X	X			-	0.900	0.100
#507	X	X	X			-	0.900	0.100
#508	X	X	X			-	0.900	0.100
#509	X	X	X			-	0.900	0.100
#510	X	X	X			-	0.900	0.100
#511	X	X	X			-	0.900	0.100
#512	X	X	X			-	0.900	0.100
#513	X	X	X			-	0.900	0.100
#514	X	X	X			-	0.900	0.100
#515	X	X	X			-	0.900	0.100
#516	X	X	X			-	0.820	0.180

Selected vertices

Copy   Paste

ALT while dragging slows down the speed

FIG 10.19

Typically, joints such as the knee or elbow tend to "deflate" and smooth out unnaturally with skinning alone. There are several tools in 3ds MAX to deal with this problem. The one I will be using is called the "Joint Angle Deformer." The effects of this deformer are calculated after all the other deformers have been evaluated, so this is usually the last step in the process of skinning.

17. First, make sure that "Vertices" has been selected in the Skin Modify Panel. Then, select all the vertices around the knee. If you aren't sure how many, go ahead and select a few more rows beyond the knee area. It's generally better to select a bit more than you think you need. A good rule of thumb is about 1/3 the distance from the joint along the bone. Next, select the bone that will be used to "drive" the deformation. In this case, the calf bone. It is generally best to select it in the Bone Dialog Box in the Skin Modify Panel to avoid deselecting the vertices.

143

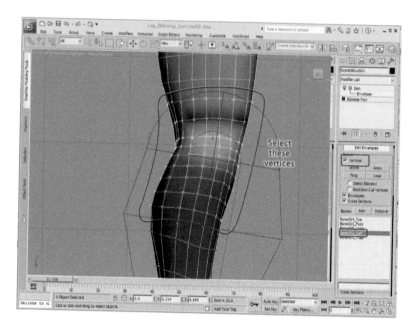

FIG 10.20

Next, expand the Skin Modify Panel by dragging its left edge to the left or scroll down and expand the "Gizmos" tab. Make sure that "Joint Angle Deformer" is selected in the rollout panel, then click the "+" button to add the deformer to the knee joint.

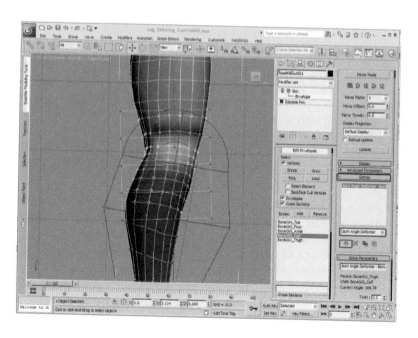

FIG 10.21

Scrub the timeline once again to see the result. You will notice a slight variation in the deformation shape. You can tweak the result in the next steps.

We will start to use this deformer to add some shape to the knee. Notice that the set of 20 control points on this deformer are red. As you bend the knee bone, the control points turn yellow. This shows that there are animation keys on these points.

Unlike time-based keys, which are linked to the timeline, these keys are based on the angle of the bone. These are commonly referred as "Set Driven Keys." As you bend the deforming bones, the points turn yellow. You can set keys along any angle, but it is best to set keys at the most extreme angles, at least to start.

18. Scrub the timeline to frame 20 (or the most extreme angle for the calf bone). Turn on "Edit Lattice" and move the points near the knee outward to create a more realistic shape. The patella helps to retain the angular shape of the knee as it bends, and it is important to show this on a realistic character.

FIG 10.22

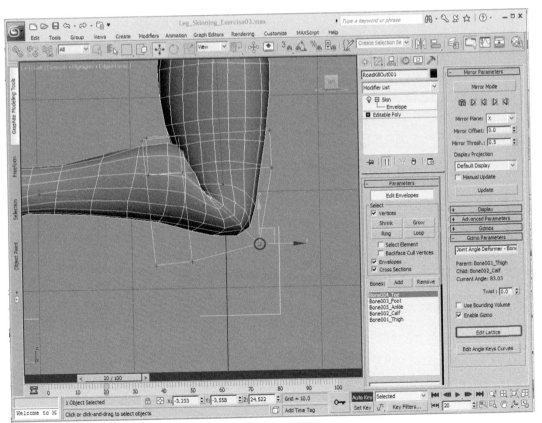

When you add move any point on the deforming lattice, all the points on the lattice turn red. This indicates that another key has been added. This one is at the most extreme angle of the Bone Deformer. Now, when you scrub the timeline, you notice that the points turn red at the most extreme angles, and in between, the points are yellow. Take care to only edit points during these extreme angles, so that you don't inadvertently add more points in between these angles.

19. Scrub the timeline back to frame 20 and make sure the points are red again. Tweak the points at the back of the knee to reduce the intersecting meshes. Now, scrub the timeline again. Notice that the tweaks you make at frame 20 (more accurately, at this joint angle) have no effect on the other angle.

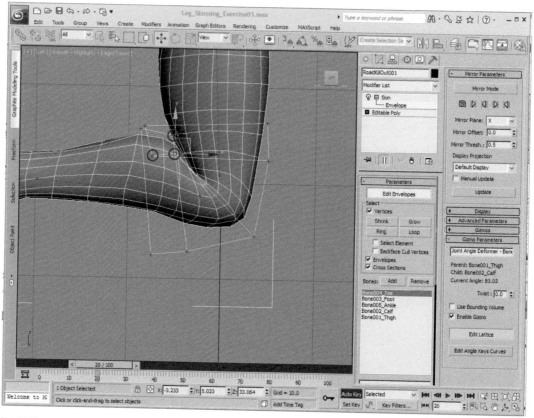

FIG 10.23

If you want to change the value, or at least view the Angle Keys, simply click on the "Edit Angle Keys Curves". This shows the values of the keys during deformation.

Perhaps, the most useful feature of this panel is to see if there are any extra keys that might have been created inadvertently. You can simply remove

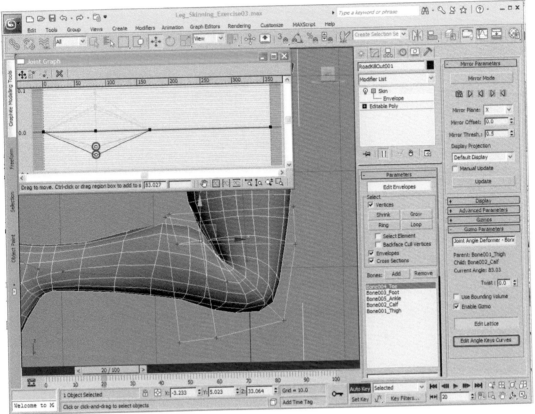

FIG 10.24

those keys by selecting them and pressing the "Delete Point" button (the red X). You can also add some ease-in to each key by right clicking and selecting "Corner," "Bezier-Smooth," or "Bezier Corner," as well as several other options.

We are now finished with this exercise. Save your work with a new file name.

Now, let's try one of the most useful tools in the Skin Panel, the "Mirror Mode". Open the "Mirror_Mode.max" file. We will be working in Perspective mode during this exercise.

I have already added a bone system to this model, in this case a biped system. Technically, there is no difference between biped limbs and any other bone system in 3ds MAX. In fact, any linked objects can be used as bones, even geometry. I have also added the Skin Modifier to this mesh. Notice the problems around the arm when the timeline is scrubbed to frame 20. This is a typical problem for these areas, and using the Skin Weight Table is one of the best ways to solve it. Use the technique we used in the knee to fix the arm.

20. Select these vertices shown in figure below and the upper arm bone in the Skin Modifier Panel. Use the Abs. Effect Rollout to make these weighted entirely to the upper arm (1.0).

147

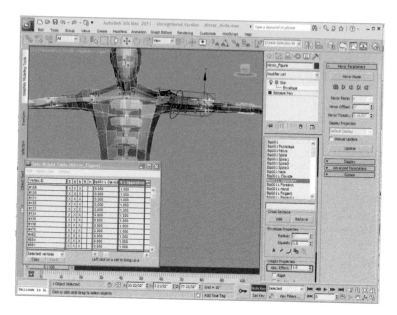

FIG 10.25

Scrub the timeline and notice how much better the arm looks.

21. Next, select the vertices one row closer to the shoulder and armpit. Change the weight to 0.5 in the Abs. Effect Rollout. Scrub the timeline and notice the improved effect. You might also want to tweak the vertex weighting of several other vertices under the arm or along the torso before mirroring the weight adjustments to the other side. It's important to only adjust the weights on one side of the character. The Mirror mode will take care of the other half.

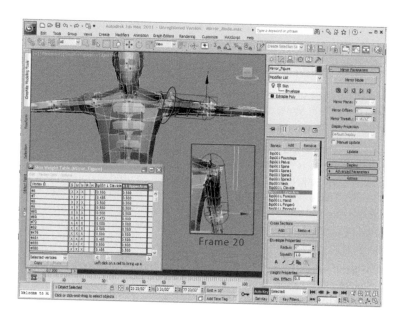

FIG 10.26

22. The next step is to mirror the envelopes. Click the "Mirror Mode" button. You will see all the vertices and bone indicators for the L Upper Arm appear in red. The mirror plane is colored orange and is located just to the right of the center of the figure.

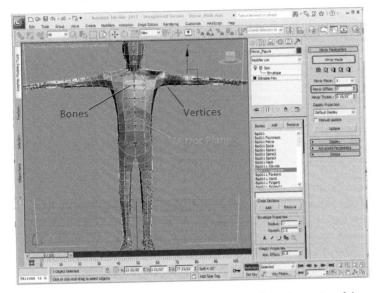

FIG 10.27

Adjust the Mirror Offset until the Mirror Plane is exactly in the center of the figure. You should switch to front view for accuracy. A setting of −4 1/2" should work. Notice that the Bone Indicators and Vertices turn from red to blue (on the character's left) and green (on the right). Typically, 3ds MAX keeps this color scheme for character rigs. Notice that the Character Studio's Biped rig also uses this color scheme.

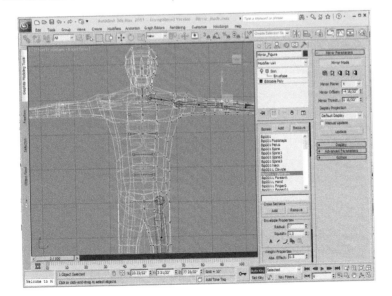

FIG 10.28

23. Now we will transfer all the weight adjustments from the left (blue) side to the right (green) side. It is customary to first transfer the envelopes, then the vertex weights. The buttons below the "Mirror Mode" button allow you to easily do this. Click the "Paste Blue to Green Bones" to transfer the envelopes from the left to the right side. The bones on the character's left side turn yellow to indicate the operation performed correctly. Next, click "Paste Blue to Green Verts" to transfer the vertex weights. The vertices on the left side should also turn yellow.

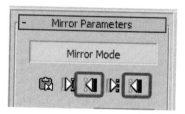

FIG 10.29

When you scrub the timeline, you should see both arms deforming correctly. This technique is a big time saver, literally cutting your work into half for every character. Transferring vertex weights only works for symmetrical characters, however. You may get unexpected results if your character is lop-sided, or the vertex count and position is different for each side. Also, because Joint Angle Deformers don't mirror, you would need to apply those deformers after the mirroring has been completed.

24. As a final touch, let's add a "Bulge" Deformer to the arm. Select the vertices of the upper arm that you wish to include in the deformation. Next, select the bending bone that will "cause" the deformation. In this case, it is the L Forearm bone. Select the Bulge Angle Deformer and add "+" button to add the deformer.

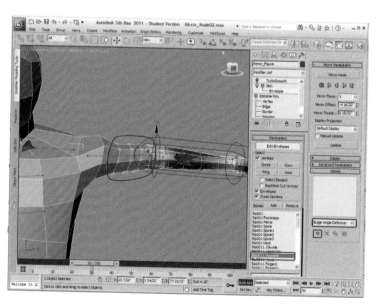

FIG 10.30

Just like the Joint Angle Deformer, you can add a key at the most extreme pose to shape the muscle. Scrub the timeline to frame 40, press the "Edit Lattice," and move the control points to push the bicep into shape. Scrub the timeline from frame 30 to 40 to show the effect. Apply a TurboSmooth Modifier above the Skin Modifier to improve the effect.

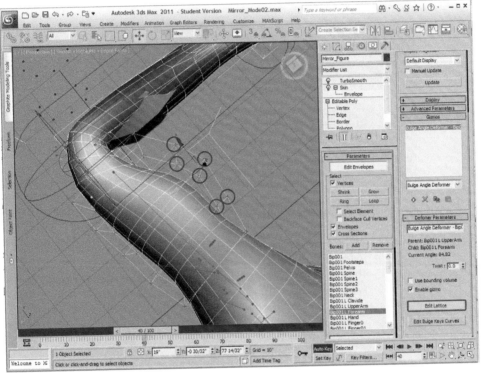

FIG 10.31

The next skin deformer is quite flexible for many different challenging situations. It is called the "Morph Angle Deformer." In a nutshell, it is a morph that is controlled by the angle of the bone. It is perfect for creating bulging muscles, as with the Bulge Angle Deformer, but more complicated deformations as well as simulating tendons. Setting it up requires a few more steps than the more basic Bulge and Angle Deformers but provides a few more options.

25. First, open up the file "Arm_Bulge_Start.max". This file will work equally well for the Morph Angle Deformer. Add a "Skin Morph" Modifier to the stack above the "Skin" Modifier. Turn off the TurboSmooth Modifier if it helps to avoid confusion. Go to the Sub-Object mode, select the vertices around the upper arm. Next, click "Pick Bone," and select the Forearm bone. This will become the bone that will drive the deformation. Click "Create Morph" button. This will set the first Morph key at angle 0.

151

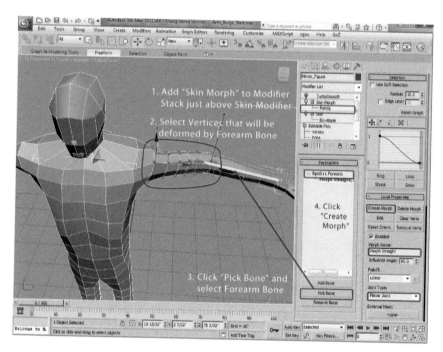

FIG 10.32

26. We have some animation for the forearm in this file. Scrub the animation
to frame 40. The arm goes down, then up, and then bends at the elbow.
This will be the next angle we will key. Click Create Morph in the Local
Properties rollout. Name the new target "Morph Bent".

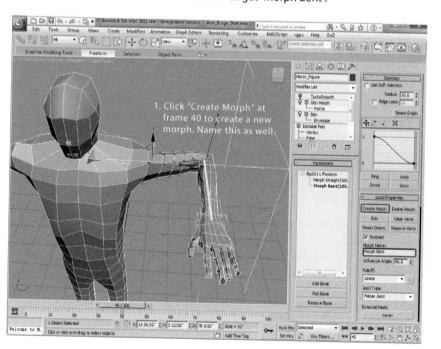

FIG 10.33

Next, click on the "Morph Bent," or the second morph in the list, and click "Edit." Move the vertices of the mesh to create a bulge shape in the arm, and a pointed elbow. Click "Edit" again to turn off edit mode. Scrub the animation back and forth to see the results. Turn on TurboSmooth again for the final effect. If you need to tweak the effect, simply scrub back to frame 40, click on the morp "Morph Bent," click "Edit" and move the vertices some more. Deselect "Edit" and test it again.

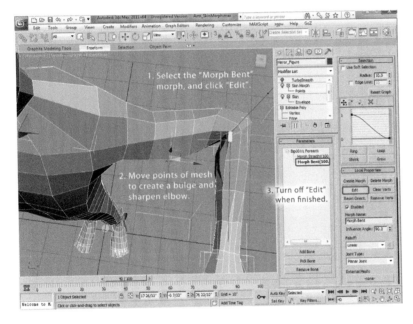

FIG 10.34

The Skin Morph is a very powerful deformer and extremely useful where most deformers will fail to give you the proper results. For the shoulder area, or the hips, you can change the "Joint Type" to "Ball Joint." This is a bit more tricky, so try to use as few morphs to get the result you need.

27. Next, let's wrap a shirt to the figure without resorting to using a cloth simulation system. If you are animating a figure with several different costumes, and the clothes are rather tight fitting, you can avoid the overhead of having to simulate the cloth simply by using the "Skin Wrap" modifier. Open the file "Skin_Wrap_Start.max". You will see the same figure as we have been using, but with a shirt object. This was made simply by copying the body mesh, deleting the modifiers, then deleting the polygons around the hand, head, and lower torso. A "Push" Modifier was applied to create some distance between the body's mesh and the shirt's. The entire mesh was then collapsed into a Editable Poly object.

Select the off-white Shirt object. In the Modifier Panel, add the "Skin Wrap" modifier to it. Click the "Add" button, and select the body Polygonal object as the deforming mesh.

153

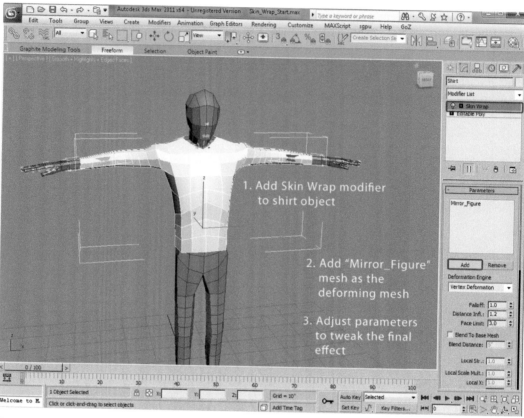

1. Add Skin Wrap modifier to shirt object

2. Add "Mirror_Figure" mesh as the deforming mesh

3. Adjust parameters to tweak the final effect

FIG 10.35

28. Adjust the parameters to tweak the final result. I found that increasing the falloff to 10 improved the results around the shoulder. You might also try an "Edit Poly" Modifier, selecting some vertices, then use a "Push" Modifier around the shoulders and areas where the body's mesh is visible.

These are simple exercises using relatively low polygon models. As you improve your skills, you can begin to tackle much larger, denser meshes. More advanced animation artists and character riggers incorporate weight painting techniques and even complex muscle simulation systems to create more realistic effects for feature films and broadcast. As game engine technology becomes more sophisticated, these systems can be incorporated into those pipelines as well. There are virtually no limits to the levels of realism that an animator is able to achieve but starting with these simple techniques can often be extremely effective.

CHAPTER 11

Camera as an Integral Part of the Scene

Richard Lapidus

Rule: Camera as the integral part of a scene

- Smoothly move a camera in your scene with path constraints.
- Use depth of field for more realism.
- Consider the line of action when using multiple cameras.
- Use a background image.

Part of the learning curve in creating a 3d scene that draws the attention of a viewer and immerses them within the world you are creating is based on a number of factors. The most important being the aspect of how you use your camera. Whenever working with a professional client, one of the first questions I'll ask them is relative to their camera moves. When viewing a poorly animated scene, typically you might see that the animator hasn't thought about the action within the scene and will simply animate the camera from start to finish trying to follow the action or show every important detail. The worst-case scenario is linking the camera to a moving object and following it through the entire scene. This leads to what I call a virtual freeze. That's where one element is stuck in the dead center of the frame and doesn't appear to move that much if at all. Not only does it kill the realism of the scene but it also is very poor composition.

The camera, like most other 3d objects, is maneuverable through space and has unique parameters. The majority of them have the same basic problem to start with, that being a very shaky and poorly moving view of their environment. A set of keyframes are easy to adjust, the problem is that if you haven't visualized in your mind how the camera is the integral link for your viewer to become immersed in the scene, it becomes more than a badly animated object.

I like to think of creating good animation from the aspect of how a person might go about creating a good photograph. There are the elements of good composition, which you can study by taking a class or doing a search on the Internet for the rule of thirds or good composition. Beyond the rules you have to be a good hunter. Here is an example of two really great photographers whom you may want to take a cue from. Those are Ansel Adams and Brassai. Each had very completely different subject matters but was masterful with their artwork because they were familiar with the environment in which they were working. Adams for example would go back to the same places year after year knowing that if he was there at the right time, the environment which he had no control over might provide him with the spectacular shot he was looking for. Brassai would wander the streets of Paris becoming familiar with the atmosphere and the people who just hung out in the streets late at night. In some respects, you have to be a hunter … waiting for the right moment. The similarity is that they have already taken time to be completely immersed in their environments and were waiting for the moment to converge. If you are not viewing your scene from the moment you start building it, you're going to lose an awareness of the 3d space in your mind. In addition, you will probably be chasing after a moving object or trying to display part of the scene that you spent a lot of time working on instead of focusing on the key point. What you're looking for is how the action moves through the scene or the message that you're trying to get across to your viewer. It's key that you maneuver your camera around through the scene and develop in your mind where things are moving around and why.

This purpose of this tutorial is to show you how to animate a camera through a scene smoothly, so that you can start to develop an awareness of the 3d scenes that you will be creating. There are other ways to animate your camera, but I like using a targeted camera controlled by two-path constraints as an exercise in seeing a scene and also a clearly defined line of action. In addition to this controlled camera we will create several other cameras which you might consider switching between in a final rendered project. One of the other great resources for developing an understanding of why you should use more than one camera to define the scene is probably sitting right in your living room. The next time you watch one of your favorite DVDs see if there aren't any extras which talk about how the movie was produced. Very quickly find that most scenes are shots with multiple views and then edited together. It's very seldom that you'll find a production that was shot start to end with just one camera. We will start with loading an old project file that I produced of a school campus. It's not a very good example of modeling by today's standards because the entire scene was created with loft objects. As a resource for discussing cameras, it provides a very nice setting for maneuvering.

1. Load the file called chpt_12_school_campus_load.max.
2. Hit the F3 Key to enter wireframe mode.
3. Create a camera anywhere in the foreground and call it 360 spin camera.
4. Hit the F9 Key and render a simple view. It doesn't need to be the same position as the one in figure below. I just wanted you to explore around a bit and get used to moving the camera up with the Pan, Dolly, and Orbit Tools.

FIG 11.1

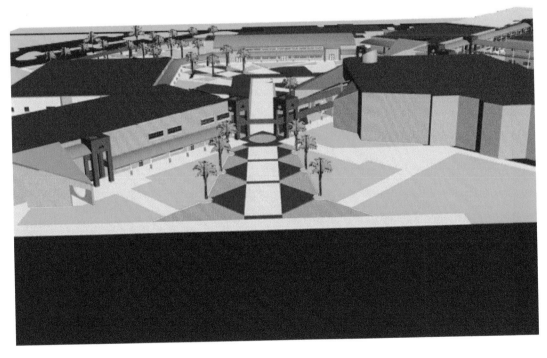

5. Hit the "H Key" or the select by name icon to find the "360 spin camera. target object".

Turn of objects to reduce the
number of displayed assets

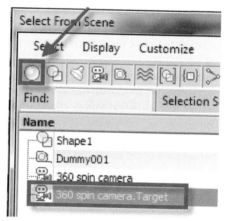

FIG 11.2

6. Drag out the Align Tool to Quick Align per Fig. 11.3 and then use the H Key to select the Dummy001 object by name. This will align camera target to the dummy, which is in the center of an interesting part of the campus.

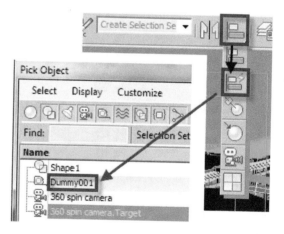

FIG 11.3

7. Switch to the top viewport and select the 360 spin camera object.
8. Link it to Dummy001. We are going to do a pull in and spin around the campus.
9. Save your file. If you like I have incrementally saved the project and called it chpt_12_school_campus_load01.max if you want to have the same exact view as mine through the chapter.
10. Make sure the Select Tool is active and select the Dummy001.
11. Lock the selection with the space bar.
12. Increase the active number of frames to 200 and move the Time Slider to frame 200.

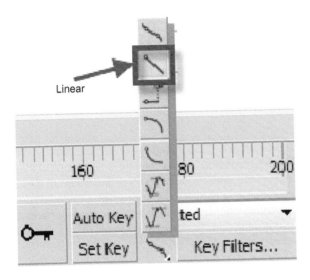

Linear

FIG 11.4

13. Change the key tangent type to linear per Fig. 11.4.
14. Turn on the Auto Key, angle snap ("S" Key), and rotate the dummy 360° on the "Z" axis.
15. Select the Camera and right click the Time Slider at frame 200.
16. Create a keyframe at frame 200 from its current position.
17. Play the animation and you see a perfect 360 looping spin, "BORING".
18. Move to frame 0 and dolly the camera out until most of the scene is in the view.
19. Select the dummy001 object and move its rotation key from frame 0 to 100.
20. Play the animation.

This is one version of the million dollar camera dolly. Not the most pleasing of camera motions on the face of the planet. I used to see this a lot in the early days of animation when someone wanted to fly into the front of a large scene they had built from a long establishing shot and then do a 360 spin around the scene. This is not very pleasing to the eyes. More importantly, it indicates a substantial problem in theory of good cinematic production. Motion does not occur without a reason. I've seen students and professionals spend weeks or months modeling a scene and then animate the camera at the last moment. The tools for helping them kill their animation are the walk-through assistant, path controlled space cameras, linking to a moving object, or even haphazardly moving the camera through the scene. Essentially the focus isn't on good composition and how you move a camera through the scene but just moving the camera, which is an animation at all, it's just motion. The other problem that arises is the fact that your focus is essentially centered in the view even though the camera happens to be moving in this instance. Without the spin to move the camera around, a straight dolly and toward the camera target would essentially be a move without changing the focus of your scene. If you have a moving object and link the camera to it, you will create what's called a "visual freeze." The best example of this was first done by one of my

159

students who built the nose of a dog and linked the camera to it. He animated the nose all over the scene as if it were a dog maneuvering around the way a dog would. What you end up seeing for several hundred frames is a dog's nose frozen in the center of the image. Try this at home and see if it doesn't become very apparent.

Hint

If you must use the walk-through assistant or animate your camera on a path with path constraints, always bring the interpolation of the path from the default of 6 steps to 100 steps. I'm so annoyed with the concept of teaching people how to make it look good with a controlled path that I decided to exclude it from print forever. Previous copies are available if you want to go down this path. Please excuse the pun.

21. Reload the file called chpt_12_school_campus_load01.max.

FIG 11.5

22. Dolly, pan, and orbit the camera, so that you're looking down the main campus entrance. Please feel free to use Fig. 11.5 as a reference.
23. Because this is the setting for an architectural walk-through or backdrop for some animation let's take a look at the mechanics of controlling the camera and some of the elements for setting a scene.

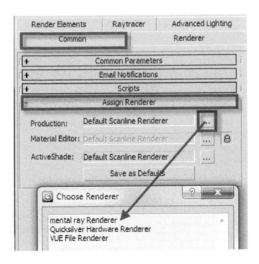

FIG 11.6

24. Hit F10 and at the bottom of the Common Panel, change the rendering type to mental Ray. This will give us a better rendering engine and also a background based on global position and time of day. Those in the next couple steps that we will put together.

25. In the Create Panel, choose the systems radio button.

26. Select daylight and drag out a compass in your scene. This will create a system that will allow you to access accurate global position relative to the sun during some part of the year. This system includes a direct light like any SkyDome, which will do a very nice job of creating outdoor lighting.

27. Click the Modify Panel and change the sunlight to mr Sun and the skylight to mr Sky.

28. When you change the skylight to the mr Sky, you will be prompted to use the mr Physical Sky in the environment map.

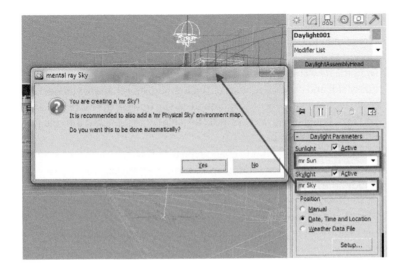

FIG 11.7

29. Hit the eight key on your keyboard to open the environment settings.

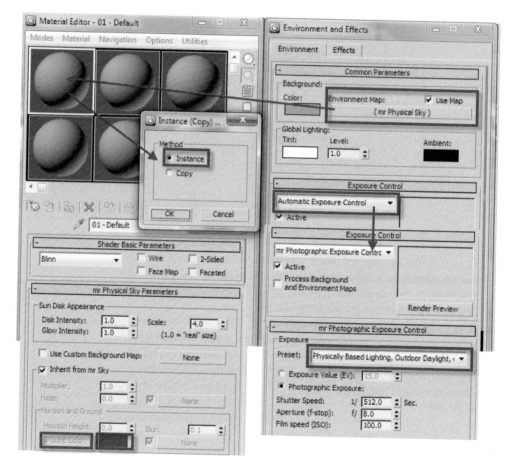

FIG 11.8

30. Please refer to Fig. 11.8 for the following steps.
31. Open a Material Editor and change to Compact mode.
32. Drag the new Environment Map mr Physical Sky into an open Material Editor slot and choose Instance as the method. Any changes you need to make to the environment background can be done in the Material Editor. You can change the size of the disk, the color of the sky, and the color of the ground for example.
33. In the environment settings, change the exposure control from Automatic Exposure Control to mr Photographic Exposure Control.
34. Choose the Physically Based Lighting, Outdoor Daylight, Clear from the Drop-Down.
35. Close both of these dialogues for now.
36. Hit F4 and enable Smooth + Highlights for the Shading mode of the camera viewport.

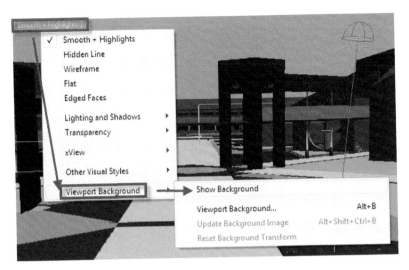

FIG 11.9

37. Left click on Smooth + Highlights and drag down the Viewport
    Background to enable Show Background and choose Viewport
    Background per Fig. 11.9.
38. Click the keyboard shortcut ALT + B to open the Viewport Background
    Dialogue. This can also be dragged out in the same procedure above
    as seen in Fig. 11.9. Enable Environment Background and Display
    Background. Click OK to close the Dialog.

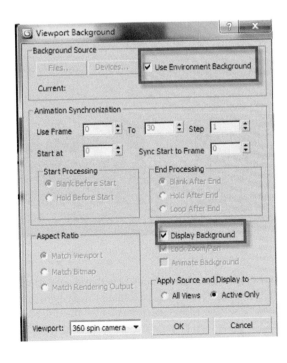

FIG 11.10

FIGS 11.11 and 11.11a

39. Render the view and you should see something like Fig. 11.11A.
40. The last thing we want to do is click the viewports Shading mode, drag across from Lighting and Shadows. Enable Hardware Shading, Exposure and Shadows in the viewport.

FIG 11.12

Your viewport should now look like Fig. 11.12 with the sky and shadows showing in the viewport. Notice how I've rotated the daylight systems North direction to about 296°. This allows you to maneuver the disk of the sun from the mr Physical Sky to be seen in the viewport. I've also sets the hours to about 7 AM and the month to July 21.

41. Hit the Key and select the Camera Target. Notice how it appears in the viewport in Fig. 11.12 when you enable select and move. Drag it up on the "Z" axis until you see the sun's disk. Hardware shaders are very cool.

Part of the process of creating an effective camera move through a scene is making sure that it's lit properly and that you are getting contrast where you need it. If you simply animate the camera through and hope that the lighting is right, the odds are against you that it will work effectively. Thinking back to the example of America's great outdoor photographer, Ansel Adams, he would go back to the same place waiting to catch the right atmosphere to take the amazing shots that he produced. If you haven't had the opportunity to view his work you owe it to yourself to investigate the amazing atmospherics and types of compositions that he put together.

The question always arises as to whether to use free or target camera in a scene. The natural choice would be a free camera because there's only one element to place in the scene and rotate into the view. I've always preferred targeting cameras because it allows me more subtle control of movements in my scene. Think about it for a second, a free camera can only orbit and rotate about its own pivot. Rotations are delineated by even numbers. Moving the targets or the camera gives you more subtle control than a rotation. A really good example of this is to create a very small scene and try to maneuver a free camera. Another way to look at it would be of a viewer wandering around through a scene, the targets can be moved back and forth as if the eyes were wandering as you move through the view.

42. Create a new targets camera in this entryway and also a dummy object.
43. Link the camera and its target to the dummy.
44. Now animate the dummy across the scene.
45. Scrub the timeline and imagine several areas that you may want to show up in the view.
46. Go back in and animate the camera target maneuvering left or right in the viewports. You can actually drag the X or Y spinner in the status line to not have to keep reselecting it and trying to grab the transform gizmo axis.
47. Another way to animate the camera that creates a very smooth move is to go in and set the target on the opposite side of the scene. Create a dummy object near the starting point of the camera and link the camera to the dummy.

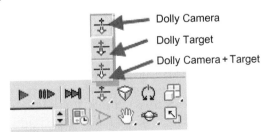

Dolly Camera
Dolly Target
Dolly Camera + Target

FIG 11.13

48. Move through time and then Dolly the camera toward the target. That would be the top Dolly fly out.

49. Now select the dummy object and move it back and forth in the top viewport as you scrub through time. Notice in Fig. 11.14 how smooth the trajectory appears for the camera. For that image, I selected the camera went into the object properties and turn on the trajectory. You can get that smooth of a motion by setting keys and you also run into sort of the same problem using a path constraint. Think of the dummy as of force pushing the camera back and forth. You can even use this concept by animating an object across your screen and then using some movement or rotation on a linked dummy to create nice subtle control.

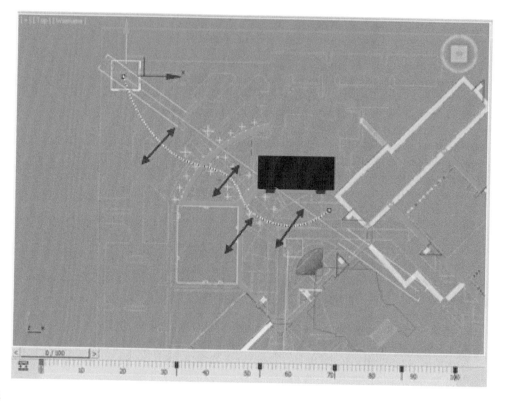

FIG 11.14

Just a few extra hints that you may want to think about while setting up and animating a camera in your scene. The first is to enable the horizon in the Modify Panel for the camera. In terms of good composition, you typically want to keep the horizon somewhere in the lower third of your composition. I can't tell you how many animations I've seen ruined where there was a still background image used with the nonmoving camera. So many people like using the nice backgrounds that ship as part of the program's maps. We've all seen them, these great images of sky with clouds. The problem is that these were shot by someone tilting the camera up into the sky in order not to catch whatever might be in the foreground or on the horizon. Subtly when I see that it feels like something's off. If you use the camera horizon as a reference, this will help you to make adjustments with the background image. You can put an instance of that image into the Material Editor from the environment background and then offset the "V" coordinates. The line of the horizon can be used, so that you can see where the image would tile and repeat in the background environments.

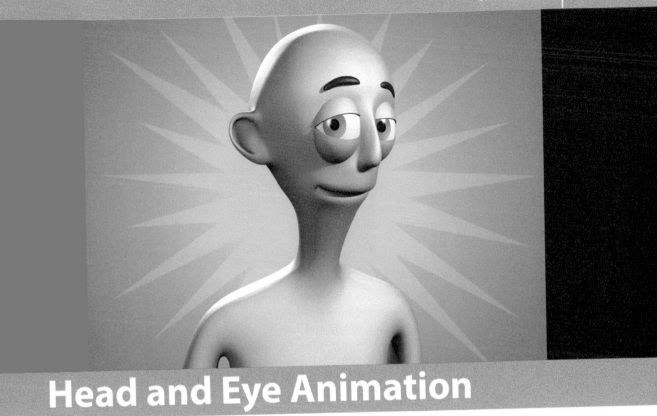

CHAPTER 12

Head and Eye Animation

Chris Tedin

Rule: Head turn, eye movement, and appeal

- Animate the head and eyes in a natural manner.
- Interpret meaning in eye movements.
- Be able to animate eyelids in a naturalistic way.
- Express emotion by animating the head, eyes, eyelids, and eyebrows.

Although your characters can express quite a bit through the movement of their body, much of the emotional expression is going to come through the head. In a medium or close-up shot, the audience's attention is focused on the face. They look for the character's reactions and interpret emotional meaning from the slightest change in expression. The face, especially the eyes, can tell a story without words. It can show what the characters are feeling during the length of a scene. In an effective animation, the audience should see the thought process and be able to know exactly when the character's thoughts or emotions have changed. The face moves the plot forward and pulls the audience into the story.

FIG 12.1

We will begin with the movement of the head. Often the head movement directs the movement of the eyes, and often it lags behind a bit. Eyes, after all, are much smaller and move very quickly. At any rate, it is much easier to animate the larger object and place the eyes where they need to be afterward. You can, of course, tweak the head motion after the eyes, if it makes sense. It is an iterative process, with constant refinements back and forth. This can often be the most difficult type of animation, since so much can be said with very small movements.

We will talk about "motivation" in terms of head and eye movement. What causes the person to move their head? Is the character surprised by a sudden sound? Is he interested in something and wants to look more closely? Is she looking away shyly, while her eyes linger, focused on the object of her interest? Think carefully about what your character is doing in the scene and that will direct the motion of the head. The speed is also crucial. A very slow turn of the head can indicate fear, especially if the eyes lead ahead, turned as far as they can, showing a lot of white. View the animation *Slow_Head_Turn .mov* to see this effect.

A very fast head motion, otherwise known as an "accent" can show surprise. Another type of accent is known as a *take*. The head turns to look at something rather slowly. The character's head then turns away, as if seeing nothing out of the ordinary. The face reacts, and the head turns quickly to look again. View *Take_Accent.mov*. More commonly known as a double-take, it can be used for comedic effect.

To create natural movements, it is important to use arcs with the movement of the head. Turning the head in a flat motion gives the character an unnatural feeling. The character is not a robot, and a linear motion would give him a mechanical look. Robotic machine joints pivot on single point of rotation, or at most, a couple. The human neck is comprised of seven cervical vertebrae, which is arched backward slightly. There are dozens of muscles pulling these bones in almost every direction. It would be almost impossible for this configuration to produce the same motion as a simple machine. Most animators add a slight dip at the middle of the human head turn. Overhead arcs are much less common.

Now, let's give it a try. We will do a few simple head movements, working on the turn of the head. We'll create this motion using three simple keys, including a nice soft arc. Open "Head_Turn_Start.max". There is a simple bust figure, fully rigged for head motion as well as some eye motion, which we will do later. The basic movements of the head and neck, as well as shoulder movements are contained in two point objects. The lower point object, called *Head_Neck_Shoulder*, contains sliders for moving those parts. The face is animated by the sliders on the *Face* object.

1. We will start out very simply, with a very basic head turn. The initial pose is a little stiff, so let's start with something a little more relaxed. It's important to give the figure some life, even if it's sitting still. Scrub the Time Slider to frame 5. It is a good idea to start your first frame of animation on any frame *except* frame 0. I use frame 0 for skinning and like to return the character to that pose to do any tweaking of the Skin Modifier. Turn on the Auto Key button and let's make a few adjustments.

2. First, angle the base of the figure by selecting the purple ellipse, body base, and rotate the "Y" axis to about −8° and the Z axis to about −8° as well. Next, select the Head_Neck_Shoulder object and use these settings:

NeckTurn	1.3	NeckNod	−1.1	NeckSide	−0.5
HeadTurn	1.0	HeadNod	−0.2	HeadSide	−0.3
LShoulderUp	4.8	RShoulderUp	0.0		

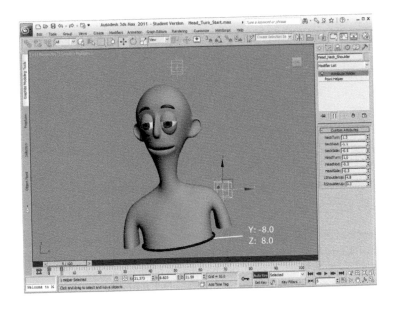

FIG 12.2

171

This has the effect of giving the character a more casual, asymmetric pose. We avoid the dreaded "twinning," where the body is symmetrical, stiff, and unnatural. We are catching him staring off into space a bit, in a relaxed manner.

3. We will add the next key, which will be at the end of the turn. We will come back and do the middle key or "breakdown" next. Scrub the timeline to frame 60. Rotate the body on the "Z" axis to about 22°, then on the "Y" axis to about 5°. We are using the world coordinates, which you can see directly under the timeline. Normally, you would use the local coordinate system for rotating body parts, but for the sake of simplicity, let's use the world coordinate system, as it is easier to simply set the absolute numbers.

It is important to rotate the body as well as the head during a turn or any head movement. Rarely the head moves without being driven by the initial movement of the body. Sometimes, the head will move before the body, especially when surprised, but usually the body moves first.

4. Next, set the values in the sliders to turn the rest of the body. You can use these values as a starting point but feel free to try different positions.

NeckTurn	−6.0	NeckNod	2.3	NeckSide	−4.0
HeadTurn	−4.0	HeadNod	−4.5	HeadSide	2.3
LShoulderUp	1.3	RShoulderUp	1.9		

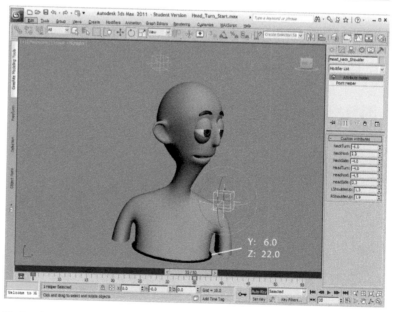

FIG 12.3

Notice that the character rig has controls for both the neck and head. Using both of these allows for some more flexible poses and movements. I have the character's neck tilted forward, but the head is tilted back. This gives him a more attentive and interested appearance, which is motivating the head turn.

If you play the timeline, the movement is rather stiff. Let's add a few things that will give him a bit more life.

5. First, let's move the Time Slider to the middle position between the keys at 5 and 35. Frame 20 will be our "breakdown" key, generally used to add some subtlety to the transition between two major keyframes. Make sure that the Auto Key button is still pressed. Only adjust the NeckNod and HeadNod values:

NeckNod: 2.5   HeadNod: 0.0

Be sure to add keys to the rest of the values as well. Simply clicking the arrows up and down will turn them red and add the keys. This is a good practice and keeps all the keys organized and set on the same frame.

6. Now, to add a little overlapping, let's delay the head movement slightly. In this way, the body leads, and the head follows the action, and the whole figure doesn't stop on exactly the same frame. This will give it a more natural feel.

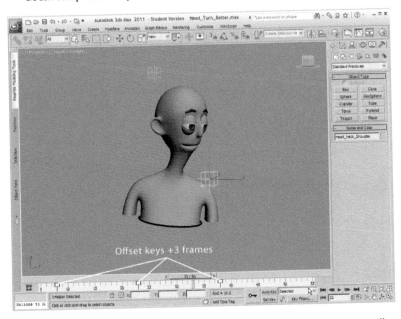

FIG 12.4

Play the animation and notice the difference. It's much more natural, but still missing something. Most people tend to blink while moving their heads. In fact, blinks are a great way to signal that something in the story is changing. If characters change their minds, they blink. If they are surprised, suddenly realize something, or change their attention in any way, they blink. Let's add a blink here in the middle of the turn.

7. Scrub back to frame 15. Select the point object over the character's head, called "Face." Key "LeftEyelidUpper" and RightEyelidUpper" by scrolling back and forth to go back to 0.0. The arrows should be framed with red to

173

indicate that a key has been set. Next, scrub to frame 17 and set both of these values to 10.0.

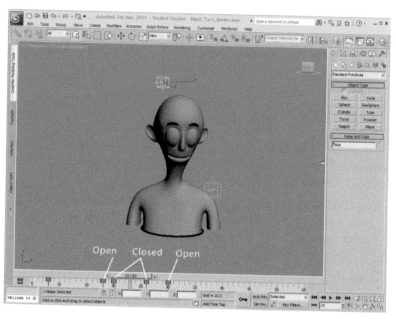

FIG 12.5

8. Next, move to frame 23, reset keys at 10.0 to keep them closed for three frames. At frame 27, set the values to 0. This should give the eyes a 12-frame blink, with a rather slow and casual speed. The eyelids close a bit quicker and open a bit slower in most cases. You could also open the Dope Sheet and offset each eyelid a frame to give them a slightly asymmetrical appearance.

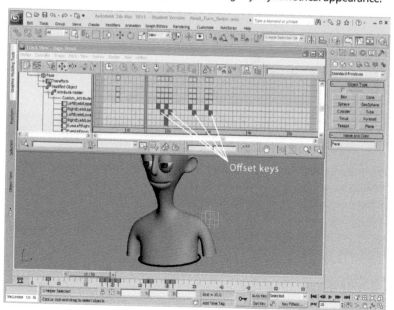

FIG 12.6

Okay, we have some more subtle motion, but it still could use a little more work. I'm going to play it back and forth a few times and have a little fun. Sometimes it is a good idea to add a little variety to the breakdown key, so that it has some nice variation compared with the main keyframes. We are going to do a little trick that will give the head a bit of "lead in." Simply tilt the head slightly into the move.

9. Scrub the Time Slider to the breakdown key, which is now at frame 23. Select the "Head_Neck_Shoulder" control and adjust the tilt of the head slightly with these values:

NeckSide: −1.75   HeadSide: −2.7

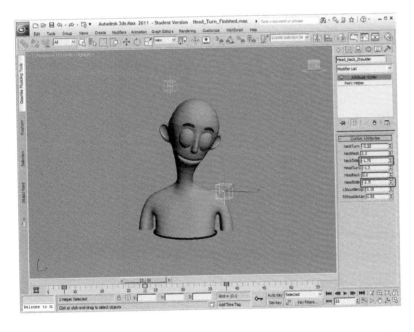

FIG 12.7

Now, play the motion to see the final effect. Feel free to play around with the pose in the middle to get even more fun and playful expressions. The art is in the motion, capturing the personality of the character between the poses.

We can only do so much with the head. It can give us an indication to what the character is thinking and feeling. No part of the face can communicate more clearly than the eyes. They speak to us by the direction they are pointing, the lids that cover them over, not to mention the brow ridge and the eyebrows. Even the pupil's dilation can speak to us about whether they are interested in their subject or not. Weary, bloodshot eyes tell the story of a late night. Bright, cheerful eyes can communicate love and affection, or perhaps just a good night's sleep. Darting eyes make the character seem

175

distrustful, while eyes that look down and to the right or left seem to indicate that a choice is being made. Eyes that look up to the right or left show that the character is trying to remember something.

Let's look at a few examples of how the eye position relates to the head and how you can use their relationships to communicate the character's attitude. For example, if a character is looking directly at you with both his body and eyes, it shows complete attentiveness. However, if the character's head is tilted away while his eyes are locked on you, it can communicate several things. If the head is looking down, it can be very submissive. If turned directly aside, he can show a level of distrust. If the head is turned up and the eyes look down the nose, it can show a condescending attitude.

FIG 12.8

FIG 12.9

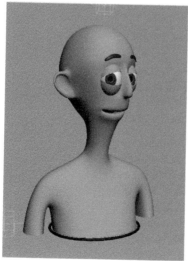

FIG 12.10

FIG 12.11

When the eyes look away and begin to focus on other things or other people in the scene, there are a few things to consider. Although it is a common practice to use things like "Look-At" constraints to direct the eyes to a single point object. Then, by moving that object around the scene, the eyes can be directly aimed at any object in the scene. Although this seems logical and sensible, the practical limitations to this setup begin to become apparent.

First, the eyes move very, very quickly. Often, they will move to a new location in one or two frames. Most beginning animators feel uncomfortable moving the "Look-At" object that quickly, so you tend to get sluggish eye movement. Eye movements are called "Darts" for a good reason. They tend to dart about very quickly. Your "Look-At" object should move around quickly.

Second, there is no real reason that the eyes have to be focused on an object precisely. In fact, it is better to have the eyes pointing in the general direction of the object. The object is 90° away from the camera in this example. If the eyes were to point precisely at the object, and if the head were turned too far, we would not even see the eyes at all, just the edges of the iris, and a lot of white. This is not very attractive. Simply turn the head a bit to show more of the face and both eyes, and turn the eyes slightly and the effect is much better. It is not precise, but the audience simply can't tell the difference. Even having the head face the camera and let the eyes point 45° toward the object works. It is nowhere near focused on the object, but it communicates much better.

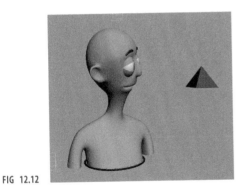

FIG 12.12

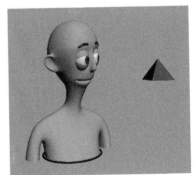

FIG 12.13

FIG 12.14

The eyelids can express quite a lot as well. They can cover up the eyes, hiding them from view. When a character is trying to be sneaky, introverted, or simply too tired to be extroverted, covering the eyes can help create this attitude. The lids can open fully and uncover the eye, leaving them bare, innocent, and vulnerable. Young children usually have very wide eyes, especially when excited or playful. No matter what expression the character exhibits, the eyelids almost never leave the iris completely exposed. Some part is almost always covered up. Usually the bottom lid covers some portion of the iris, and if the character is showing alertness, it is the upper lid that moves off the iris. Below, the first character has a moderately alert expression. The next character has a normal expression. The upper lid covers a bit of the iris, but no part of the pupil is covered. If that happens, the character looks half asleep, as in the last example.

FIG 12.15

FIG 12.16

FIG 12.17

Let's first look at how the lids work as the eye moves around the eye socket. With any given expression, the relationship stays relatively constant while the eyes move around. When the eye rotates upward, both lids follow, almost covering the same part of the iris. Don't make it too precise, however. That would look unnatural.

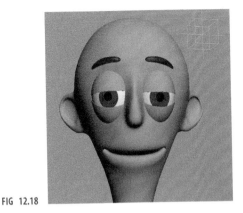

FIG 12.18

FIG 12.19

FIG 12.20

I have set up this character rig to move the eyes with a few sliders, one for the up/down direction, and the other for the left-right direction. Let's play around with a few eye movements and try to create naturalistic motion. There are a few things to think about when moving the eyes. First, the eyes move very quickly, often within a few frames. If the eyes are panning across a scene, they will jump several times across the arc of the pan. The eyes tend to lock on single objects one at a time, and seldom slide across any part of the scene. Try it yourself. Turn your head slowly across the room and see if you can get your eyes to slide. Difficult, isn't it?

Now, let's try a more simple task. Let's keep the head still and pan the eyes across the scene. This is a little easier, since moving the head would require the eyes to stay in one place, requiring the animator to reverse the motion of the eyes to keep the illusion that they were staying still. We will try that after this first example.

1. Open "Eye_Pan_Start.max." Scrub to frame 5 (the beginning) and push the eyes all the way over to the right by sliding the *EyesLeftRight* slider to 10.
2. Then, create several more keys every 10–15 seconds, adjusting the *EyesLeftRight* incrementally each frame, approximately 5 units, until the eyes stop over at the other side. Also at each frame, move the eyes upward

179

a little, then downward to create an arching motion. Use the *EyesUpDown* slider and make sure you use the same frames as the *EyesLeftRight* movement. Your results should look like this, with a keyframe at every 10–15 frames.

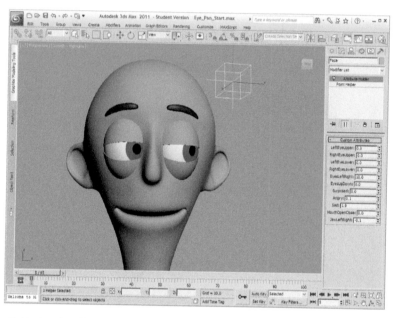

FIG 12.21

3. Notice that the eyes still slide across the frame. We need to copy each key and slide it over to just before the next key (2 frames), so the eyes hold for those frames. You can simply shift-drag a frame to copy it.

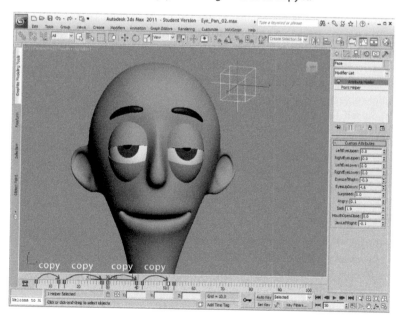

FIG 12.22

4. Now, let's adjust the eyebrows so that they follow along the movement of the eyes. Use the *LeftEyeUpper* and *RightEyeUpper* sliders to keep the upper lid in the same part of the iris, just above the pupil. Use the same keyframes we created for the movement of the eyes. Next, use the *LeftEyeLower* and *RightEyeLower* to do the same with the lower lid. The lower lid doesn't have to follow as accurately as the upper lid, however. You can make its motion follow the eyes a little less closely in most cases.

Now let's take this simple movement and use it for some more expressive facial animation. Let's show the character's thought process while trying to make a decision. We'll incorporate some subtle head movement with some eye darts. Each movement of the eyes will give the audience a glimpse into the mind of the character, bringing them into the story and allowing the audience to see things from the character's point of view. We'll use a little of the eyebrows as well, to add some accent to the expression.

1. Open "Face_Expression_Eye_Darts_Start.max". Make sure the timeline is set to frame 5 and the "Auto Key" button is pressed. Now, let's give him a starting expression. Making a decision takes some time, so let's not rush things too much. We want the expression to be meaningful to start out with, and gradually develop so that there are noticeable and specific changes to his expression.
2. I start by looking down and away from the camera. I take three moves for the eyes to get to that position. The first move is at frame 30, and the next is at frame 60. I stutter the movement of the eyes, so that they seem less confident. Especially in the first part of the animation, where the character is most confused or challenged by the decisions, the eye movement is in small increments. I set another key at frame 90 with an extreme look to the right. Right before a large move, I set a key in the opposite direction. This acts as an anticipation of the move and makes the move seem that much stronger.
3. It may not be technically realistic, but moving the eyes side to side while looking down often communicates a decision-making process. Let's begin moving the eyes to the other extreme position by setting keys at various random points along an arc moving from the character's right to the left. I set keys at frame 145 and 153 to keep the motion relatively incremental, creating some nice variation in the timing. It is important not to set keys at regular intervals for these eye darts. If they are set at even spacing, the movement appears very mechanical and regular. Finally, at frame 195, the eyes are completely to the character's left. If you notice, the eyes are directed more toward the camera now, and the audience is more engaged with the character.
4. Now, we will zigzag and move the eyes up a bit, at frames 250 and 290. Finally, at frame 330, we will pull the eyes back to the center, just as he is starting to come to a realization or final decision. I pull the eyes down a few frames, then pop them up, widen the eyelids, and raise the eyebrows for the final effect. He has come to the decision at frame 412.

5. Again, if we play this back, the motion of the eyes is slow and steady. To move the eye from one position, then hold it, and then to the next position, you need to copy each key you have made and slide it up to the left of the next key. It might be easier to zoom in on the timeline at the bottom of the screen. Hold down the CTL-ALT buttons and slide with your right mouse button to expand or contract the right side of the timeline. The CTL-ALT left button will expand and contract the left side. Control-Alt middle mouse button will slide the timeline backward and forward. If you zoom into the first few frames, you will be able to copy much more easily.

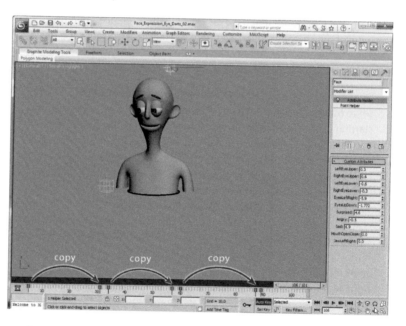

FIG 12.23

6. If you look at the figure below, it shows each eye position holding for a certain number of frames, then moving quickly to the next keyframe. This should be your final result. Open Face_Expression_Eye_Darts_Finished .max to see the final results.

I have also added some expression in the eyebrows, as well as some head movement. Feel free to experiment with this technique on your own. Record yourself with a webcam and see if you can follow along with your own eye motions.

Now, let's have a bit of fun and put some of these techniques to practical use. One of the staples in comedy is called the "double-take." When an actor looks at something for a moment, looks away, reacts, and then snaps quickly to the object in obvious surprise, the audience feels the actor's instant moment of reaction. It is almost a cliché; however in comedy, it can be very amusing. Add a beverage, and it becomes a "spit-take."

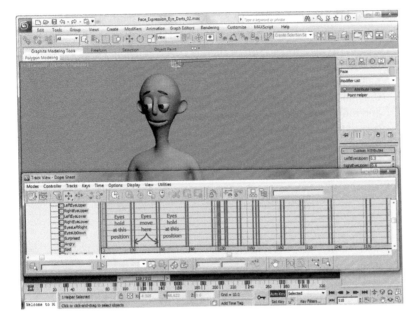

FIG 12.24

Let's try this out. Begin by opening up the file "Head_DoubleTake_Start.max." The opening expression at frame 5 is pretty bland, so it's a pretty good starting point. The final expression is going to be one of surprise and shock, so a blank expression will provide a nice contrast.

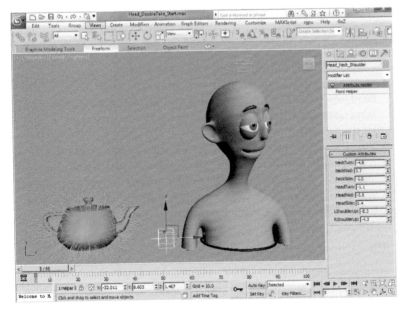

FIG 12.25

1. Let's adjust the position of the head away from the object (in this case a furry teapot) that will surprise him. You can use the amount in the figure above. The eyes should also be slightly closed and pointed off in space.
2. Now, move the Time Slider to frame 50. This will give him a second and a half to slowly turn and "discover" the teapot. Later, we will add a blink in the middle of the turn, as well as a slight dip. Make sure "Auto Key" is on, and turn the head and neck to face the teapot. Drop the eyes down to look at the teapot. Remember to adjust the eyelids to follow the eyes, so that the top eyelids still cover the top of the iris. We need to make sure he stays disinterested, and keeping the tops of the iris covered allows us to express that.

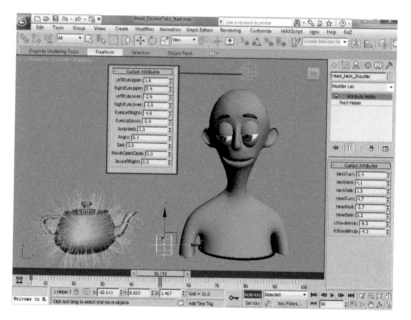

FIG 12.26

3. Remember that we only want him to casually look over at the teapot. The head moves over just enough to allow the eyes to glance over. The head takes quite a lot more effort than the eyes, so he is expending little effort for this first look.
4. Now, just as slowly, he will look away. You might be able to simply copy the keyframes back from frame 5 to a new keyframe at frame 80. The look away is slightly quicker, but we will pause it at frame 80 for a second or so. We will be adding some more keyframes, so use the "time configuration" button, and extend the animation to about 150 frames.

Tip

To make keyframing easier for the individual custom attributes, you can select the "Key Filters" button and select "All." Now, when you click "Set Key," it will key all the parameters for the two green control objects.

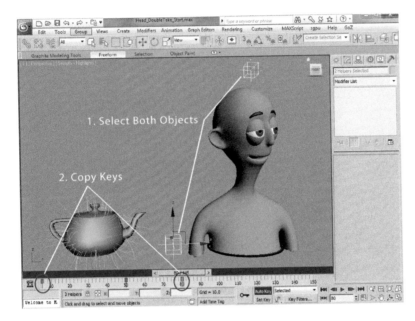

FIG 12.27

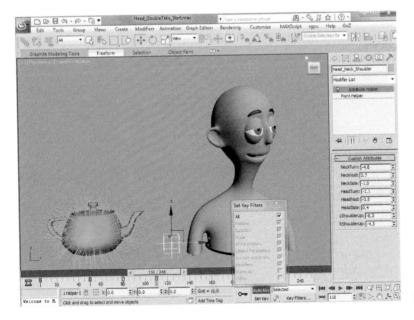

FIG 12.28

5. Move the Time Slider to frame 110. Select both objects and the blue "BodyBase" circle under the character. Click the Set Keys icon (not the "Set Key" button, but the one with the Key icon) to set keys for everything. This will hold the pose for a second, allowing him to realize that he just saw something strange. At this key, adjust the eyelids a bit to open them up.

185

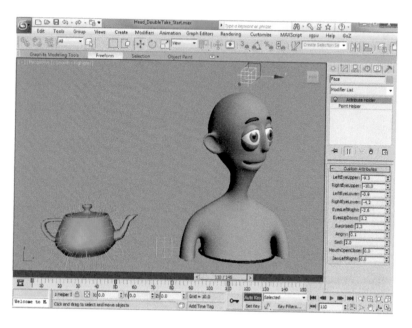

FIG 12.29

6. Now, the quick turn at the end will be done very fast, with no blink in between. Let's try 8 frames to see how that looks. I rotated the "BodyBase" circle −12° in the "Z" axis to give the whole body more energy as well.

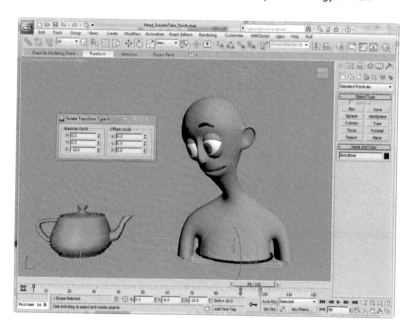

FIG 12.30

7. I think that speed is about right. Do a "Grab Viewport/Create Animated Sequence File" under tools to preview the motion so far. The reaction time looks a little slow. Select all the green control objects and the blue

"Body Base." Select the keyframes at frames 110 and 118 and drag them to frames 90 and 98, respectively.

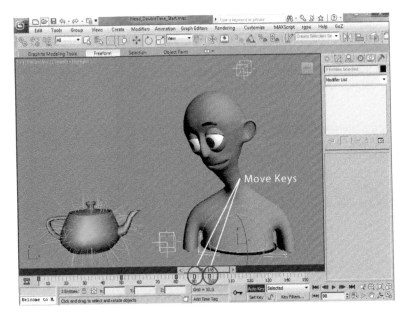

FIG 12.31

8. The motion is much better and timed out about right, but it still looks mechanical. Let's fix this by adding a slight dip and blink at the first head turn. Move the Time Slider to frame 25, about midway through the first turn. Lower the head by a few degrees by adjusting the NeckNod and HeadNod values slightly. Do the same at frame 65.

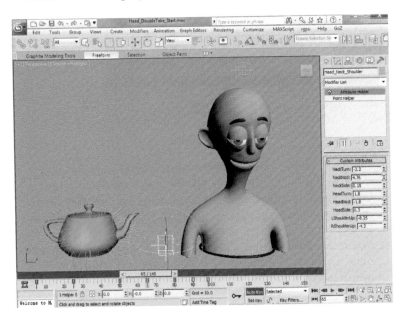

FIG 12.32

187

9. Now, let's add a blink around those same frames. Remember to add two keys on each side of the blink, so the eyes stay closed for a few frames. This will give the eyes a "lazy" look. A single frame blink is too quick for this particular example. You may need to open up the Curve Editor to make sure your blinks are timed properly. Since we set a key earlier at frames 25 and 65, we will need to make sure the eyes stay closed. Referencing the Curve Editor is important. You can find the keys under "Modified Object>Attribute Holder>Custom_Attributes."

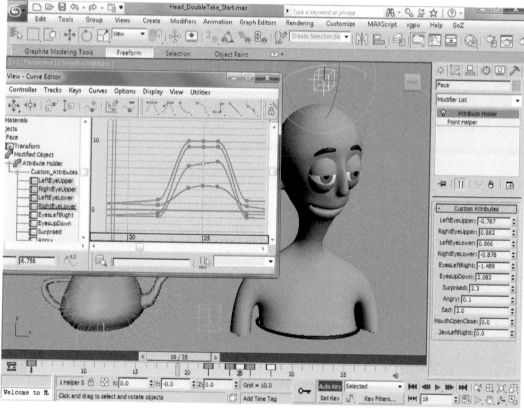

FIG 12.33

10. The reaction at the end of the second head turn is a bit too slow. Let's move the keys for the eyelids from frame 80 to 83, and the other key from frame 90 to frame 86. This will speed up the "eye pop," giving him a stronger reaction. Also, increase the eyebrows "Surprised" value to 10 at frame 86. This will increase the effect.
11. Now, I really don't like having an object come to a dead stop, so let's add some "overshoot" to the final turn. Since it comes in so fast, it looks more natural to have it flow past the final key and bounce back a bit. At frame

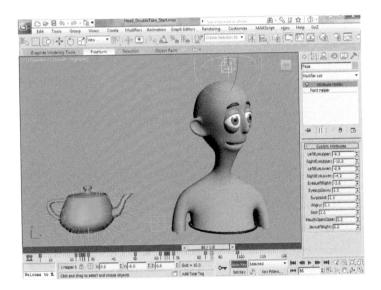

FIG 12.34

102, use the NeadNod, NeckSide, HeadNod, and HeadSide to bend the head a little forward. Then, copy the key at frame 98 to frame 106 and that should bring the head to a proper rest.

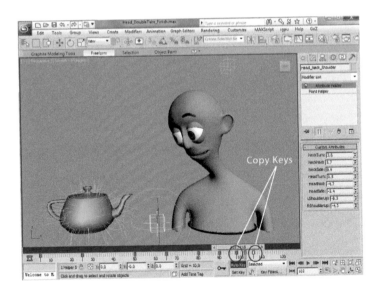

FIG 12.35

Of course, these are just quick guidelines to get a "base" animation. Spend some time with a webcam and try making some of these double-take movements yourself. Time the sequences out and try to emulate the motion. After that, do another pass with exaggeration and "snap" to give it that extra cartoon effect.

189

CHAPTER 13

Secondary Motion and Breaking Joints

Chris Tedin

Rule: Secondary motion and overlapping motion

- Animate limbs with sequential breaking joints.
- Create cloth simulations with realistic effects.
- Create hair simulations using cloth system.
- Use spring controllers to simulate body jiggle.

Creating natural, believable movement is one of the most challenging jobs in the industry. Humans move with an amazing level of complexity and with an almost infinite variety. Factors such as age, gender, size, physical build, emotion, and physical language all play a part in each individual's movement and timing. Understanding takes a great deal of observation. Professional animators watch people as they move for hours at a time, often videotaping where appropriate, such as public places. Old men getting up from a picnic bench, feeling the weight of their bones, aches and pains from an injury long ago, can be a great inspiration for a short film. In contrast, a room full of 6-year-old children happily playing hide and seek could fuel the creativity of any ambitious animator. Anyone or anything can be a great subject for animation, as long as the artist approaches them with loving care and attention.

Tail Wag

This chapter will look at a group of animation techniques that are lumped into a large group: "secondary motion." In the broadest sense, secondary motion is any movement that comes after the motion that is initially directed by the character, animal, machine, or object. For example, when a fat character jumps up and down, the belly will tend to wiggle after the primary motion has finished. When a walking woman wearing a long dress suddenly stops, the gown might flow around her for a few seconds before coming to a rest. We will also talk about the concept of "breaking joints," which can be seen in a wagging tail. The base of the tail might move first, while the tip follows behind a fraction of a second, like the action of a whip. Fish and whales demonstrate this motion effectively while gliding and darting through the water. Even humans, such as a ballet dancer, gracefully extend their shoulders, arms, wrists, and fingers in a beautiful flowing sequence, avoiding the abrupt sudden stop of the entire arm. In fact, this "breaking" is common in almost any human movement and is something to keep watch for while observing your subjects.

1. We will begin by creating this "breaking joint" movement using a simple wagging tail. Open the "Tail_Wag.max" file to work along with this section. Maximize the top viewport and double click the first bone in the viewport. This selects all the bones in the rig.
2. Next, click the Curve Editor button on the Main toolbar. When the editor opens, click "Modes" on the Menu Panel and change it to Dope Sheet. The bones are listed on the panel on the left, indented to indicate their parent-child relationship.

Notice how all the keys in the rig are lined up on every 10th frame.

FIG 13.1

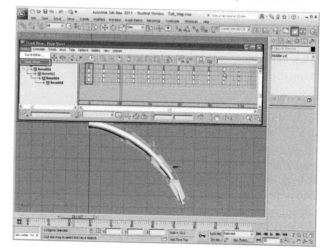

3. Double click Bone002, which is the second bone in the hierarchy. Notice that the first bone disappears, and only Bone002, Bone003, Bone004, and Bone005 remain in the Dope Sheet Editor. The Editor's filter has been set to show only selected and animated objects. All other objects disappear. This is to keep things simple for the animator, but those settings can be changed if you wish.

4. Move all the remaining keys on the Editor 2 frames to the right. This will delay their motion slightly. Notice how the keys on the bottom panel under the Time Slider also move slightly. This compact view of the Dope Sheet shows all keys for the selected objects but compresses them onto a single timeline. It is best to use the full Dope Sheet until you get more experience and use the compact viewer for animating single objects.

5. Next, double click Bone003 and move their keys a few frames to the right. Repeat this for the remaining bone, Bone004. You can ignore the last bone, which is the tip, and is not animated.

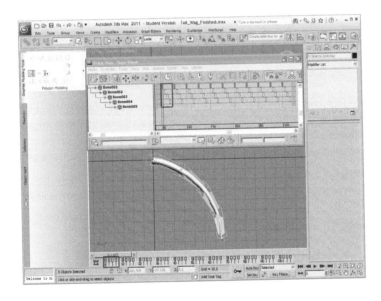

FIG 13.2

6. Now, close the Dope Sheet and play the animation. You can see how the motion is much more fluid and "soft". Open "Tail_Wag_Finished.max" to see the final result. You can also use this technique to simulate a more fluid whipping motion or fish-like motion by simply moving each set of keys a bit more (perhaps 3 frames), and the effect is much more extreme. Open "Tail_Wag_Fish.max" to see this result. Notice that by simply moving a key can have a big effect on the final look of the animation. Of course, if you want a more spring-like effect, more like a whippet than a golden retriever, you could delay the keys a single frame. The choice is yours.

This is a simple technique, and the effect is easily achieved. Take this to another, more nuanced example, and you can see how this technique still works very effectively.

7. Open "Secondary_Fishing_Pole_Start.Max", an arm casting a fishing pole. Scrub the timeline a bit, or play in real time and you will see a fairly typical "pose to pose" motion. The entire motion is contained within 5 keys, spaced out in gradually increasing speed.

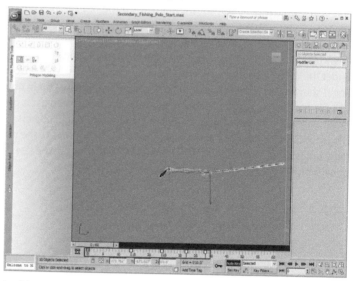

FIG 13.3

Not bad for a first round of animation, but the motion in the arm is rather stiff. Notice that we've added a little "overshoot" to the arm motion. This is where the arm moves a little past the final key and bounces back to its final resting pose. We will use the same technique as the tail to add some flexibility and naturalism.

8. Double click the elbow. Select all the keys in the timeline below the viewport. If you wish, open up the Dope Sheet to manipulate the keys instead. Slide the keys over 3 frames to the right.

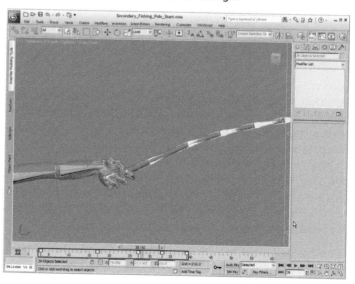

FIG 13.4

194

9. Next, double click the palm of the hand to select all the bones in the fishing pole as well. Slide these keys over 4 frames. Play the animation and notice how much more natural the motion has become.

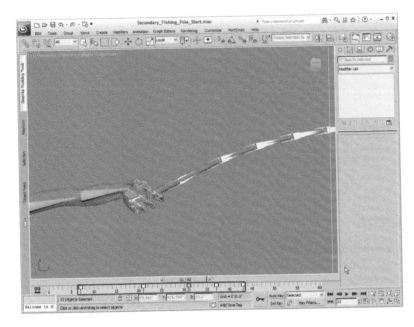

FIG 13.5

To create more of a whip-like motion, you could delay the bones slightly along the length of the pole. This creates a much softer effect, more appropriate for a riding whip or a softer bamboo fly-fishing pole. Double click BoneWhip01 and move the keys over 1 frame. Next, double click BoneWhip04 and move 1 frame, then BoneWhip07 and move 1 frame. Selecting every third frame makes the motion much more subtle. Delaying each and every bone sequentially would create an action that is much too slow and unrealistic, but might be perfect for delaying a large bullwhip.

Open the Layer Manager and unhide the Mesh layer. Hide the bone layer and play the animation to see the final result. If you look at the Dope Sheet, you notice I moved all the keys for the fly rod back 3 frames while keeping the delay along the length, just to give it a bit of snap. I realized that it started to flex a bit before the arm moved down to its full resting position, more like a spring. Double check the timing on all of your motions to be sure it looks correct. There are seldom any hard and fast rules about these motions, and different materials will act in completely different ways. Close observation is always important, and do some tests to compare their motion. Use the Tools>Grab Viewport>Create Animated Sequence File to play these animations in real time. Use the "Rename Sequence File" to save different tests for comparison.

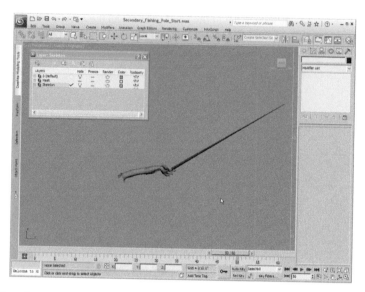

FIG 13.6

Cloth

Animating realistic clothing has been the challenge for film studios for many years. In the early days of computer animation, clothing was hand animated using bone systems and deformers. In the last decade, there have been a number of simulation systems created specifically to handle the challenges of cloth. 3ds MAX has a very robust and flexible system to deal with cloth. We will use it for the next exercise.

Open the file named "Secondary_Cloth_Skirt_Start.max". Here you will see a rather abstracted young woman going through a few fanciful dance moves. She is built with few polygons so that the simulation will run a bit quicker.

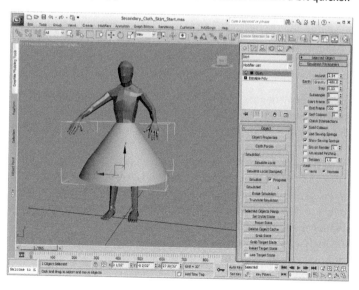

FIG 13.7

The skirt has a moderate number of polygons. The more polygons that a piece of clothing has, the longer it will take to run the simulation. However, the results won't be acceptably realistic unless there are enough to describe the folds and creases. It depends on the situation, and you can add polygons in areas that you know will have more folds, such as elbows, armpits, and the inseam of pants. We will run this simulation with a fairly low poly count but feel free to add more polygons to this mesh and run it again for better results.

1. Click on the skirt object and add a Cloth Modifier to it. This is a pretty complex modifier, with a great deal of parameters you can adjust, so you might want to pull the Modifier Panel out to see all the settings. Click on "Object Properties" and you will see the main Cloth Simulation Panel. Select the "Skirt" object in the object list. Click the Cloth setting and select the Cloth Properties Preset rollout, and select "Satin."

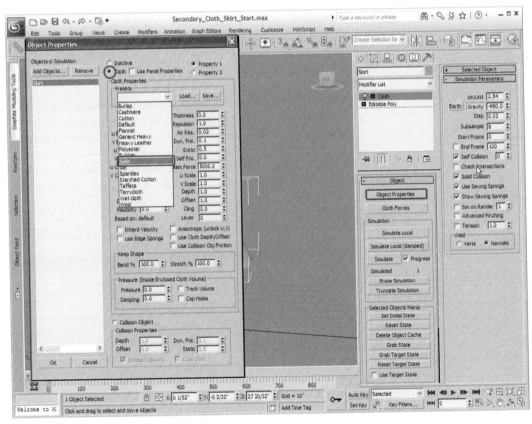

FIG 13.8

Next, and equally important, add the woman's mesh to the simulation. On the upper left corner click "Add Objects"… and add "Figure" to the simulation. It's important to understand that every object in the cloth simulation is actually part of a single modifier. All elements you want to add to the simulation should be added using this panel, rather than adding a new modifier.

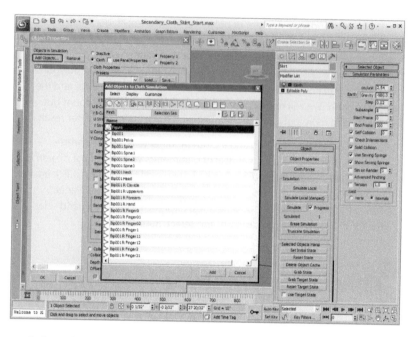

FIG 13.9

2. Once the "Figure" mesh has been added, click "Collision Object" to make this mesh a collision mesh. Set the offset to 0.7. This is the distance that the skirt will be kept away from the body mesh. Too far, however, and it will be pushed away from the waist far too much.

3. Now, turn on the Sub-Object mode of the modifier and select "Group." We need to bind the waist of the skirt to the "Figure" mesh, and we need to

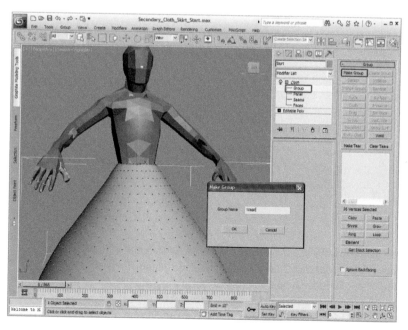

FIG 13.10

198

make a selection of the mesh into a group. Select the top row of vertices and select "Make Group." Name this group "Waist."

4. Now, with this group created, now it needs to be assigned to an object. In this case, it will be the surface of the dancing figure. Click "Surface," and select the figure's mesh. The group is now assigned to the figure's mesh and will now stick to it during the simulation.

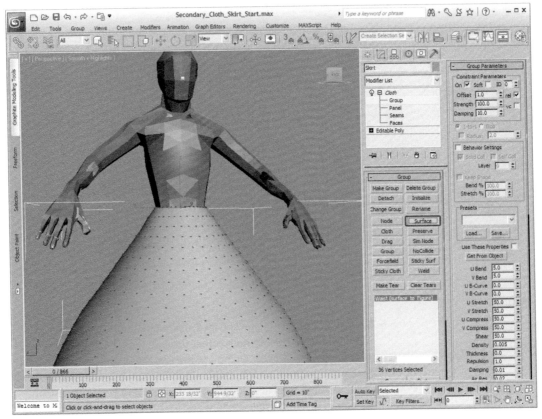

FIG 13.11

5. Much of the realism of cloth is related to the scale of the simulation. Setting the cm/unit to the right amount is important. Too small and the cloth looks like a napkin. Too large, and it acts like a huge tarp. Set this simulation to 3.0 for now. Turn on self-collision and click "Simulate." Watch as the cloth drapes slowly down to the woman's body. Stop the simulation after a few frames by clicking "Cancel" or pressing the Esc button on the keyboard. If you click "Simulate" again, the simulation will continue where it left off. Press the Play button and watch the simulation in real time. Feel free to add a TurboSmooth on top of the mesh. It adds a nice smoothing effect to the skirt without adding any calculations to the simulation.

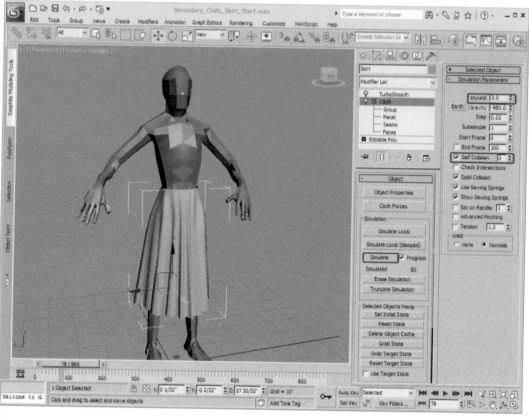

FIG 13.12

6. Now, click "Simulate" again and let the simulation run a bit longer. Watch and see if the leg mesh comes through the skirt. If it does, simply increase the subsamples. Doing so increases the simulation time a great deal, so do this with care. It is normal for the leg mesh to peek out of the cloth mesh from time to time, especially during quick movements. Increasing the Subsample amount and perhaps the Collision Offset may help fix this.

7. As this simulation runs, the simulation data that is created (which stores the movement of the cloth object) is stored in a temporary cache file. You can save this file to your hard drive and apply it to the same mesh later. This allows you to save several simulations and compare them later for the best results.

8. Simply open up the "Selected Object" rollout and click the "Set..." button. A Dialog box appears and allows you to create the cache file. Save this file with a name that best describes the movement. I saved this file as "Skirt_Dance01.cfx". Next, click "Save" to save the effect to the cache file. Any changes to the effect can now be saved to this cache file with the "Save" button. You can also switch simulation cache files by clicking "Import..." and loading up the new cache file.

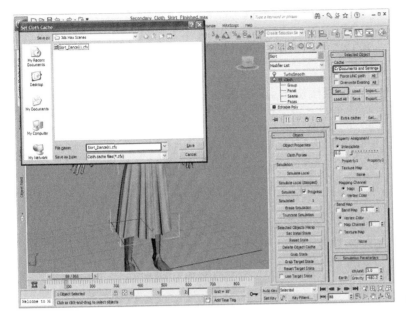

FIG 13.13

Once you have saved this cache file, test the result by clicking "Erase Simulation." Then, click "Import…" and load the file. The cloth will simulate properly.

9. Now, for some extra flourish, let's add some wind to the effect. This is very easily done. First, click on the "Space Warps" tab in the Create Panel. Create the wind object and turn it 90°. I have turned mine to the left a bit, but you can turn it any direction you like.

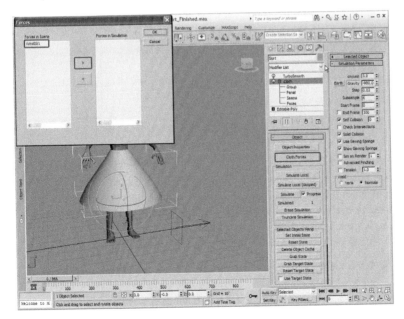

FIG 13.14

10. Then, open up the object's Cloth Modifier. Click the "Add Forces" button. You should see the wind object in the left panel. Select it and click the right arrow to add it to the simulation. That's it. Delete the simulation by clicking the "Erase Simulation" button and resimulate it. You should see the effects immediately.

11. If the effect is too much, simply stop the simulation, select the wind object and lower the Strength amount (I set mine to .35), erase the simulation and resimulate. You can also animate the direction of the wind, add turbulence, and change the frequency for even more subtle motion.

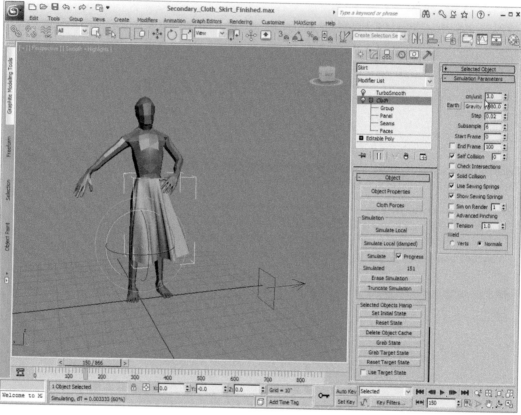

FIG 13.15

Now, let's add a ponytail to the character. Although we will be using the Hair and Fur system in 3ds MAX, we won't be using its built-in deformation system for this example. The results are fairly good, but not for something like a ponytail object, which behaves much more like a single cloth mesh, rather than individual strands, which is how the Hair and Fur system generally simulates with its dynamic system.

12. Open the file "Cloth_Hair_Start.max". This is basically where we left off with the skirt simulation. I have added a few objects, however. There are a series of lines with a Hair and Fur Modifier added. This can be easily done

by creating a single line, copying it over a few times. Then, select one of the lines, click the Attach button, and select the other lines one at a time. The order in which you attach the lines is important, because the hairs will be added in between each line in that exact order. I already attached them together and added the Hair and Fur Modifier, but feel free to do this yourself if you wish.

13. Next, add a "Skin Wrap" Modifier to these lines. This modifier is automatically placed below the Hair and Fur Modifier, since Hair and Fur is considered a "World Space Modifier" and is always added last on the modifier stack. Now, the hair will follow the motion of the HairSimulationMesh object.

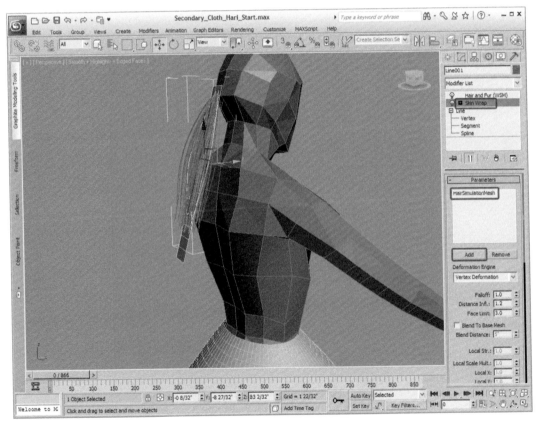

FIG 13.16

Now, all we need to do is add the "HairSimulationMesh" to the cloth simulation. Since we have already added the skirt object and finished the simulation, we can add a new Cloth Modifier to this object. As long as the hair and skirt aren't going to be colliding, they can be simulated separately. This will speed up the simulation significantly and prevent the time-consuming resimulation of the skirt object.

14. Add a new Cloth Modifier to the "HairSimulationMesh" object. Just as before, open the Properties for the object, and make it a Cloth object.

15. Add a new object into the scene, select the Figure, and make that a Collision object.

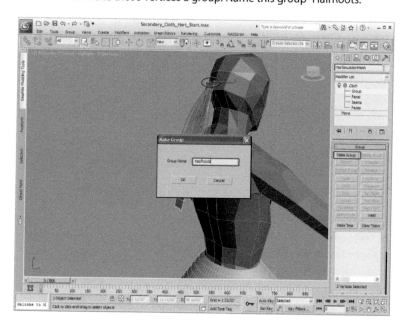

FIG 13.17

16. Next, select "Groups" in the Sub-Object mode of the Cloth Modifier, select the top vertices of the "HairSimulationMesh," and click the "Make Group" button to make those vertices a group. Name this group "HairRoots."

FIG 13.18

204

17. Then, click on "Surface," then select the "Figure" mesh to assign this group to the "Figure" surface. Get out of Sub-Object mode.

18. Open up the Properties Panel again, and adjust the settings of the Ponytail a bit more. I found these settings to work pretty well for a start. The "cloth" object needs to be a bit stiffer and heavier to act like hair. Finally, open the "Forces" Panel and add the wind force.

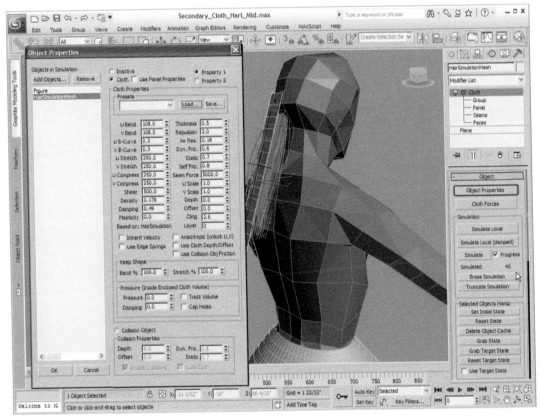

FIG 13.19

19. Run the simulation and check out the final results. You can hide the HairSimulationMesh if you like to see how the hairs move by themselves.

Spring Constraints

Many objects can be effectively simulated with a very simple constraint called a "Spring Constraint." It simply constrains two objects together, so that if one object is moved, the other object is pulled along as though on the end of a long spring. The Spring Constraint can be adjusted in terms of tension and mass, which creates variations in the motion of the "following" object. One of the best ways to use this kind of constraint is to simulate a large belly.

1. Open the file called "Secondary_Belly_Start.max" and you will see a file very similar to the one we used for the skinning exercise, but this one gained a bit of weight. I have added a few bones to the middle of the belly mass, with the pivot point near the back of the spine so that the belly jiggles in a more vertical direction. I created an IK system for the end of the bone and constrained the goal of the IK to a point object. I have also placed a point object above this bone, which is linked to the lower spine of the biped system.

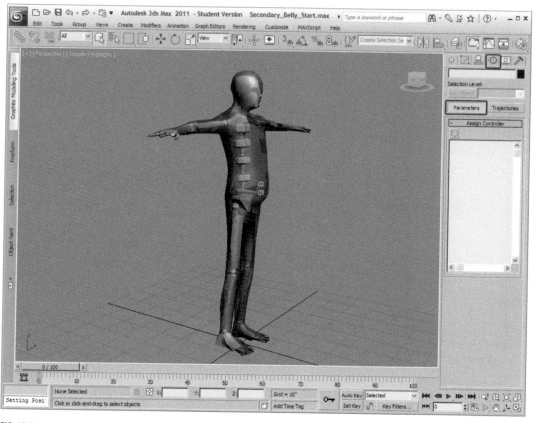

FIG 13.20

The character mesh's skin includes two additional bones and is weighted so that when they move, the belly will move with them. Scrub the Time Slider a bit and you will notice that the end of the bone has not been linked to the biped, so it doesn't move in space. We will change that next.

2. Select the green point object that is on the end of the bone. Be careful not to select the cross-shaped goal object of the IK system, which is blue. Open up the Motion Control tab on the Command Panel. Click the Parameters button, select the "Position" controller, then "Assign Controller", and finally select "Spring" as the controller type.

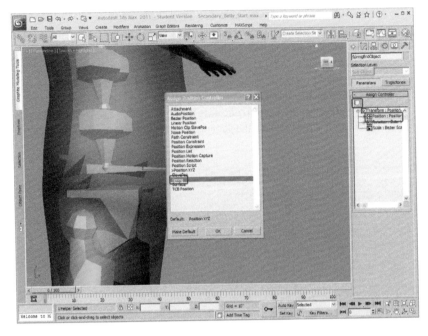

FIG 13.21

3. Once this is selected, the Spring Controller Property Panel appears. Click the "Add" button and select the top point object. There should now be two objects in the list below. Each object has its own influence over the motion of other object.

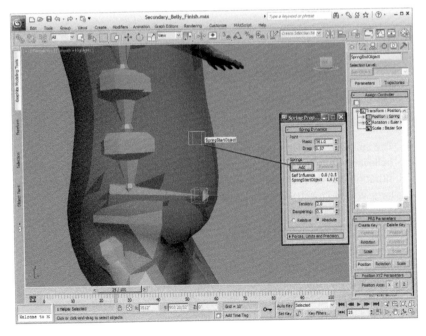

FIG 13.22

4. Currently, the object itself, called "Self Influence," has as much control as the top object. Let's change this. Select the "Self Influence," and make the "Tension" amount 0.00. Next, select the "SpringStartObject" and set the Tension to 1, the Dampening to 0.5, the Mass to 500, and the Drag to 0.6. Play the animation again and notice the change in the movement of the belly mass. If you change these numbers around, you can change the behavior of the belly. Generally, if you decrease the Mass, increase the Tension, and decrease the Dampening, the jiggling will appear faster and less massive.

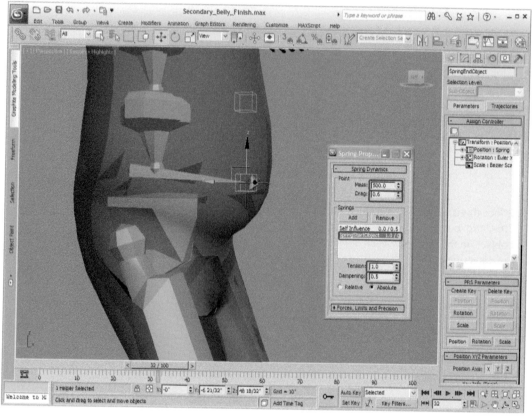

FIG 13.23

The Spring Controller is one of the most useful controllers for creating believable simulations. It can be used for a wide variety of applications. Any situation that calls for a swinging motion can use this controller. Imagine a large walking mech vehicle, with hoses and dangling weaponry, each part moving individually with its own weight and timing. This can create a very convincing effect if used carefully.

Now, let's combine the Spring Controller and the "Tail Wag" demo and create a more elaborate system. The advantage to this tail system is that it is completely adjustable by the animator. The animator can keyframe the rotation of each of the bones in this system, and the computer will add the secondary wag on top of this primary movement.

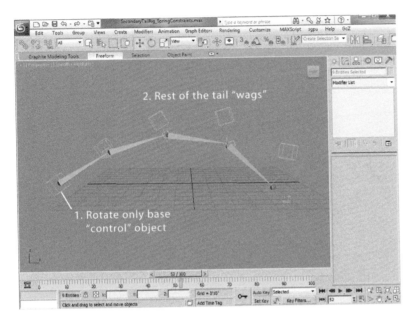

FIG 13.24

Open the file "SecondaryTailRig_SpringConstraints.max" to see the final file. Rotate the base point object and set animation keys, and then play back the animation to see the final results. The Spring Controller delays the animation cycle through each of the point objects (the smaller ones, which contain the Spring Controller) each offsetting the delay, creating a whip-like motion.

1. Begin by drawing five bones in the viewport. Use the front viewport so that they align properly. Use Create>Systems>Bones on the right panel.

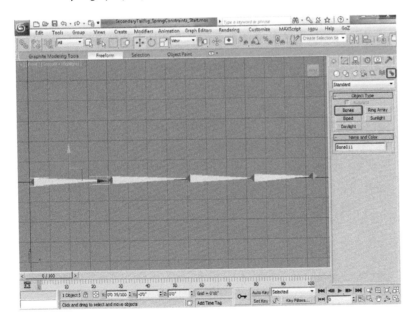

FIG 13.25

2. Next, select the base of each bone, click on the menu Animation>IK Solvers>HI Solver. With this tool now active, click the base of the first bone. A dotted line will appear. Next, click on the base of the second bone.

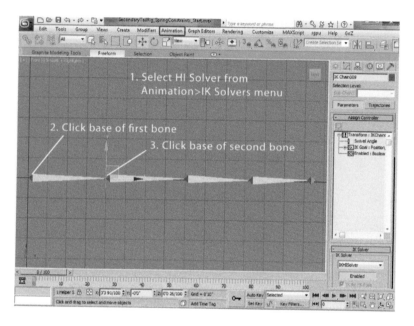

FIG 13.26

3. Repeat this process for the rest of the bones. You should have an IK system at the base of each bone, each extending to the base of the next bone in the chain.

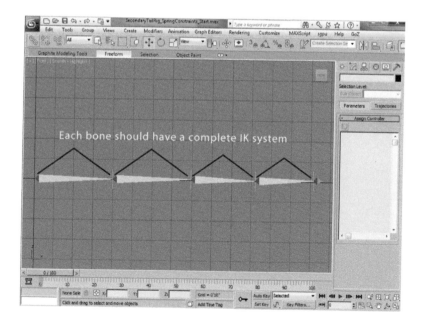

FIG 13.27

4. Next, create a point object and use the Align Tool to align it to the IK Goal
   of the first IK object.

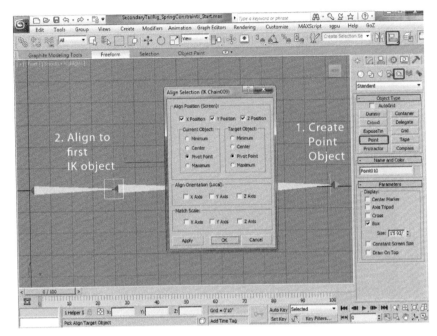

FIG 13.28

5. Repeat this process for the rest of the bones. You should have point
   objects at the location of each IK Goal.

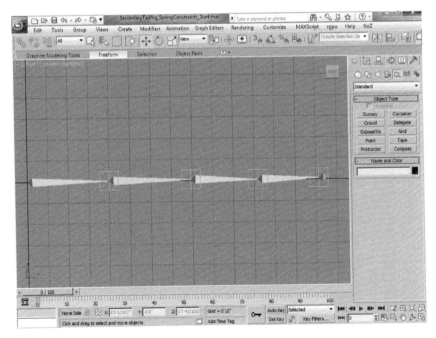

FIG 13.29

6. Link each IK Goal to the nearby point object. Use the Link Tool in the upper left command panel.

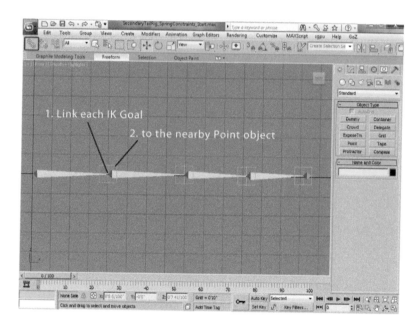

FIG 13.30

7. Next, create a new set of point objects; these are a little larger, at each location, with an extra one at the base of the first bone. Use the Align Tool to align them to the smaller point objects. Feel free to color-code these objects with a slightly different color to avoid confusion.

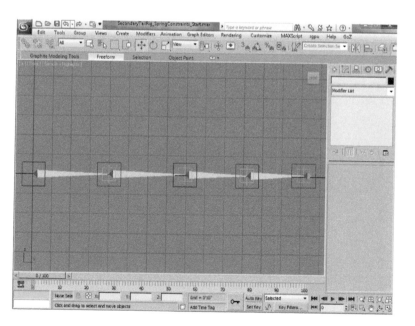

FIG 13.31

8. Now, we will use the Spring Controller to delay the motion of the little point objects relative to the larger ones. Click each of the smaller point objects (be careful not to select the IK Goals by mistake. It would be a good idea to hide these by using the Display Panel and selecting IK Objects in the lower selection set. The goal objects will disappear, but you won't need to select them anyway.)

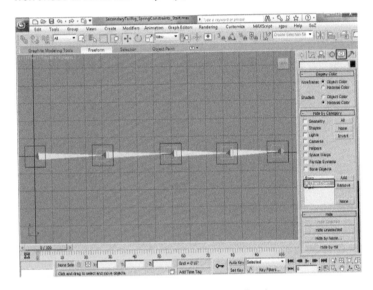

FIG 13.32

9. Select the small point object at the end of the first bone.
   (a) Open up the Motion Control Panel.
   (b) Select "Position: Position XYZ" controller.
   (c) Click "Assign Controller" button above.
   (d) Click "Spring," and then click OK.

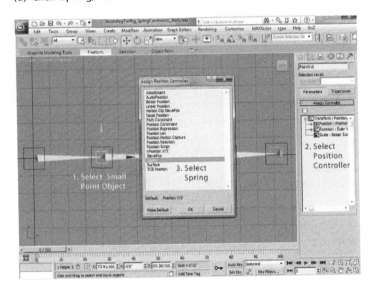

FIG 13.33

213

10. The Spring Parameters window will now appear, and you can adjust the values for the Spring Controller. For now, increase the drag to 2.

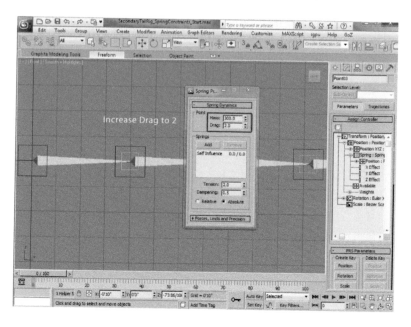

FIG 13.34

11. You can always open this parameter panel by double clicking the Spring Controller in the "Assign Controller" Outline Panel, or by clicking "Spring" in the "Position List" and adjusting the parameters in the "Spring Dynamics" tab below.

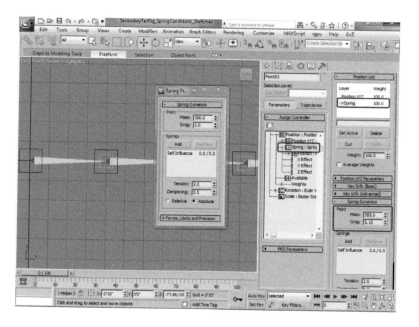

FIG 13.35

12. Now, link each of the large point objects together into a hierarchy. Use this diagram to show the linking order. This is very important to get right, or the system doesn't work properly.

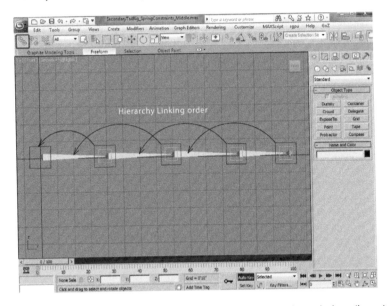

FIG 13.36

13. Now, set a few rotation keys for the base point object and watch the tail wag!
14. If you wish, you can pose the tail before simulation. Simply move the large point objects into the pose positions and run the simulation again. The simulation will work for those new positions. You can also animate the position of the large point objects, and the simulation will be added to that animation.

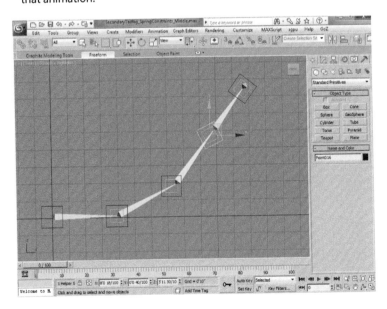

FIG 13.37

Some animators prefer having complete control over every aspect of a character or object's motion during an animated sequence. However, as scenes become more complex and more software sophisticated, many large animation and visual effects companies have set up entire departments to handle simulations and secondary motion. Many large visual effects studios are even developing their own simulation software. Many of the simulation systems operate in a very similar way to the techniques we have demonstrated here.

CHAPTER 14

Animating with the Morph Modifier

Richard Lapidus

Rule: The use of overlapping action

Rule: Weight and drag

After Completing This Chapter, You Will be Able To:

- Use the three states of animation: anticipation, action, and reaction.
- Add weight to a character.
- Animate with the Morph Modifier.

Of all the tutorials that I've written, this one was most designed to solve a lot of problems in teaching 3ds MAX. One of the most intrinsic benefits to working with 3ds Max is the versatility of what you can do with the Modify Panel. After teaching this program for a number of years and collaborating with other instructors, it became apparent that a lot of people were not using the full

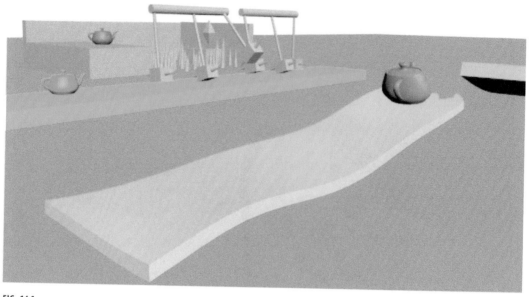

FIG 14.1

range of modifiers. The other thing that I've noticed in looking at a variety of resource materials is that there has always been very little application of animation in the traditional sense as applied to learning a software program. The approach that I took with this tutorial was to give my students a look at 17 different modifiers that could be used to enhance the fluidity possible when creating motion, weight, and timing of their animations.

For professionals, the choice of a tool is very often driven by ROI and for students, it's how quickly the tool can enhance the quality of their creative process. Unfortunately, when there is such a steep learning curve for the new user, it sometimes becomes frustrating to see them end up focusing more on learning the tools than on how to effectively utilize them. The concept of morphing dates back to the original DOS version of this program. Although the tools have changed, you still have the basic concepts of having an object change based upon the position of the vertices of the target objects. My first morph was to have a basketball net swish as the ball went through it. By today's terms, it was very primitive relative to using space warps or a dynamic simulation using soft bodies. Regardless of how sophisticated your tools are your animation can still be effective if you take the time to study some real motion and figure out how much you can use. What we want to accomplish with this exercise is for you to use as many of these modifiers as possible to create the illusion of some life in this sheet and that it is cognizant of the surrounding.

There are a few rules that you need to be aware of when working with the Morpher Modifier. The first rule is that all morph targets must have the same number of vertices as the object of the Morpher Modifier on it. The basic starting point for this is to use a static pose for your Morpher object and then create clone copies of it to adjust. As long as you are adding or changing the basic topology of the object, your morph targets should work as well.

The basic click through on my morphing teapot tutorial ended up being too long to include as part of this chapter. We will start out this project with the finished morph targets. The three_obstacles.max is the one my students use for animating. It allows them to choose from three types of hazards to maneuver through. Good news. You will find a PDF version of the basic set up and an explanation of the 17 modifiers on the website (www.tradigital3dsmax.com). In the second phase of this tutorial, we will be exploring timing ways and motion involved in creating the illusion that this teapot is in a dangerous and precarious set of circumstances. Keeping in mind that I'm approaching this type of animation from a problem solving standpoint. The second half of this tutorial, which you will be working through in this chapter, shows how to maneuver your object through one of three obstacles.

When I originally wrote up the tutorial using these 17 different modifiers to create the morph targets, I didn't have in the back of my mind what the teapot would be doing. What I mean is that I had not contemplated how the teapot would actually move. A lot of my students will click through the tutorial and then pick one of the three obstacles in animating it without adjusting how the morph targets move or are animated. This is just something to keep in the back of your mind. If you like the idea of creating an animated object, then please feel free to take creative license with how you use these modifiers. Where this tutorial has always fallen short is in having the majority of my students rarely explore using morph targets and the timing involved in keying these objects to create a more realistic animated character. So that's where we are going to focus in this chapter. I will, however, point out a few of the key parameters for some of the different modifiers so that you can understand a little bit better the infinite variety possible when adjusting objects.

1. Load the file morph_3_obstacles_morph_targets.max.
2. Drag the Time Slider or click the Play button.

When viewing the scene through more teapots, you will notice that there are three obstacles available for you to choose from. There are also three basic cameras already in place for each one of the obstacles. The camera called "cam morph teapots" should be active when the scene loads so that you're getting a good view of several of the modifiers that happen to be animated, as well as the swinging spikes in the gauntlet portion of the scene. The goal is to give you the opportunity to work through having your object jump over an obstacle, maneuver through moving objects, or simply over a surface after avoiding a piece of missing range to continue on the other side.

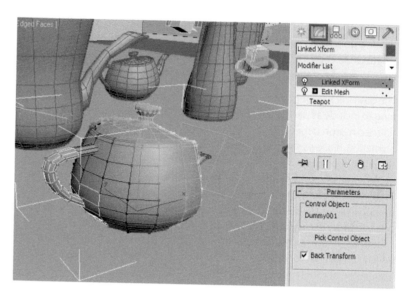

FIG 14.2

3. Hit the "H" Key and select the teapot named a "linked xform".

There is an Edit Mesh Modifier with a soft selection of vertices being passed up the modifier stack to the linked Xform Modifier that has a control object of an animated dummy. As you play the animation, you will notice that the dummy is actually rotating back and forth on a curve. This was accomplished by moving the pivot of the dummy somewhere inside the teapot. This gives the spout wiggle a more realistic and curved motion. Here's something else you could try if you like the idea of controlling just part of the object. How about a nervous shake to just the lid? This could easily be accomplished by adding a noise float in the Motion Panel to the control object. Since there are three Euler XYZ tracks by default, you could control each axis a little differently. Your Ramp in and Ramp out parameters within the Noise Float work just like limits.

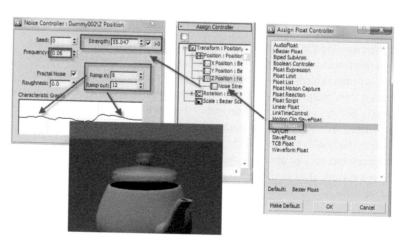

FIG 14.3

4. Select a teapot named squeeze.

Notice in the Modify Panel that there is a limit effect parameter that allows you to control the upper and lower extents of the modifier on the whole object. If you hit the "+" indicator next to the Squeeze Modifier, the basic two sub-object components are gizmo and center. By default, the gizmo covers the entire extent of the object, and the center controls the focal point of the modifier. The Center will always be aligned to the object's axis when added to the stack. We looked at this in chapter 2, Working with Kays and the Dope Sheet. By changing the position of the gizmo, you're adjusting the projection of the modify. If the direction for one of the morph targets is not to your liking, try going into the sub-object of the modifier and rotating the gizmo 180 degrees. There are literally unlimited variations of the changes you can make to these objects.

5. Select the object name "Morph object".
6. Increase the length for the active timeline with a CTL+ALT+right mouse drag so that you have 300 frames.
7. Drag the timeline and notice that a few of the objects continue moving beyond frame 100. Some of the objects have an out of range parameter repeat added to modifiers.

FIG 14.4

8. In the Modify Panel, you will notice that the "Morph Object" already has the Morpher Modifier added. You will add these to the other morph objects in the obstacle courses. Drag the percent spinner for the FFD and the Stretch targets to 100%. Notice how the object will interpolate through itself. You have to be careful in using multiple morph targets so that the positioning of vertices doesn't add up to moving through the object.

Note

Right clicking on the spinner will "Zero Out" the spinner. Click up once and down once with the Auto Key button on; this will set a value at current state. Since the Key Tangent Type is set to "Linear" in the file, you will not get over interpolation with the keying of these spinners. After testing out animating a variety of percentages of Morph Weights, you may want to change this to the default or another tangent type to your liking.

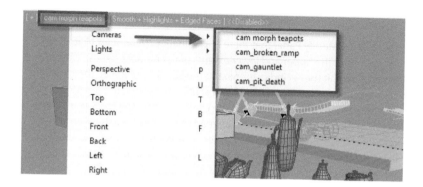

FIG 14.5

9. Change the camera view and select the "cam_broken_ramp" camera.
10. Select the teapot sitting on the ramp called "broken_ramp_teapot_morph". Assign a Morpher Modifier to it.

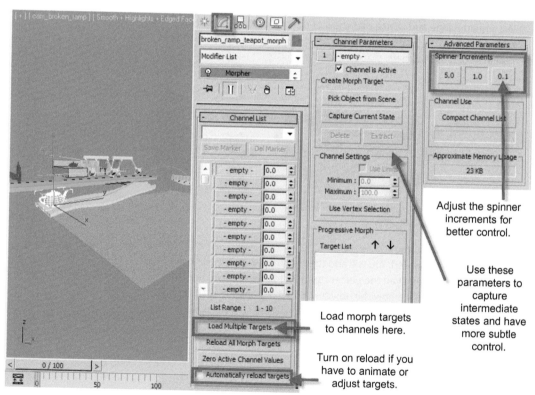

FIG 14.6

11. Click the "Load Multiple Targets" button and select all the teapots in the Select by name list. Do not include the "Morph Object".
12. In the Advanced Parameters, you may want to change to 0.1 for the Spinner Increments for more subtle control.

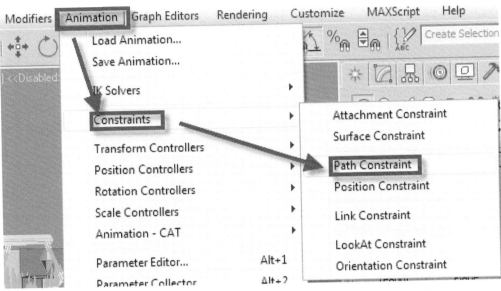

FIG 14.7

13. Create a dummy and align it pivot to pivot to the "broken_ramp_teapot_ morph" object.
14. Link the teapot to the dummy and then with the select tool, reselect the dummy.
15. Go to the Animation Menu>Constraints>Path Constraint and select the spline that is near the dummy object.
16. Save your file incrementally. There is a copy called morph_3-obstacles_ ramp_dummy.max saved at this point for you.

There is a trap in moving an object directly to a path without a buffer like a dummy object. The object will now move with the dummy as its parent as you animate the path percentage along the path in the Motion Panel. The other option is to add a list controller as we will see in the next chapter so that you can have addition Move Transform control. We will look at those options later on. Take a moment to drag the Time Slider and notice how the object moves smoothly from beginning to end of the active segment. This is nice control, but not how something that is living might maneuver in the real world jumping over a broken ramp. Special note to the guys who wrote the plug-in called "Glue". You can find it at www.itoosoft.com. After building this ramp, I had a few students who wanted the object to smoothly move over it. Glue will allow you to project a spline onto the surface of an object. Nice free plug-in along with several others you will find on their site.

17. Let's first animate the teapot over the jump by keyframing the dummy's percentage along the path, then add and mix the morph channels. Go to the Motion Panel and then drag to about frame 50.
18. Turn on Follow and Bank. The dummy will rotate 90° but follow the path more smoothly.

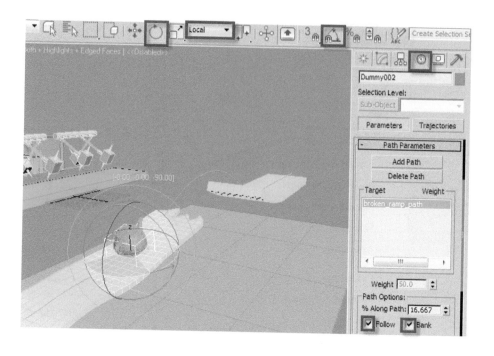

FIG 14.8

19. Enable Angle Snap with the "A" Key, select the Rotate Transform, and change the reference coordinate system to Local. Now rotate the dummy −90°.
20. Enable the Auto Key button and then click the "% Along Path" button in the same area indicated in Fig. 14.8 by up and down one click. This will set the position of the teapot at around 16.6% along the path.
21. Now move to frame 82 and drag the percentage to 10% along the path. The teapot will move out from the start, go up the ramp a bit, and then move back.
22. Drag the Time Slider to around frame 115 and note the percentage along the path. Mine reads around 24. Move to around frame 150 and the teapot should be in mid-air above the gap in the jump.
23. Let's drag the percentage to 24 at frame 150. The teapot will now move slowly toward the ramp from 82 to 150.
24. At frame 200, drag the percentage to around 20%.
25. Drag the timeline again to pick the percentage along the path so that the dummy will be in mid-air above the jump. Mine is reading about 40%.
26. Move to frame 250 and set the percentage to 40%.
27. Select the keyframe at frame 300 that represents the end of the path. When it highlights "white", meaning that it is selected, delete it.

Looks like we have run out of time to have this teapot come to the realization that it is not going to make it and will fall. I love killing teapots. You can either add more keys or compress what you already have to make it work faster.

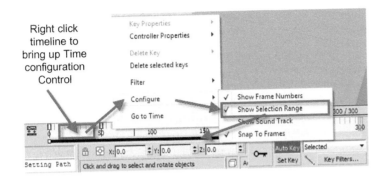

Right click
timeline to
bring up Time
configuration
Control

FIG 14.9

28. Drag a marquee around all the keys, right click the timeline, and enable Show Selection Range in the Configure Menu.
29. Move the cursor over the right side of the Range Bar for selected keys so that there is one arrow. Now drag the right end of the range to frame 200. This will make all the action happen a bit faster.
30. Select the teapot and right click the Time Slider at frame 200. When the Create Key Dialog appears, hit OK to set Position, Rotation, and Scale Keys at frame 200.
31. Move to frame 225 and rotate the teapot on the "Z" axis about −150°.
32. Move to about frame 214 and rotate it up about 15° on the "Y" axis.
33. At frame 250, rotate it down on the "Y" axis about 45°.
34. At frame 300, move it down on the "Z" axis below the plane.

Wait … it is falling too soon without realizing it is in peril. All objects in the cartoon world are not affected by gravity until they are aware of their situation.

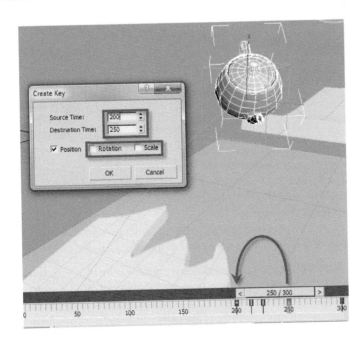

FIG 14.10

225

35. Move back to frame 250 and right click the Time Slider. Disable rotation and scale. Set the Source Time to frame 200 and Destination Time to frame 250.

Play the animation and you will see the object does two chugging moves to get up the ramp and then finally hangs in space before falling. Please feel free to add additional rotation keys or more time to your liking to animate this object moving through the obstacle. Oh noooooooooo! Something is wrong. If you haven't gone exploring around the scene, the mistake I built into the file may not show up until rendering time. The path for the dummy object does not fit the ramp properly. That's not the only problem … but it's the first I want you to fix.

36. Switch to the top viewport and marquee select the teapot with ramp portion of the scene. Now right click and enter Isolation mode.
37. Switch to the left viewport and zoom in on the ramp. The teapot is floating.

This is a common mistake that might not show up until rendering time. It looked good from the camera view, but if you don't get into the habit of viewing your scene from different views, these kinds of mistakes can go hidden until after the scene is rendered.

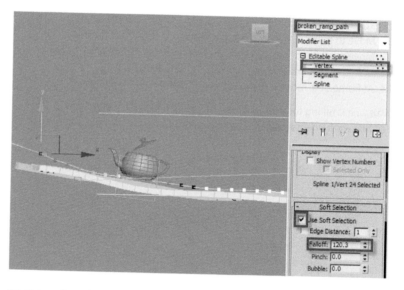

FIG 14.11

38. Select the spline called "broken_ramp_path" and enter the Vertex Sub-object level in the Modify Panel.
39. Select the vertex near the end of the ramp, enable Use Soft Selection, and set the Falloff to around 120.
40. Move this vertex down until most of the vertices are near the ramp. It won't be perfect, but we will fix that. Exit sub-object.

Using paths for modeling and animation is a great way for objects to fit neatly together. In the intro levels of my classes, we use a tutorial called "Creating a Rollercoaster." It was written for a class years ago to cover lofting, path constraints, and snapshots. By using the same path in different functions, my students start to develop a sense of the correlation between modeling and animating. In this case, they like to use it, but something still seems a bit off. Given an object without legs or wheels, how should it maneuver a ramp and fly through space? You could adjust some of the morph targets and animate the lower half of the object. The limits or passing a sub-object soft selection would work very well for this. Let's see if possibly a little animation could be used to fix the problem. Without adding a list controller to the dummy, its position is controlled by the path. The buffer of using a link would allow for moving the teapot, but that could cause some problems if you decide to start changing the animation at a later time. Let's try something new so you can get a sense of different possibilities with the program. With a link, any changes to the parent's transforms are passed to the child in the tree. What if we blocked some of what was being passed down the chain? If we scale the dummy, the teapot will scale. In a scale function, the transform gizmo moves in addition to changes in the size of the objects. What if we block inheriting the scaling? The transform gizmo for the teapot will move, but its size will remain the same. I came up with this idea over 10 years ago when animating logos flying in on nice soft curved trajectories.

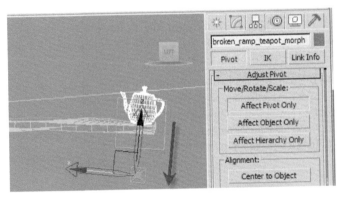

FIG 14.12

FIG 14.13

41. Select the teapot and go into the Hierarchy Panel.
42. In the Pivot selection, enable Affect Pivot Only, and move the pivot down below the teapot so that it isn't lined up with the dummy.

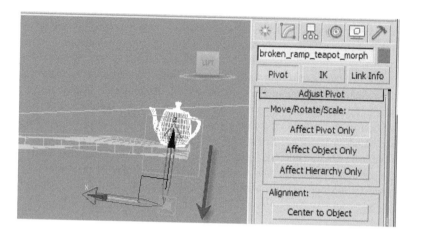

FIG 14.14

43. Turn off Affect Pivot Only when you have to move it below the object.
44. Go to the Link Info Panel and in the Locks area, turn on Scale X, Y, and Z, and turn off Inherit Scale X, Y, and Z.

To make this a little easier to navigate and animate, let's show you how to create a Slider to control the scale of the dummy object. Sliders can basically be "wired" to any object parameter to give the current viewport a floating control. When finished working with it, you can easily hide it in the Modify Panel or hide it as a helper in the Display Panel.

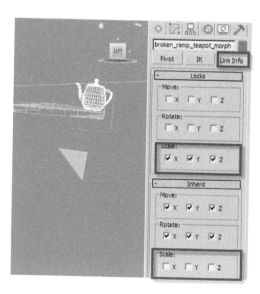

FIG 14.15

45. Go to the Create Menu>Helpers>Manipulators and choose Slider.
46. In the Modify Panel, call it "Scale Dummy Z".
47. Set the Minimum Value to −0.5 and the Maximum Value to 2.0.

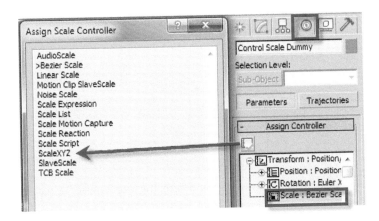

FIG 14.16

48. Reselect the Dummy Object and go into the Motion Panel.
49. In the Motion Panel, select the Scale Transform and click the Assign Controller button.
50. When the Dialog appears, choose Scale XYZ. This will split the scale track into three separate tracks.
51. Right click the Slider in the view and choose Wiring from the Quad Menu.
52. Choose Value in for the Object and when a marquee line appears, left click the dummy.
53. Drag across from Transform to Scale to "Z" axis. The Wiring parameters will appear. If you choose the wrong one, it can be fixed easily right now. See Fig. 14.17.

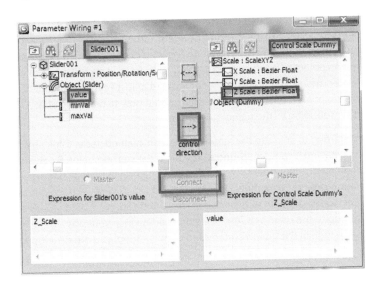

FIG 14.17

229

54. Make sure the Slider has Value selected on one side, and the "Z" axis for the Control Scale Dummy is on the other.
55. Click the direction of flow arrow to point from the Slider to the Dummy.
56. Click the Connect button and minimize the Dialog. Don't close it until you see it is working properly.
57. Enable Select and manipulate in the Toolbar.

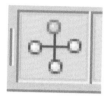

FIG 14.18

58. Now drag the Slider arrow back and forth. The teapot moves by scaling the dummy.
59. Move to frame 0 and turn on the Auto Key.
60. Right click the timeline and set the filters to Object. This way the keys you make to the Sliders parameters will show up in the timeline.
61. Drag the Slider so that the teapot is sitting on the ramp.
62. Scrub time and look for places where you want the teapot to be floating in the air. This usually happens on the far side of a bump in the path.

Animating by hand in the traditional sense with a 3d program requires a little bit of investigation by the animator on a number of levels. Like a cell animator, we have to study our subject as to how it moves, carries its weight, and reacts to its surroundings. We then take it further by taking some area and exaggerating it so that we get the response that we want from our view. Typically in the 3d scene, we might find ourselves limited in trying to get the exact details and scales of objects and not really think about how it might function. In this situation of this scene, I provided you with three dangerous elements for an inanimate object to navigate. Although we've only looked at one of them in this chapter, I want to use your imagination as to how you will get an object to jump over something dangerous like a spiked pit or maneuver through swinging obstacles. Instead of just keyframing your object to go from point A to B, you want to think about how to make the object look like it's responding to the scene that it is in.

When starting to animate the teapot through its next obstacle, think about possibly having it wander around a little bit at the starting point. By giving your animation sometime to set itself up, you are providing that stage of animation called anticipation. How might we do that? Well, with the pit scene, imagine you're standing at the edge of the Grand Canyon. Would you walk straight up to the edge or might you stop short an inch your way up slowly. With a change in the timing and rhythm of the motion, you can develop a more organic feel to the movement of your objects. In the third portion of the scene, which happens to be one of my favorites, you might have your objects stop short and then start to sway back and forth trying to pick up the timing of one of the pendulums as he gets ready to maneuver that portion of the obstacle. I've had some of most interesting solutions to these problems solved by my students over the years.

CHAPTER 15

Tricks for Automating Motion and Controlling Timing

Richard Lapidus

Rule: Weight in motion

Rule: Timing

After Completing This Chapter, You Will be Able To:

- Create a link setup using multiple objects.
- Use a Link Constraint to weigh between multiple objects.
- Use an Attachment Constraint to have an object stick to another object's surface.
- Link to world for free-form animation between links.
- Without linking, get the hands of a biped to move with another object.

We want to create a complex linkage so that over time, an object can appear to smoothly move along two different surfaces. This tutorial will show you how to sync the movement of an object to basically follow two moving

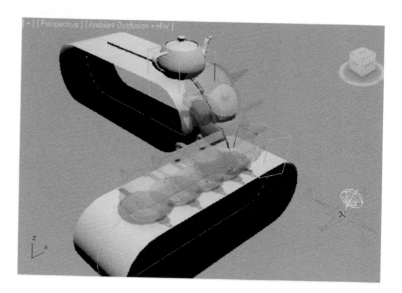

FIG 15.1

surfaces and also give you a segment of time to hand animate it. The objective is to have two different parent objects (dummies) that are attached to moving surfaces controlling the position of a teapot. Since an object can only be linked to one object at a time, or be a child to one parent in a hierarchy chain, a link constraint will allow us to get around this traditional limitation. Constraints are typically used to control one or more transforms of an object by giving up the "hand-keying" control to have the object animated by other more complex assemblies or motions. Although this is a very powerful tool, it is necessary to sometimes have the option of making adjustments by hand. This tutorial will show you how to assign control of an object's transform and then also how to adjust it by hand when you want.

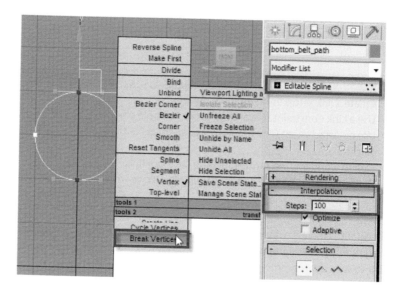

FIG 15.2

1. Reset 3ds MAX and enable the front viewport.
2. Go to Create Shapes and create a circle with about 100 radius.
3. Go to the Modify Panel and set the interpolation to 100 from the default of 6.

For splines that will be used as controllers for moving cameras, objects, or deformations, it is always best to use the highest interpolation value possible. There will be at least 600 steps along the whole length of the spline, which can be used for moving or deforming an object along the length. The default number of 6 will look smooth from a distance but will cause objects to have a lot of "jerky" stepping going around the curves. If you have ever tried one of the walk-through assistant tools that places the scene camera on a spline for a fly-through, you may have noticed that the camera snaps in a funny way through a curve. I've made a number of architects very happy in showing them how the default values of spline interpolation causes the problem with their fly-through animations.

4. With the circle still selected, right click the screen or the name of the object in the top of the Modify Panel and convert it to an editable spline.
5. Call this object "bottom_belt_path".
6. Go to the Edit Menu and clone the object as a copy, call it "wheel_control".

Whenever creating an object that I want to reuse again, I will typically incrementally save the file since I will be destroying the original or make a clone of it. This object will be used later on to create a fly wheel with crank to control the belts. We won't be moving the pivot of the path object, so you could snap the new object back to the paths pivot. I like to plan ahead a few steps and avoid having a spinning object in this location that does not match up perfectly. You may want to use the technique covered in biped's which constrained the feet to also constrain the hands.

7. Use the "H" Key or select by name and reselect the spline called "bottom_belt_path".
8. Go to the Sub-object Vertex level, select both vertices in the center and then right click the screen. When the Quad Menu shows up, break the vertices.
9. Go to the Sub-object Spline level, select the right half of the circle, and then move it on the "X" axis about 500–600 units. This will be the path for our belt when completed.

Hold and drag from one vertex to another. Notice how the cursor changes for the command you are in.

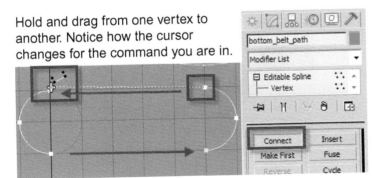

FIG 15.3

10. Go to the Sub-object vertex level, scroll the Modify Panel down, and choose connect.
11. Drag a line from the top left vertex of the left half circle to the top vertex of the other half.
12. Repeat this for the bottom so that the path is completely closed again.
13. Turn off Connect and then turn off the Vertex Sub-object level.
14. Using the Shift Key, move the path up in front viewport on the "Y" axis and leave some space between the two. Put in as much space as you like depending upon how much extra drop you want when an object moving off the top belt will fall onto the bottom belt.
15. When the Clone Options Dialog appears, make sure you choose clone and call it "top_belt_path".

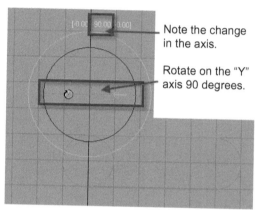

Note the change in the axis.

Rotate on the "Y" axis 90 degrees.

FIG 15.4

16. Hit "A" for angle snap and rotate the path 90° degrees on the "Y" axis. (This would be "Z" if you are in the perspective view.)
17. Change to the perspective view and pan or zoom extent the view.
18. Create a plane object that is about 160 units in length and by 800 units in width.
19. Call this object "top_belt".
20. Go to the Modify Panel Drop-Down Menu and choose World Space Modifiers: Path Deform (WSM).

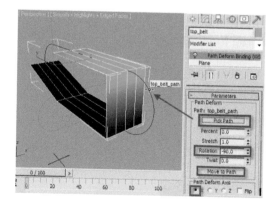

FIG 15.5

Make sure that you choose the one with a WSM after the name. There is also a Path Deform Modifier that works in Local Space on the Object, not World Space. The WSM works just like a space warp but between 3d objects. If you add the wrong one, delete it with the Delete icon in the modifier stack or right click and cut it. Chapter 14 goes extensively into working with the modifier stack and animating sub-object parameters. In my applied animation classes, we typically will work through the morphing exercise first to give a newer animator the opportunity to explore deforming objects more extensively.

21. Click the Pick Path button in the Parameters Panel of the modifier.
22. When it highlights, click on the top_belt_path. It will move to the path and look deformed.
23. Click the Move to Path button.
24. Choose "X" as the Path Deform Axis.
25. Set the Rotation to −90°.
26. Go to the Plane Level in the Modifier stack.

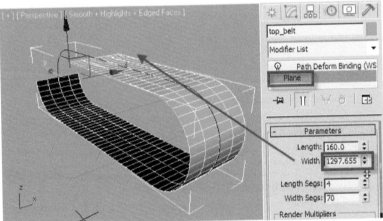

At the Plane Level of the modifier stack, drag on the width spinner and increase the width until the belt fits all the way around. The width in your project will depend on how your path is.

FIG 15.6

27. Drag the Length Spinner higher until the end of the plane meets.
28. Now increase the Width Segs to 60–70 so that the plane has more flexibility.
29. Increase the width to somewhere between 1300 and 1600, so that it wraps all the way around the path.

Depending upon your math skills, you could have easily figured out the length of the plane first to fit around this spline. Since there is some degree of variation in path lengths possible, I find it easy by just dragging the spinner and "eyeing it up." The other possibility is to get it close and then adjust the stretch value at the Path Deform Binding (WSM) level.

237

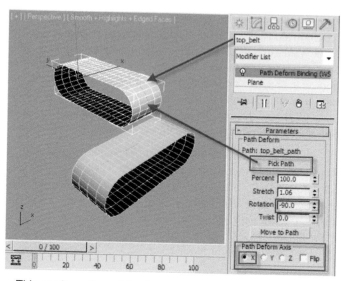

This configuration of the Path Deform Binding (WSM) always seems to work.

FIG 15.7

Align to "X" axis, rotate –90 degrees

30. Go to the Edit Menu and clone this object as a copy. Give it the name "lower_belt".
31. Go to the Modify Panel and you will notice that the WSM Binding has cloned with the object including the assignment of the "top_belt_path".
32. Click the Pick Path button and select the "bottom_belt_path".
33. Click the Move to Path button so the plane is aligned to the lower path.

Orbit around your view and make sure an object that would be falling off the top belt could fall on the bottom belt. If you select the plane and the spline, they will both move together without distorting. See Fig. 15.8 for the relative location of the paths and planes.

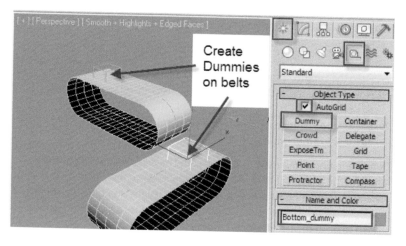

Create Dummies on belts

FIG 15.8

34. Go to the Create Panel\Helpers and select Dummy.
35. Turn on Autogrid and create one on the top belt.
36. Call it Top_dummy.
37. Create another on the bottom belt. Call it Bottom_dummy.

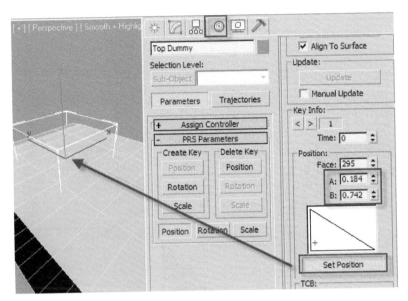

FIG 15.9

38. Select the Top_dummy and go to the Animation Menu. Drag to
    Constraints and select Attachment Constraint.
39. When the marquee line appears, click the top_belt object to assign it as
    the attachment.
40. You are sent into the Motion Panel. At frame 0, Click the Set Position
    button and then click and drag near the center of the belt at the far end
    as shown in the picture. Use the A and B position to fine tune. Turn off Set
    Position.
41. Select the Bottom_dummy. Add an Attachment Constraint to it as well.
    Check position from top viewport so the second dummy has a starting
    position far enough down the belt relative to the first.

FIG 15.10

239

42. Create a teapot with the Autogrid on relative to the Top_dummy. Quick align it if you like.
43. Hold the CTL and Alt Key and drag with the right mouse button on the timeline to increase active viewable time to about 200 frames.

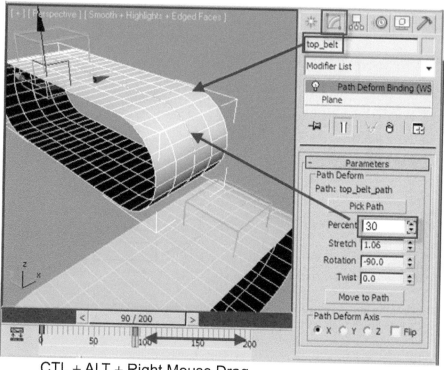

FIG 15.11 CTL + ALT + Right Mouse Drag

44. Select the top belt and go into the Modify Panel.
45. Turn on the Auto Key, move to frame 90 and adjust the percentage along path so the dummy moves across the top of the belt to a position of looking like it will fall off. I used about 32%. If your spline is reversed depending on how you connected it at the vertex level in a prior step, you may have to use 70%.
46. Select the bottom belt and go to frame 140. Click the percentage along the path spinner up and down one click.
47. Go to frame 200 and increase the path percent so the dummy moves across the belt to a precarious position. I used about −32%. If the object looks like it is moving the wrong way, try 120%.
48. Turn off the Auto Key.
49. Go to frame zero.
50. Select the teapot, go to the Animation Menu, and add a Link Constraint.
51. Click the Add Link button if it is not active and select the "top_dummy".
52. Go to frame 90 and click Link to World.

53. Go to frame 140, click Add Link and select "bottom_dummy".
54. Turn off Add Link.

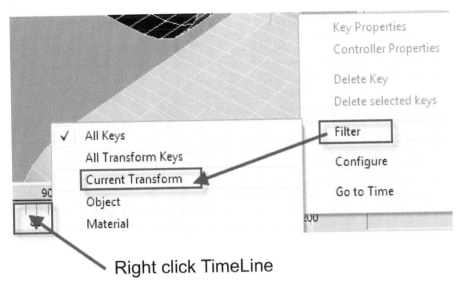

Right click TimeLine

FIG 15.12

55. Right click the timeline, choose filter, and drag to current transform.
56. Turn on the Auto Key.

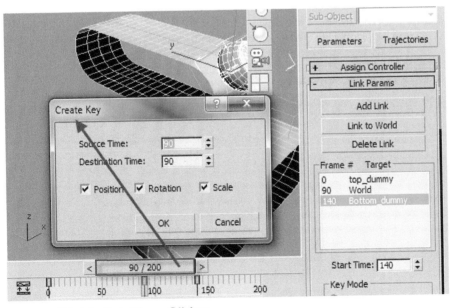

Right click Time Slider

FIG 15.13

57. Go to frame 90 and right click the Time Slider. Set a position and rotation
   key.

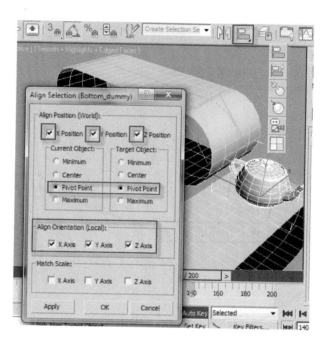

FIG 15.14

58. Go to frame 140. Select Align and then click the Bottom_dummy.
59. Make sure that X, Y, Z are all on, choose pivot to pivot, and then turn on X, Y, Z for Align Local.
60. Hit OK. Adjust rotation as needed.
61. Activate the left viewport.
62. Right click the teapot and turn on Trajectory in the Object Properties.
63. Drag the Time Slider between frames 90 and 140.

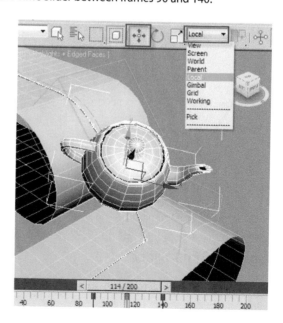

FIG 15.15

64. The teapot will appear to move through the top belt a little.
65. Turn on Select and Move, and change the Reference Coordinate System to Local.
66. Move the teapot away from the belts along the "Z" axis at around frame 110–112.
67. Play the animation.
68. Create a star spline with Radius 1: 95, Radius 2: 85, and 19 points. Call it "gear".
69. Add an Extrude Modifier with an amount of about 25.
70. Align this object locally to the "wheel_control" spline.
71. Create a tube with the Autogrid on relative to the "gear". Radius 1: 7, Radius 2: 8, and Height of about 150.

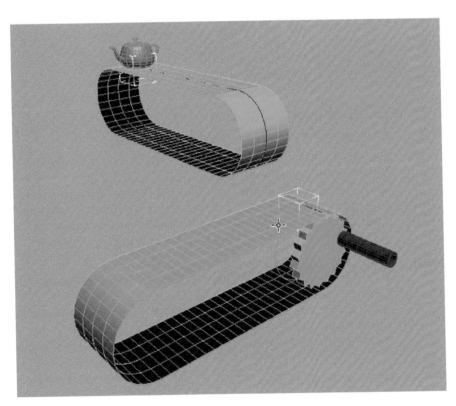

FIG 15.16

72. Add an Animation Link Constraint and choose the "gear" as the first link.
73. Right click the timeline and in filters, select object.
74. Select the "lower_belt" and the percentage keys of the Path Deform Binding (WSM) will appear on the timeline.
75. Marquee selects all the keys and when they turn white indicating the keys are selected, delete them.

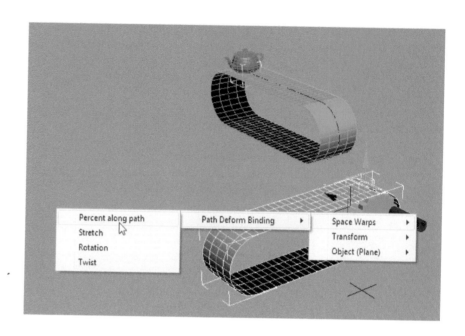

FIG 15.17

76. Hit F9 and render your scene.
77. Select the belts and add a shell modifier to each.

You can see through the plane because these objects only render one side. There are a few ways to get around this. The object can be slightly modified by adding a shell modifier to give it some thickness. Without adding complexity or geometry, several different types of materials may be added. A standard material with two sides will work, but a double sided material that will put two different materials on the front and back would probably be more realistic.

If you haven't saved in a while, this is a good time. Also do an edit hold in case the axis is wrong in the next step. We want to control the speed of the belt by the rotation of the turning of the gear. This is done with wiring. Think of wiring as what happened in a clone operation with instances except with more control. If you want to have a character walk up and attach his hands to the handle and move with the crank, this is a nice way to interactively control both.

FIG 15.18

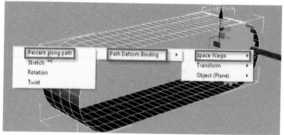
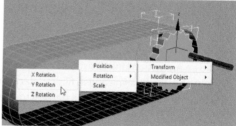

Virtually any parameter can be "wired" together. The trick is to start back-up your file first because some parameters may require a different axis, numeric value or controller for the keys.

78. Select the "lower_belt", right click it, and choose Wiring from the Quad Menu.
79. Drag across from Space Warps to Path Deform Binding to Percentage along Path.
80. Once the parameter of the belt has been chosen, move the cursor over the "gear" and repeat the steps to choose the "Y" axis of the rotation.

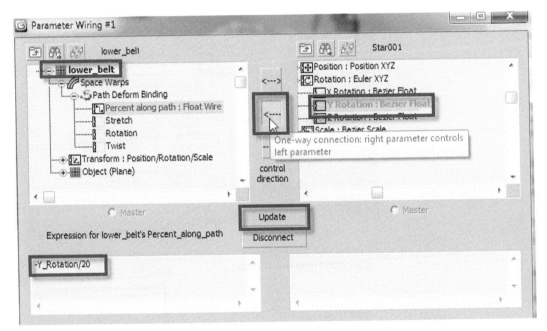

FIG 15.19

81. Select the direction arrow in the center to point from the controlling object toward the object you want to receive the control. Hit the Connect button. In Fig. 15.19, it says update. Once you have wired two parameters together and tested it, any changes need to be updated. In Fig. 15.19, the expression has changed to –Y_Rotation/20. I basically put the /20 to divide values of the degrees of rotation being passed to the percentage of the path by a much smaller number. If you don't change it and update the value, it will move way too fast.
82. Select the "gear" and rotate it on the "Y" axis.

If you want to lock the rotation orientation just to the "Y" axis, you will have to lock it down in the Hierarchy Panel Link Info Section. I created my circle in the front viewport, which pointed the "Z" axis 90° from that view. When the gear was aligned to it, the "Z" axis of the object was aligned to the same orientation. In world space, the gear rotates on "Y" but its local orientation is "Z". Unless the objects pivot is aligned to the world, the two won't match up. As per Fig. 15.20, go lock the "X" and "Y" rotations.

With Local Reference Coordinate active, the "Z" axis shows as the local axis for rotation. We are wiring relative to the world which means the "Z" is the axis left unlocked.

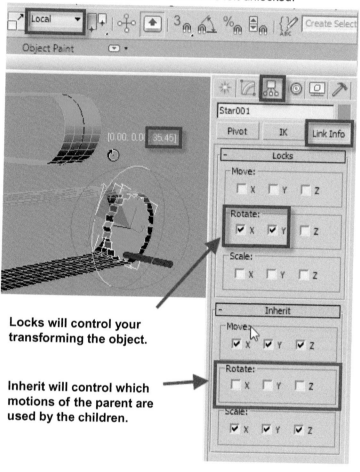

Locks will control your transforming the object.

Inherit will control which motions of the parent are used by the children.

FIG 15.20

83. In the Locks Panel, turn on the "X" and "Y" locks for Rotate, leaving the "Z" axis available for it to be rotated by a character turning the wheel in its hands. This will allow you to rotate on just one axis as a spinning gear would normally turn.
84. In the Inherit Panel, turn off the X, Y, and Z Rotate check boxes.
85. Repeat the same steps for the Tube001 object.

By turning off the Inherit Rotate controls for the Tube001, it will move in space with the gear but not inherit the rotation. If you bind the hands of a biped to the tube, you would see that hands maintain the same orientation and revolve through the wrists. By turning off the Locks of the "Z" axis like you did with the gear, there is always the option of adding some rotation to the tube so that you can show some struggling of the biped to turn the wheel.

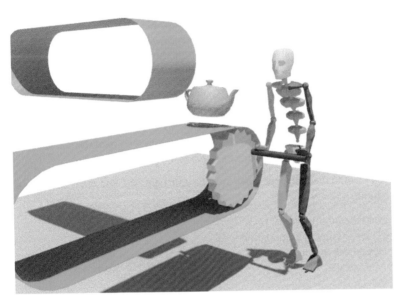

FIG 15.21

86. Create a biped about 600 units tall or what you think is a good relative height for your scene.
87. In the Name Selection box, create a set for the bip01 com object.
88. In the Motion Panel, go into Figure mode and rotate the biped 90° so it faces the crank as shown in Fig 15.21. Don't worry about the pose at this point.
89. Turn off the Figure mode.

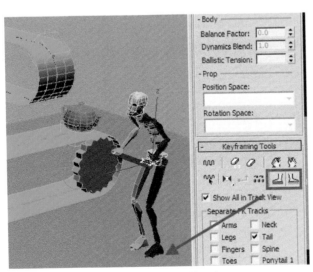

Anchor the feet allows you to position the biped001 parent object so the feet don't move.

FIG 15.22

You want to position your biped so it is a little bent over and ready to turn the handle. By anchoring the feet, you can move the main parent of this rig, biped001, and have the feet stay in position. Otherwise the feet would move through the floor.

90. Select the feet and in the Keyframing Tools Panel, turn on Anchor Left and Right Leg.
91. Select the four spine objects and bend them to give the back some arch.
92. Move and rotate the hands so that they rest on the top of the crank.
93. Select the Bip001 com object and move it down slightly.

You want to position your biped so it is a little bent over and ready to turn the handle.

94. In the Key Info Panel, set a key.
95. Set another at around frame 135.
96. Go back to frame 0 and now we will get the hands to move with the rest of the crank.

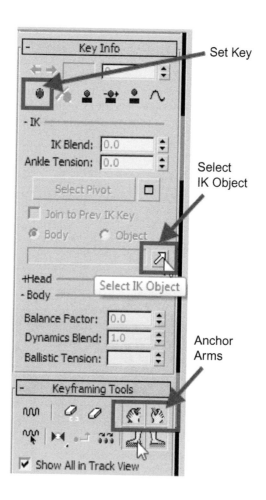

FIG 15.23

The next step is to have the hand move with the crank and get the arms moving inversely and will require using the Key Info and the Keyframing Tools Panel. We need to select the object to have the hands follow in the Key Info Panel and then anchor them in Keyframing Tools.

97. Select Left Hand which is blue and click the Select IK Object Arrow in Key Info as per Fig. 15.23.
98. Click on the Tube001 object.
99. Now click the Blue Anchor Arms Icon in the Keyframing Tools Panel. You will see that the name Tube001 appears as the target object in the naming field of the Select IK Object. The radio button that is set to body by default is set to object.
100. Repeat these steps for the right hand.
101. Scrub the timeline and notice how the hands will move for a certain number of frames and then the tube object will rotate out of reach.
102. To finish this project, simply scrub through time and add some extra bend keyframes to the spines and a little vertical and horizontal movement to the bip01 object.

CHAPTER 16

Animated Visibility

Richard Lapidus

Rule: Setting a scene

After Completing This Chapter, You Will be Able To:

- Animate an object out of view with the step-key tangent.
- Use the slice modifier to make an object appear or disappear.
- Utilize animated gradient ramps.

In traditional cell animation, it's easier to make characters or things disappear. The object is simply not on film from one frame to the next or it is gradually faded out. The first is referred to as the pop-off screen solution. With the pop-off solution in traditional animation a character might fall in a hole, duck behind a tree much thinner than itself, or be hidden in a puff of smoke. In the early days of 3d animation, to have something disappear quickly, it would need to be animated off screen in one frame with an animated key or have an animated material map working. The problem with keying it off screen typically meant doing some extra adjustments to the TCB controlling the motion. In a 3d scene, although it's just electrons, we need to control getting a "physical" 3d mesh within the scene. This chapter will cover a variety of interesting ways to do that using the tools inherent to controlling its presence with animation.

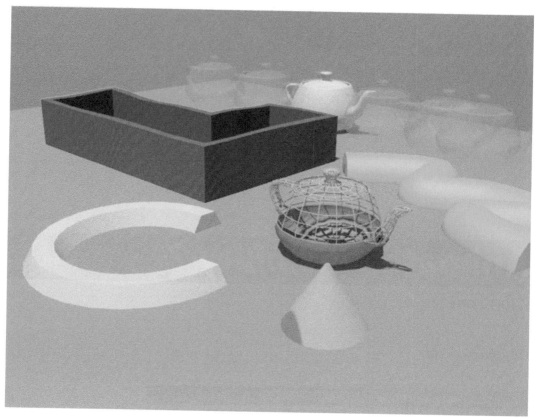

FIG 16.1

Animating an Object Out of View with the Step-Key Tangent

The first solution will demonstrate the pop-off concept and show you a little trickery with the key tangent types. It is simple to set the key tangent to step and move the object off the screen. This will keep it in place maintaining state until the next keyframe is encountered.

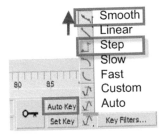

Tangent Types
for Keyframes

FIG 16.2

1. Load the file called chpt_17_visibility_start.max.
2. Select the blue teapot callved "Pop-Off".
3. Make sure the Key Tangent is set to the default of Smooth.
4. Enable the "Auto Key".
5. Animate the teapot moving across the screen at frame 50.
6. Set the Key Tangent to Step (third flyout down) and then move it off the screen at frame 75.
7. Right click the object and turn on its trajectory in the display properties.
8. Turn off the Auto Key.
9. Go to the Tools Menu and choose snapshot.
10. When the Dialog appears, enable range and set the number of copies to 10.
11. Hit OK and then choose the copied teapots with the "H" Key (pop-off001-pop-off010).
12. Right click the screen, and choose Object Properties from the Quad Menu.
13. Turn off Receive Shadows and Cast shadows. Hit OK to exit the Object Properties Dialog.
14. Add a standard gray material to the objects with two-sided rendering enabled on and the opacity set to around 25%.

Notice how the teapot moves across the screen for 50 frames, sits there for 25, and then pops off at frame 75. Looking at its trajectory, there is an apparent straight red line after frame 75 without any white dots representing the frames between your animated keys at frames 0 and 50. This is the crudest method for getting an object out of frame, but it does represent a motion we typically take for granted. Take a look at the second hand on your watch, it maintains state until the next state and then snaps into position. As we do need to use mechanical motions occasionally, it is still a noteworthy mention.

Keying is a fine art, which you undoubtedly will want to be practicing through many of the exercises. Let's take a quick look at keying some of the built-in features for slicing an object at the parametric level before we move onto modifiers. Some of your parametric objects like the torus have built-in Slice features that can be animated as well. In the next few steps, we will animate the slice values of the torus to make it grow over time. We use this effect sometimes in reverse to do a quick reveal of an object instead of making it disappear. You can always swap the keys to accomplish this.

Animating Parametric Slicing

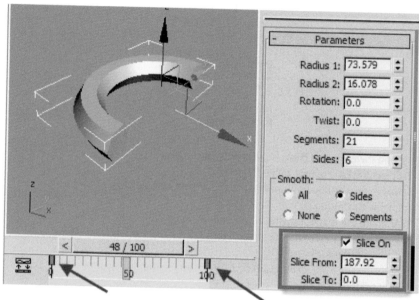

FIG 16.3

Slice from 360 at frame 0 and 1.5 at frame 100

15. Select the torus object.
16. Set your Key Tangents back to default interpolation (top one).
17. Go to the Modify Panel.
18. Make sure Auto Key is off.
19. Turn on Slice Check box in the bottom of the panel.
20. Turn on Auto Key and go to frame 100.
21. Animate the Slice From value to 1.5 and the Slice To value to 0.0.
22. Go to frame 0.
23. Set the values to 360 for Slice From and 0.0 for the Slice To value.

Several other primitive objects like the cone, sphere, cylinder, and tube will allow for this type of animation at the parametric level. These can be used in combination with other modifiers and compound objects to create very interesting animated cutting effects. We will explore one variation of this next.

The process of using animated modifiers happens to be one of my favorites for gradually making an object build or hide over time. In this case, we will use an animated Slice Modifier. I've used this to show the building of a shell over time or removing part of an object when it is being disintegrated without using special extensive particle systems. I originally came up with the idea for my architectural clients to demonstrate a sort of time lapse in creating a building on site. Once my animation students started to get the idea ... it became one of their favorites as well.

Animating Slice Modifier

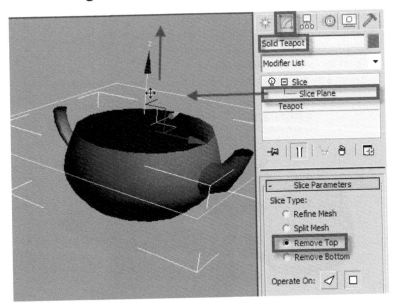

FIG 16.4

24. Make sure Auto Key is off.
25. Select the teapot called "SOLID Teapot".
26. Go to the Modify Panel.
27. Add a Slice Modifier.
28. Go to the sub-object and choose the Slice Plane.

Note

The Slice Plane modifier will be aligned to the Transform Gizmo (axis) of the object along the "Z" axis. It basically is a planar mapping projection that can be not only moved, but rotated as well. Things don't always neatly need to be sliced from top to bottom. You may want to experiment with adding a few rotation keys offset from the position key to create a little more realism. In the next few steps, we are going to animate this up over time along the "Z" axis so that the object appears to have a portion of the mesh on either side of the slice gizmo removed. Ever seen a character duck behind a thin tree or appear out of nowhere from behind something, this is how you would do it easily! It's like pulling a rabbit out of hat. Something really big can appear to be in a very small space.

29. Set the Slice type to remove top.
30. Turn on the Auto Key.
31. Move the Time Slider around frame 80.
32. Move the slice plane above the teapot on the "Z" axis about 80 units so the teapot is completely revealed.

255

33. Turn off Auto Key.
34. Turn off the sub-object slice plane.
35. Go to the Edit Menu and choose the Clone command (CTL+V).
36. Choose Copy as the type and call the new pot Wire Teapot.
37. Choose Remove Bottom for the Slice Type.
38. Open the Compact Material Editor.
39. Assign a material and turn on Wire and Two Sided in the Shader Basic Parameters area.

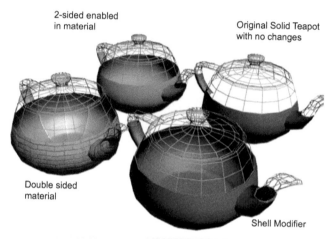

2-sided enabled in material

Original Solid Teapot with no changes

Double sided material

Shell Modifier

FIG 16.5

Note

Step 38 has three alternative solutions you can use to make your object appear to have an inside surface of the original object. By default, if you rendered at around frame 40, you would be seeing through the backside of the teapot because the normals are only rendering the outside surface. Using the Cap Holes Modifier will basically try to close off any opening created by missing faces. Capping will sometimes fail if you are doing heavy modeling and don't leave the program clean areas to close off. Since we are not doing lid modeling, I chose to skip showing it in Fig. 16.5. The Shell Modifier, which is my favorite, will create an offset surface to the inside or outside that you can control parametrically. In addition, you can assign the multi\sub-object IDs for use with a multi\sub-object material. This is really one of the best solutions because it allows for an extra material to be assigned easily to the lip surface of the moving cut of your object. Essentially, this will allow for the illusion that there is a material in-between the outside and inside surface.

40. Reselect the solid teapot object and assign it a double-sided material, a Cap Holes, or Shell Modifier.

One of the first modeling techniques in the early days of 3d was the compound loft object. Although there are numerous other techniques to draw on today, there are still a few benefits to this old work horse, which makes it worth mentioning. The Sweep Modifier was a great replacement for lofting if you only needed to use one single shape projected along a spline. What keeps lofting unique is the ability to interpolate to different shapes along the percentage of the path and also make deformation changes of scaling and twisting, for example. In this next disappearing act, we will explore animating the scale of the shape along the path with a scale deformation. When you get the hang of this, you will easily be able to animate a gradient map in a very similar way.

Note

Please refer to the bottom of the next page when doing the next several steps. From left to right along the bottom of the scale graph, you will see that the percent runs from 0% to 100%. This represents the percentage along your path from where you first click (0%) to the end of the spline (100%). Even if you use a close path, it runs from left to right. If we used a circle as a closed path, it increases in percent from the far right vertex in sub-object counterclockwise back to the beginning. You would want to adjust your spline objects in sub-object with an Edit Spline Modifier to reverse the path or pick a new first vertex to start the motion, or in this case deformation, at a different point along the spline. Refer to the chapter called Chapter 4 Deforming objects for a more in-depth explanation of spline objects.

The end result is shown in Figure on the next page as well with the graph. Just a few comments for those of you who have never worked with lofting in 3ds MAX. This graph, like most other representations of data, has a percentage that runs along the left side, which shows a default range of −100 to 100. This represents the size of the shape as it travels along the path. Along the top is another that runs 0 to 100. This represents percentage along the path (which can be an open or closed path). The goal is to position enough points that can be animated in order to create the illusion that the object grows over time.

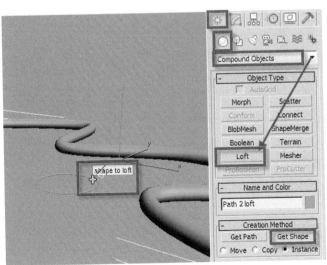

FIG 16.6

41. Select the object called "Path 2 loft".

Note

The rendering of this spline is on for easy selection.

42. Go to the Modify Panel and turn off Enable in Renderer and Viewport. You will find these in the Rendering Panel of the object.
43. With it still selected, switch to the Create Panel.
44. Choose Geometry and the change the drop-down menu from Standard Primitive to Compound Objects.
45. Choose Loft and select Get Shape in the Creation Method Panel.
46. Select the "shape to loft" circle and then turn off Get Shape.
47. Switch to the Modify Panel so that you have access to the Deformation Panels at the bottom of the Modify Panel.
48. Choose the Scale Tool.

FIG 16.7

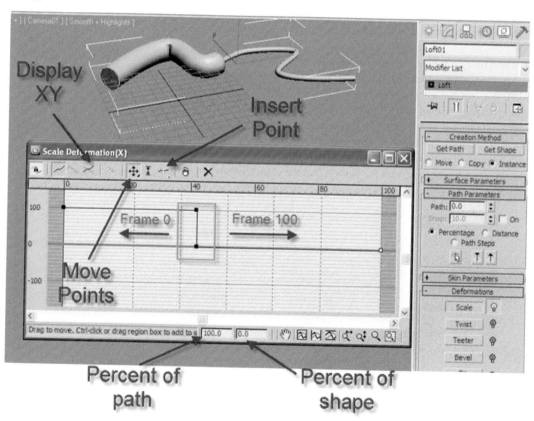

Refer to Fig. 16.6 for the icon intensive operation below.

49. Turn on Display XY axis (red and green crossed icon).
50. Click Insert Control Point (red line with yellow star).
51. Add two vertices.
52. Choose Move Control Points (looks like Move Transform icon).
53. Click the third point and zero out the shape percentage number. Set the position to 50%.
54. Click the second point and give its position 50% the scale value 100%.
55. Select the fourth point and give it a zero shape value.

Note

We are creating this step of two control points at frame 50 so that you can easily select them for animating to the end of the path at frame 100 and then back to frame 0 without grabbing the control points at either end of the path percent.

56. Go to frame 100.
57. Turn on Auto Key.
58. Slide the center two keys to the right. (There is a flyout for the move control to limit to one axis.)
59. Move the Time Slider to frame 0.
60. Slide the two keys to the far left.
61. Turn off Auto Key.
62. Scrub the Time Slider and you will notice the object disappears over time.
63. Save the file incrementally. I've saved it at this point with a file called chpt_17_visibility_04.max just in case you missed a step and want to examine my file.

I actually used this in an animation for one of my colleagues to demonstrate the trajectory of a fixed point on a rolling wheel. For his students studying calculus, it was difficult for them to visualize what this path would actually look like, much less to draw it accurately on dry erase board. In the Motion Panel, in the trajectory area, you can actually create a spline from an object's trajectory. That's how I create this animation.

FIG 16.8

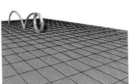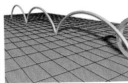

Growing an Object over Time with an Animated Extrude

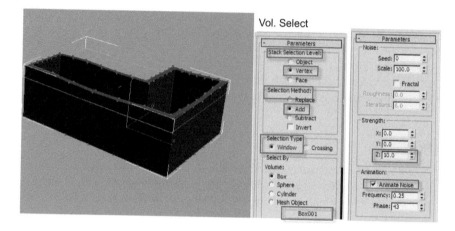

FIG 16.9

This one is similar to what we did with the torus but uses an Extrude Modifier. You could also build a wall with a slice, but it is worth learning this method to give you more flexibility and things to try. After demonstrating this in my class recently, we added a Volume Select Modifier and animated the top edge so that it ungulates as it grows. Animating modifiers can really breathe some life into your work. The Noise Modifier has a parameter for animating the effect based on frequency and phase, much as you would see in a number of space warps. Actually, noise can work in object space level as a modifier or in world space level as a space warp.

64. Select the spline object called "Line02" and add an Extrude Modifier.
65. Make sure your tangent control is set to linear.
66. Go to frame 50 and turn on the Auto Key.
67. Increase the amount spinner to 120 units and turn off the Auto Key.
68. Go to frame 0, switch to the top viewport and create a box about the size as the outline for the spline.
69. Note that my values were Length 220, Width 350, and Height 15.

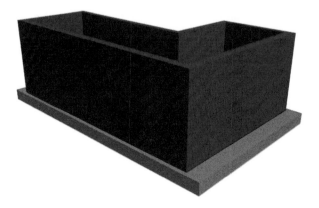

FIG 16.10

70. Hit the "F3" Key to enable wire frame shading.
71. Go to frame 50, enable the Auto Key and move the box up on the "Z" axis so the top edge intersects the top of the wall that has extruded over 50 frames.
72. Turn off Auto Key. Check from the front viewport that the box intersects the top of the wall from at least frames 30–50. See Fig 16.11. The box will be used to make a moving selection of the top of the wall.

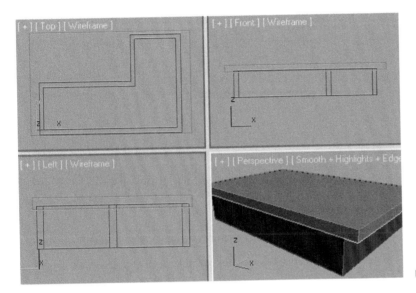

FIG 16.11

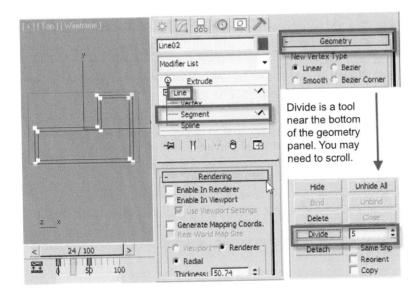

Divide is a tool near the bottom of the geometry panel. You may need to scroll.

FIG 16.12

73. Select the object called line02 (extruding wall).
74. Change to the top viewport and go into the sub-object segment level of the line in the Modify Panel.
75. Select all the segments, pan down the Modify Panel, set the Divide number to "5", and hit the Divide button.

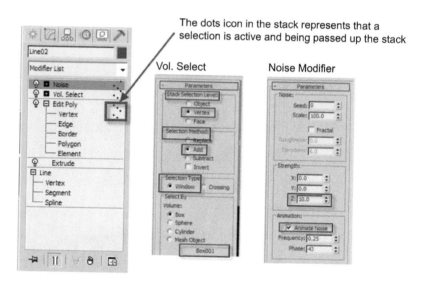

The dots icon in the stack represents that a selection is active and being passed up the stack

FIG 16.13

76. Turn off sub-object. Switch to the front viewport and add an Edit Poly Modifier.

We need to add the Edit Poly Modifier in order to get out the Vertex Sub-object components of this wall object. Note from Fig. 16.13 that there are dots next to the Sub-object Vertex level. This represents that a selection has been made at that level and left open to be passed to the Vol. Select Modifier above. The Vol. Select Modifier allows us to make a choice of what will be selected based upon another object's volume intersecting the object. Although we are maintaining the selection the whole time, you could animate a smaller object intersecting the wall intermittently to create the illusion that one is reacting to another. I will typically demonstrate this with a ball hitting a surface which also has a displace space warp and a Flex Modifier added to get some bounce back as one object hits another.

77. Go to the Vertex Sub-object level and choose the top row of vertices.
78. Add a Volume Select Modifier without turning off sub-object.
79. In the Vol. Select Modifier, enable Vertex in the Stack Selection Level.
80. Enable Add in the Selection Method area.
81. Click the None button in Select By and choose the animated box (Box001).
82. Add a Noise Modifier. Put a value of 10 in for the "Z" strength and turn on Animated Noise.
83. Select the box, right click it and hide selection, and play the animation. That is gnarly!
84. Incrementally save your file as chpt_17_visibility_05.max.

So far we have been looking at ways to physically affect the objects with various modeling and editing functions. The next one is similar to the loft but will use an animated material in order to make the cone disappear. I like to teach this one a step or two away from the loft example to reinforce the concept of animating the keys in a graph. In this case, we will animate the flags left and right in a gradient map. Refer to Fig. 16.14 for the next set of steps.

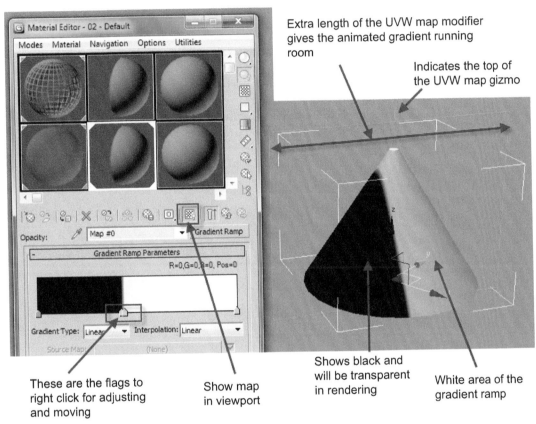

Extra length of the UVW map modifier gives the animated gradient running room

Indicates the top of the UVW map gizmo

These are the flags to right click for adjusting and moving

Show map in viewport

Shows black and will be transparent in rendering

White area of the gradient ramp

FIG 16.14

Animating a Gradient Ramp

85. Make sure Auto Key is off.
86. Select the cone and add a UVW map modifier.
87. Set the Alignment Axis to "Y".
88. Set the Length to 60 units and the Width to 80 units. This will give your animation some running room.
89. Open Material Editor and make sure you are in Compact mode.
90. Assign another material to the object.
91. Add a gradient ramp to the opacity channel.
92. Turn on Show in the viewport.
93. Double click the center flag and turn it to pure black: 0, 0, 0.

94. Move your cursor near the white flag in the gradient area and drag a flag to near the center flag.
95. Do not overlap them.
96. Turn on the Auto Key.
97. Move the Time Slider to frame 100.
98. Move the center two flags to the right (do not overlap them).
99. Move the Time Slider to frame 0.
100. Move the flags to the left.
101. Turn off the Auto Key.

Hopefully these sets of exercises for controlling the visibility of your objects will give you a few good ideas for some areas of animating the properties of 3ds MAX, which you may not have been familiar with. There are other variations that you may want to explore as well. In post production, alpha channels, for example, can be used to hide and reveal layers of assets. You might want to consider adding Material IDs and Object IDs to your objects in order to select them for easier keying.

Gallery

DAVID DRZKA

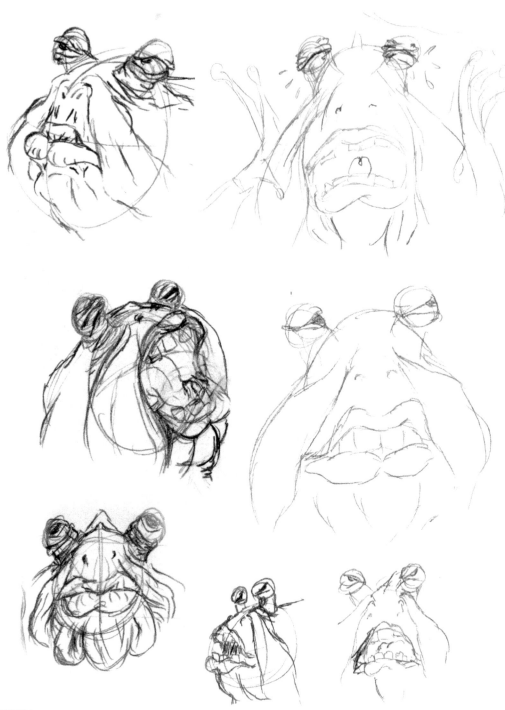

GEORGE BERLIN

GEORGE BERLIN

GEORGE BERLIN

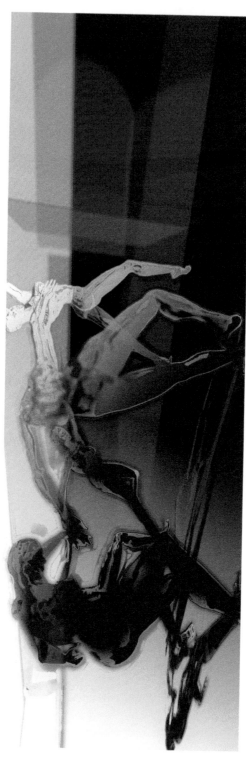

RICHARD LAPIDUS

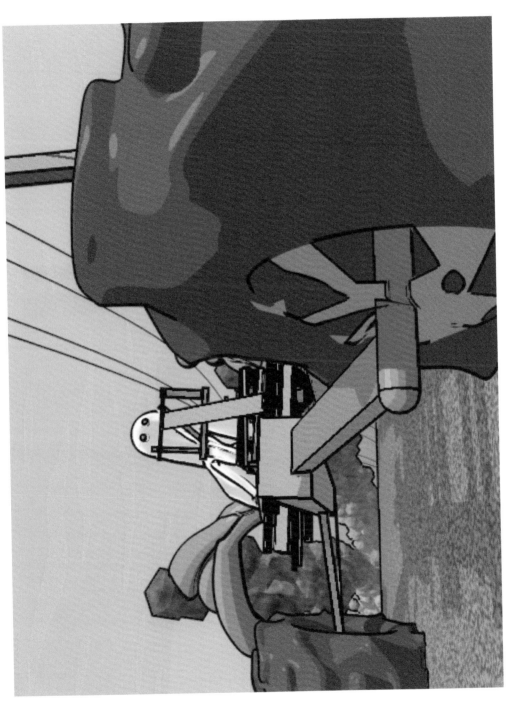

TOMAS ZAVECKAS

Index

Page numbers followed by *f* indicates a figure and *t* indicates a table.

275

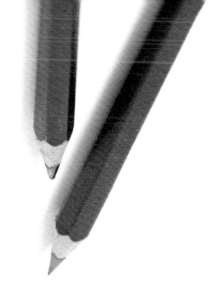

tradigital Series

Focal Press adds a new star to its brightening constellation of superb Animation titles: The *Tradigital* series. *Tradigital* titles bridge the gap between animating with a particular software tool and applying the twelve principles of animation to your work.

ISBN: 9780123852229

ISBN: 9780240817309

ISBN: 9780240811581

The 12 basic principles of animation were introduced by the Disney animators Ollie Johnston and Frank Thomas, who wanted to codify the efforts of the leading Disney animators from the 1930s onwards to produce more realistic animations. The principles mainly teach animators how to create characters that look like they are adhering to the basic laws of physics. The principles also deal with more abstract issues, such as emotional timing and character appeal.

Visit the series webpage at http://www.focalpress.com/tradigital, and check out the next pages for more about Tradigital Maya and Tradigital Blender.

Lee Montgomery presents *Tradigital Maya* which shows animators how to use the Maya controls, while applying the classical principles of animation and core techniques. Part of the new *Tradigital* series, the companion site for *Tradigital Maya* can be found at www.tradigitalmaya.com.

Finally a book that bridges the world of software instruction with the classical principles of animation - for animators. **Roland Hess** offers the only artistic guide to applying the principles of traditional animation with Blender's tool set. Part of the new *Tradigital* series from Focal Press, the companion site for *Tradigital Blender* can be found at www.tradigitalblender.com.

Printed and bound by CPI Group (UK) Ltd, Croydon, CR0 4YY

21/10/2024

01777057-0006